If *P*, then *Q*

'*If P, Then Q* is recommended reading for all who want to work in this surprisingly rich field'

Australasian Journal of Philosophy

'Some delightfully insightful comments on the probability account of conditionals, on the Ramsey test, and especially on possible world semantics . . . It also provides a healthy dose of humbling realism'

Journal of Philosophy of Science

'Undergraduates will find the book useful as a resource. It covers a lot of ground mentioning most of the issues and positions that need to be addressed in a course on conditionals, and it has an excellent bibliography.'

Theoria

'This interesting book covers a great deal of ground . . . the expository chapters are clear, accurate and sympathetic . . . The book has many interesting examples and stimulating arguments, as well as concise and reliable exposition of what has been said about conditionals over the years. This is a good place to learn about conditionals or to have one's ideas about them challenged'

Notre Dame Journal of Formal Logic

'a useful starting point for a course on conditionals. The introductions to the issues are clear and well-illustrated with examples.'

Dialogue

'very useful . . . The writing is clear and non-technical, but without any sacrifice of rigor.'

Choice

'an often provocative, sometimes original, philosophical discussion of sustained interest'

Canadian Philosophical Review

'a useful book about conditionals . . . includes a clearly and engagingly written historical survey of the literature on conditionals'

Philosophy and Phenomenological Research

'I can recommend Sanford's book as a thoroughly well-informed, intelligent and original contribution to the field'

Philosophical Books

Since its publication in 1989, David H. Sanford's *If P, Then Q* has become one of the most widely respected works in the field of conditionals. This new edition includes a new preface, a supplementary bibliography, and a new chapter covering developments in the field since the first edition appeared.

Part One gives an historical overview of the history of philosophical treatments of conditionals from the Stoics to the present. In Part Two, Sanford puts forward his own treatment of conditionals, defending the position that we should explain conditionals by reference to dependence rather than the other way around.

David H. Sanford is Professor of Philosophy at Duke University.

If *P*, then *Q*

Conditionals and the Foundations of Reasoning

David H. Sanford

Routledge
Taylor & Francis Group

LONDON AND NEW YORK

First published 1989
by Routledge
11 New Fetter Lane, London EC4P 4EE

Simultaneously published in the USA and Canada
by Routledge
29 West 35th Street, New York, NY 10001

First published in paperback 1992

Second Edition published 2003

Routledge is an imprint of the Taylor & Francis Group

© 1989, 1992, 2003 David H. Sanford

Printed and bound in Great Britain by MPG Books Ltd, Bodmin, Cornwall

British Library Cataloguing in Publication Data
A catalogue record for this book is available from the British Library

Library of Congress Cataloging in Publication Data
A catalog record for this book has been requested

ISBN 0–415–28368–X Hbk
ISBN 0–415–28369–8 Pbk

Contents

Contents

vi

Preface

This book is directed to students of philosophy at every level and their teachers. Chapters I and II provide a selective account of about two thousand years of the history of logic combined with an introduction to the basic vocabulary used to discuss conditionals, inference, and validity. Historians of ancient and medieval logic will find that the only original historical scholarship in these chapters is their own. Teachers of elementary logic, however, and writers of logic textbooks, may find that my discussions of invalidity, which occur first in Chapter II, conflict with their own pedagogical practice.

Chapters III and IV deal with the history of the subject in the late nineteenth and early twentieth centuries. While I am indebted to historians who write on this period, I have not been wholly dependent on them. My version of how Russell ran together 'material implication' with 'the material conditional' does not appear elsewhere, so far as I know.

Chapters V, VI, and VII cover some later twentieth-century treatments of conditionals. While I still attempt to deal with the subject historically, much of the work discussed is quite recent, and it is difficult to achieve historical distance.

Although Part One of the book, Chapters I–VII, makes no attempt to appear neutral, it does attempt to present a wide range of views. Part Two is devoted to my own views, and I discuss other philosophers mainly to advance this end. Parts One and Two together mention quite a few positions and arguments by other philosophers; and I could mention many more, including the programme of the philosopher who once asked me, 'You are going to write a whole *book* about conditionals?'

According to modern legend, a child's book report began 'This book told me more about owls than I wanted to know.' Readers told more about conditionals here than they want to know may be dismayed to learn how much remains to tell. I mention many contemporary articles and chapters on the subject, and several recent books, only in passing. Others I do not mention at all. The Bibliography was rather longer in an earlier version, although it was never close to being comprehensive. All the publications it lists in the current version meet one of these three criteria: they are mentioned in the Notes; they are recent publications by authors who are already listed; or they are publications of mine on which I have drawn. Anyone who has published on conditionals and feels neglected by me can at least take comfort that he or she is in company that is large and good. An attempt to recognize every distinctive contribution would result in telling more than almost anyone wants to know.

During the 1982–3 academic year, I combined a sabbatical leave from Duke University with a fellowship from the National Endowment for the Humanities to pursue a project entitled 'Time, cause, and explanation: studies in asymmetrical dependence'. As part of this project, I wrote papers that eventually appeared as Sanford 1984a, 1984b, and 1985, plus a long paper entitled 'Conditionals and dependence'. When Professor Ted Honderich sent out requests in 1983 for proposals for this general series and included conditionals as a possible topic, I decided to let the ideas of 'Conditionals and dependence' be the core of a book.

I am grateful for invitations that allowed me to read preliminary studies to philosophical audiences of great ability. I delivered papers entitled 'Conditionals and dependence', differing somewhat from the original and from each other, to the Corcoran Department of Philosophy at the University of Virginia and to the Department of Philosophy at Syracuse University. I delivered 'How an acceptable conditional can fail the Ramsey test' to the Creighton Club, the New York State Philosophical Association, and 'Various visions of possible worlds' to the New Jersey Regional Philosophical Association. 'Circumstantial validity' was submitted and accepted on the programmes of the North Carolina Philosophical Society and the Society for Philosophy and Psychology. I owe thanks to the many generous acute philosophers who made suggestions and criticisms, and I want especially to thank Ernest Adams, Jonathan Bennett, James Cargile, Alvin Goldman, David Lewis, Brian McLaughlin, Peter van Inwagen, Barry Loewer, and John Rust. Loewer and Rust served as formal commentators. My Duke colleague Paul Welsh read a version of the entire manuscript and saved me from many errors.

The Duke University Research Council has continued to help defray some of the material costs involved in the preparation of this book. Karen Simon and Frances Finney of the Duke Department of Philosophy have helped me enormously in preparing all the drafts of the manuscript and in patiently guiding me, from around Chapter XI onward, into the world of word processing. Frances Finney and William Beach helped me a great deal in correcting proofs and preparing the index.

I thank Kate, Daria, and Anne for sustaining me in a thousand ways.

I dedicate this book to, or to the memory of, three of my teachers in the Detroit Public Schools: Alice Hanning, Wilfrid B. Marshall, Jr, and J. V. Simon.

David H. Sanford
1989

Preface to Second Edition

A recent web search, July 2002, for the first edition of this book produced the following title: *If P, Then Q: Foundation of Logic and Argument*. In fact, no book with this subtitle was ever published. An editor at the time would accept my proposal, *If P, Then Q*, as a main title only if the word 'foundation' appeared in the subtitle. He suggested 'Foundation of Logic and Argument'. I thought this sounded too much like 'Foundations of Mathematics', a phrase with an accepted meaning that misrepresents the contents of the book. We compromised on 'Conditionals and the Foundations of Reasoning'. This subtitle remains to indicate the extent of identity between the two editions.

'Foundations of Reasoning' does not have a fairly precise meaning. If it had one, I don't know whether I would agree that reasoning has foundations. An alternative subtitle represents the content of the book more clearly: *Theories of Conditionals, Past and Present*. This hypothetical subtitle adapts the name of the series in which the first edition appears, *The Problems of Philosophy: Their Past and Present*, edited by Ted Honderich. Like other books in this series, *If P, Then Q* has two parts, one historical and one presenting the author's views.

Part One presents concepts and vocabulary that are central in current theoretical discussions of conditionals. I organize this presentation historically. The first two chapters move quickly, from the Stoics to 1879. Historians of ancient and medieval logic will find that the only original scholarship in these chapters is their own, but I am responsible for the choice of topics. Although Johannes de Celaya is not a well-known figure, for example, I refer to his notion of *contravalidity* to subvert what still seems to be common practice in introductory logic courses. Every instance of a valid argument form, but not every instance of an invalid argument form, is a valid argument. No alert person would infer from this the falsehood that every instance of an invalid argument form is an invalid argument. Text-book writers do not believe this, explicitly, but many continue to write chapters or sections entitled 'Proving Invalidity' that encourage their readers to believe it. I think that notion of *contravalidity* helps explain an asymmetry between *valid* and *invalid* argument forms.

Chapter III opens with Frege's 1879 *Begriffsschrift* and moves on to the truth tables in Wittgenstein's *Tractatus* and Grice's theory of conversational implicature and its use in defending a truth-functional account of ordinary-language conditionals. The remaining historical chapters, IV to VII, never look back. Chapter IV describes the twentieth-century revival of modal logic. Chapter V concentrates on how Nelson Goodman and Roderick Chisholm focussed philosophical attention on the importance and difficulty of understanding counterfactual conditionals. Although Chapter VI both moves rapidly from one author to another for the sake of providing more historical information and, like all the chapters, is quite concise, I intend it to tell a coherent, unified story about the relations between conditionals and probability in which the work of Ernest A. Adams is central. I believe that I invented the particular form of illustrative diagram I use in Chapter VI, and also the form of diagram I use in Chapter VII. (I certainly did not invent the idea of using diagrams which probably would not have occurred to me without the examples by Ernest Adams and by David Lewis.) The possible-world semantics for counterfactual conditionals proposed by David Lewis and by Robert Stalnaker is the major topic of Chapter VIII which also outlines some variations of and some putative problems with possible-world approaches.

There are various logical relations between the points I make in Part Two. I think the discussion of inference in Chapter VIII is independent of the main points in the following chapters. A philosopher who agrees that Chapters IX and X present some genuine difficulties for currently accepted theories is not thereby forced to accept the views I present in Chapters XI to XIV. Considering logical relations going in the other direction, I would say that one's sympathy with Chapters XI to XIV, themselves far from monolithic, does not require accepting the negative points in Chapters IX or X. Chapter XV presupposes relatively uncontroversial material about invalidity from Chapters VI and VII.

Here is a summary of some of the main points in Part Two.

Chapter VIII distinguishes inference from implication and adapts W. E. Johnson's distinction between constitutive and epistemic conditions of inference. Some philosophers develop theories of *entailment*, so called to distinguish it from the ordinary strict conditional, so that, for example, a contradiction does not entail just anything, and a necessary truth is not entailed by just anything. I claim that the epistemic conditions of inference typically block an inference from a contradiction or to an arbitrary necessary truth. A theory does not need to revise the constitutive conditions to explain the oddness of the 'paradoxes of strict implication'.

Chapter IX returns to the Ramsey test I explained in Chapter VI. I claim that there are conditionals about which we are much more confident than we are about how to employ the Ramsey test. Assuming the if-clause, we have little idea what minimal revision of our beliefs would or should result although there are some conditionals with the same if-clause about which we have no corresponding uncertainty.

Chapter X returns to the theories of possible worlds I outline in Chapter VII. After revealing a potential ambiguity in Leibniz's phrase 'the best of all possible worlds', I try to say something original and useful about the so-called modal realism of David Lewis. This view is, in brief:

> The actual world is the one and only world in which we live and move and have our being. No one who inhabits any of the vast number of other worlds is strictly identical to any of us, no matter how similar, but these worlds are no less real than the single world that is actual from our point of view.

As Lewis quite knew, and calmly accepted, very few are able to accept this view; and I am not one of the few. Philosophers have devoted much effort to responding to Lewis's impressive case for the reasonableness of modal realism. My Chapter X response is relatively short and simple. I describe the theory of modal super-realism. All the more-or-less similar individuals that occupy distinct possible (but real) worlds according to modal realism exist, vastly far apart, in this actual world. The hypothesis of modal super-realism, I claim, works (almost) as well as the hypothesis of modal realism to account for counterfactual conditionals and other modal notions. Difficulties with modal super-realism are therefore also difficulties with modal realism.

Chapters XI to XIV attempt to make a positive contribution to understanding conditionals. This approach grew out of my earlier research interest in temporal asymmetry, causal and explanatory nonsymmetry, and one-way dependence in general. An example of a one-way dependence that is neither causal nor temporal is this: 'Snow is white' is true because snow is white, and not the other way around; snow is not white because 'snow is white' is true. A single example of one-way dependence such as this does not show that the relation in question is asymmetric. The asymmetry of 'explains' requires that in any case whatever, if *A* explains *B*, then *B* does not explain *A*.

The whiteness of snow is a necessary and sufficient condition of the truth of 'snow is white'. The truth of the sentence is not a condition of the color of snow, and thus is neither a necessary nor a sufficient condition. 'Condition of' is a nonsymmetric relation. In this case, it is a one-way relation. I reject the principle that '*A* is a necessary and sufficient condition of *B*' is equivalent to '*B* is a necessary and sufficient condition of *A*', although this is a consequence of the standard treatment of 'necessary condition' and 'sufficient condition'. I claim that the standard treatment of these relations leaves out the actual or possible dependence of the existence or occurrence or nature of *A* on its conditions.

Initially bewildering many students, the standard classroom doctrine also maintains that corresponding sentences of the forms *if p, then q* and *p, only if q*, are equivalent. I say the bewilderment is justified. *p, only if q* typically requires that *q* is a necessary condition of *p*, while *if p, then q* accommodates a wider range of relationships of dependence and independence. The same moral applies to the phrase *if and only if* (see the brief dictionary entry *iff*, Sanford, 1995). Chapter XIII distinguishes several patterns of dependence which might ground a conditional of the form *if p, then q*.

Causation and temporal succession are examples of objective dependence, independent of anyone's beliefs, perceptions, theories, problems, or interests, except, of course, when these things themselves are successively related. Explanations are typically less objective in this way. Admitting that there are several patterns of explanations associated with acceptable conditionals, Chapter XIV defends the view that a pattern of objective dependence itself often grounds a pattern of explanation.

As Chapters VI and VII explain, the argument forms *contraposition* and *hypothetical syllogism* are invalid for ordinary-language conditionals. But many particular instances appear to be perfectly valid. Chapter XV addresses the problem explaining the validity of these instances.

The second edition contains a Supplementary Bibliography that, with a couple of exceptions, covers the period 1987–2002. The additional Bibliographical Remarks function primarily as a guide to the new bibliography. It engages with a few substantial issues briefly without making an attempt to acknowledge, expound, and criticize my own earlier suggestions and much of the most important and influential work about conditionals that appeared since about 1987. There are, of course, many different ways, larger and smaller, I could have started to revise the first edition, especially the Notes. I decided against making any of these because of a combination of wisdom, expediency, uncertainty, and sloth, the relative proportions of which I am ill suited to estimate. The unaltered text of the first edition, pp. 1–265, reappears here.

My thanks, acknowledgements, and intellectual history in the Preface of the First Edition are not repeated here. I am grateful to Jonathan Adler for organizing a session discussing the first edition sponsored by the Association for Informal Logic and Critical Thinking and presented in conjunction with the 1990 Eastern Division Meetings of the American Philosophical Association. The two speakers were philosophers of extraordinary ability, accomplishment, and generosity, Robert Stalnaker and Vann McGee. Stalnaker, 1992, and McGee, 1993, published versions of these contributions, and other a number of other reviews, make points that deserve attention. I would not improve the book, in my opinion, if I lengthened it in response to the criticism I think I can handle and revised it to evade the rest.

I am also grateful to the National Endowment for the Humanities and National Humanities Center during the 1989–90 academic year for enabling me to pursue research on 'Causation and mechanism'. Two results of this research are Sanford, 1994a and 1994b, which I hope bolster my claims about the direction of causation in Chapter XVI.

I dedicated the first edition to three early teachers. The second edition is not revised enough to justify a rededication, but I want anyway to mention two later teachers who had a big effect on me. Norman Malcolm and Max Black did not appear to their graduate students at Cornell to operate as a team, but they did so anyway in at least one respect: they both attempted to pass on philosophical interests, accomplishments, and techniques that flourished at Cambridge University in the first half of the twentieth century. An article by Malcolm that grew out of conversations with Wittgenstein is one of the subjects of Chapter IX. Black is responsible for my interest in W. E. Johnson's treatment of inference (Chapter VIII).

Introduction
Conditionals in Everyday Life
and in Philosophy

A conditional sentence typically has a main clause and at least one if-clause. Often there is just one if-clause. For example:

> If it were done when 'tis done, then 'twere well it were done quickly.
> If our newspaper was delivered this morning, the neighbours' dog took it.
> If happiness is activity in accordance with virtue, it is reasonable that it should be in accordance with the highest virtue.

Conditional sentences with several if-clauses are common.

> If you quit smoking, and if you don't also change your eating and drinking habits, you will probably gain weight.

> Yet, they, should the last scene be there,
> The great stage curtain about to drop,
> If worthy their prominent part in the play,
> Do not break up their lines to weep.

Conditional sentences have received concentrated, if intermittent, theoretical attention since antiquity. The attention during the past forty years has been intense. I shall presently sketch the main developments, early and late, and also discuss how conditionals play central roles in many philosophical theories. In the first part of these introductory remarks, I show how someone with no knowledge of the history of the treatment of conditionals and no prior acquaintance with philosophical topics that lead to

1

an interest in conditionals can still see how conditionals pose a theoretical or philosophical problem. Conditionals play a central role in our everyday thinking about the world and in our deliberating about how we should try to act. One need not have other philosophic concerns to appreciate their importance. One can become puzzled by conditionals without first developing a taste for philosophic puzzles.

Many creatures make their ways in the world without consciously considering any possible alternatives for action. Highly sophisticated and intelligent human activities, for example, rapid, clever conversation, occur unaccompanied by any prior conscious laying of plans about how best to act. People who ponder at length before acting can end up opting for a stupid and disastrous alternative. The practice of deliberation nevertheless continues to enjoy good reputation, and not merely because it appears to be uniquely human. Many projects and accomplishments would be impossible without it.

Deliberation involves the conscious consideration of alternatives for future action. A student entering college and contemplating a career in medicine might consider all the following:

> If I want to be admitted to a good medical school, I have to get decent grades in physics and organic chemistry.
> If I take physics, I need to take calculus first.
> If I go to medical school, I will have to borrow lots of money. On the other hand, I can end up earning much more than a teacher or a musician if I become a doctor.
> If I become a doctor, I will frequently have to go without much sleep, especially during my residency.

The consideration of conditionals like these is essential to deliberation. It will be useful to adopt some terminology for talking about the parts of a conditional sentence.

In a conditional sentence such as:

> If you become a doctor, you will make a lot of money,

the first clause, *you become a doctor*, is often called the *antecedent*, and the second clause, *you will make a lot of money*,

2

is called the *consequent*. Occasionally the old-fashioned grammatical terms *protasis* and *apodosis* are used instead of *antecedent* and *consequent* respectively. With this particular example, and many others, *antecedent* seems to be an appropriate term in two different ways. The antecedent precedes the consequent in the conditional sentence. Moreover, if the sentence is true, what the antecedent is about, your becoming a doctor, will be or would be prior to what the consequent is about, your making a lot of money. If you become a doctor, the sentence suggests, you will become a doctor before making a lot of money. You will make a lot of money as a consequence of practising medicine. The consequent is thus as well-named as the antecedent.

The well-entrenched terms *antecedent* and *consequent* are not likely to be replaced soon in the teaching of elementary logic. They nevertheless can hinder theoretical understanding of conditionals. In the first place, the order of the so-called antecendent and consequent is often reversed in conditional sentences. The order of the clauses in our example can be changed without producing any change in meaning:

You will make a lot of money if you become a doctor.

The antecedent is the clause in the scope of *if*, not necessarily the clause that begins the sentence. In the second place, the terms suggest a thesis that is sometimes explicitly advanced, that a real relation of antecedence or consequence corresponds to the antecedent and consequent clauses of a true conditional sentence.[1] What the consequent describes depends on, is a consequence of, what the antecedent describes. What the antecedent describes comes first. A look at some examples, however, reveals that the order of priority can be reversed:

If I take physics, I need to take calculus first.
If the digital clock display blinks, then the power has been interrupted.
If the annual growth ring of a tree is narrower than normal, the rainfall that year was less than normal.

In the second half of this work, I will devote more attention to the different patterns of dependence that can relate what is described by the clauses of a conditional sentence. The terms *antecedent* and *consequent* are appropriate only to one of several patterns of dependence. These terms have been common in logic and philosophy books for some time, and they occur frequently in this book as well; but I also use some alternative terms that are shorter, more accurate, and less theoretically loaded, namely *if-clause* and *main clause*. An if-clause is a clause in the scope of *if* no matter where it occurs in a conditional sentence. A main clause is one not in the scope of *if*, one that can stand by itself. When one deliberates whether to do so-and-so, one tries to decide, among other things, what will result, what might result, what cannot result, what must come before, and what cannot come before, if one does so-and-so.

A conditional can bear on future action, however, even though neither its if-clause nor its main clause concerns something that is potentially within the agent's control:

If a hurricane hits this beach, as one did in 1955, most of these houses will be destroyed.
If interest rates go up, the market value of a bond declines.

Even though it is not up to you whether a certain beach house is destroyed by a storm or whether a certain bond declines in value, it may be up to you whether you become the owner of the house or bond.

We use conditionals to decide what to do. We also use conditionals to decide what to believe, whether or not the belief is immediately relevant to any prospective alternative for action. Much of our inference from evidence is naturally cast in conditional form. By observing a certain kind of electric clock, one can infer whether or not there has been an interruption in the power. By observing the cross section of a tree, one can infer something about the relative amounts of rainfall in successive seasons past.

All the examples of conditional sentences we have considered so far have been declarative. Non-declarative conditionals are familiar in everyday life and in literature. Commands, requests, advice, and principles of action are often given by conditional imperatives:

4

If you see her, say hello.
If your soil is mostly compacted clay, work in some granulated gypsum.
If music be the food of love, play on.
If anyone would sue you and take your coat, let him have your cloak as well.

Exhortations and questions can be posed in a conditional form:

If the neighbours' dog didn't steal our newspaper, who did?
If I forget thee, O Jerusalem, let my right hand forget her cunning.
If Winter comes, can Spring be far behind?

Non-declarative examples such as these are commonly neglected by theoretical treatments of conditionals, and I shall continue this tradition of negligence. A conditional imperative, after all, seems to pose no vexing problem. I am not advising you, for example, simply to work some granulated gypsum into your soil no matter what. My advice is hypothetical rather than categorical. If the specified condition obtains, that is, your soil is mostly compacted clay, then my advice is operative. Notice that I have just used a declarative conditional to explain the function of a non-declarative conditional.

Questions and imperatives can be sound or silly, appropriate or irrelevant, and so forth. They cannot be true or false. Declarative conditionals, however, like declarative sentences generally, are naturally regarded as being either true or false. This immediately poses a puzzle.

Truths correspond to reality. Falsehoods don't. 'The cat is on the mat' is true if and only if the cat is on the mat. There is no apparent problem in understanding what state of affairs must actually obtain for 'The cat is on the mat' to be true so long as it is obvious in the situation which cat and which mat are being referred to. 'Someone let in the cat' is somewhat more complicated since there may be no particular person referred to by 'someone'. It is still clear enough what kind of situation must obtain if 'Someone let in the cat' is true: Either Tod let in the cat, or Lucy let in the cat, or Charles let in the cat, or. . . . Consider now the conditional 'Someone let in the cat if the cat is on the mat.' What sort of situation or state of affairs makes it true? We know how to draw a picture of a cat on a mat, or a cat not on a mat, and of a mat with no cat on it. How can we draw a picture of a conditional state of affairs: if the cat is on the mat, then such-and-such? Given an event description, an event so described either occurs in a certain vicinity during a certain period, or it does not occur. There is no such thing as the conditional occurrence of an event. Declarative conditional sentences about occurrences are therefore not about conditional occurrences. What are they about? What in the world makes a declarative conditional sentence true?

Theorists who deny that conditionals are literally true or false still have a question to answer about the acceptability of conditionals. We distinguish acceptable from unacceptable conditionals; and if the difference cannot be explained by reference to the distinction between truth and falsehood, it must be explained some other way.

The theoretical problem of accounting for conditionals can thus be motivated independently of prior theoretical concerns. Logic, the philosophy of reasoning, and the philosophy of language, which we have just approached through everyday examples, focus attention on the nature of conditionals. Many philosophical concerns in addition to logic and the philosophy of language, for example, the treatments of causation, freedom, and physical existence, provide additional motivation. Conditional accounts of causation and of freedom occur in consecutive parts of David Hume's *An Inquiry Concerning Human Understanding* (1748). The following passages also illustrate how, in Hume's hands, innocent phrases such as 'that is' and 'or in other words' can effect a startling transition:

Similar objects are always conjoined with similar. Of this we have experience. Suitably to this experience, therefore, we may define a cause to be *an object, followed by another, and where all the objects similar to the first are followed by objects similar to the second.* Or in other words *where, if the first object had not been, the second never had existed.* (Section VII, 'Of the idea of necessary connexion', Part II)

By liberty, then, we can only mean *a power of acting or not acting, according to the determinations of the will*; that is, if we

6

choose to remain at rest, we may; if we choose to move, we also may. Now this hypothetical liberty is universally allowed to belong to every one who is not a prisoner and in chains. (Section VIII, 'Of liberty and necessity', Part I)

Hume is clearly on to something when he introduces these conditionals. The acceptability of a conditional such as 'If Judy tried to jog three miles, then she would – or at least might – have jogged three miles' appears to be necessary for the acceptability of 'Judy could have jogged three miles; she had the power, liberty, and freedom to do it.' Similarly, the acceptability of a conditional such as 'If James had not taken the vitamin C, then his cold symptoms would not have disappeared so quickly' appears to be necessary to the acceptability of 'Taking the vitamin C caused James's cold symptoms to disappear.' Conditional accounts of causation are part of today's philosophical orthodoxy. Although conditional accounts of freedom receive somewhat less attention right at present, they were intensively discussed for much of the century.[2]

Most if not all of the properties we ascribe are dispositional. Solubility, the standard philosophical example, is the disposition to dissolve. If a soluble substance is put in a suitable solute, it dissolves; if an insoluble substance is put in a liquid of the same kind, it does not dissolve. To have a certain property is typically to behave a certain way if the conditions are appropriate. Some philosophers have held that even physical existence is dispositional. A famous statement of the view that came to be known as *phenomenalism* appears in J. S. Mill's *An Examination of Sir William Hamilton's Philosophy* (1865):

I believe that Calcutta exists, though I do not perceive it, and that it would still exist if every percipient inhabitant were suddenly to leave the place, or be struck dead. But when I analyse the belief, all I find in it is, that were these events to take place, the Permanent Possibility of Sensation which I call Calcutta would still remain; that if I were suddenly transported to the banks of the Hoogly, I should still have the sensations which, if now present, would lead me to affirm that Calcutta exists here and now. (Chapter XI, 'The psychological theory of the belief in an external world')

Mill's permanent possibility of sensation is the abiding truth of conditionals relating circumstances of sensing with the character of the resulting sensation. (Note that these conditionals, and also those involved in conditional accounts of causation or freedom, have false if-clauses.)

We shall survey a number of attempts to explain what makes a conditional acceptable or true, whether or not its if-clause is false. The explanations are confined to three historical periods, each marked by original innovation and rapid development in logic generally, not just in the treatment of conditionals. The ancient period consists roughly of the fourth and third centuries BC. The modern period begins in the second half of the nineteenth century and continues – we should like to think – to the present. Separated from these two epochs by long periods of stagnation and decline in logic and the philosophy of logic, the medieval period contains many important logical discoveries and much subtle discussion related to conditionals.

The problems of studying ancient logic and of studying medieval logic are in one respect very different. On one hand, many ancient logical treatises are irretrievably lost. Our information is based on second, third, or fourth-hand reports written hundreds of years after the original work. Many medieval books and manuscripts on logic, on the other hand, are there waiting to be retrieved. As medieval historians keep making new discoveries, the medieval period of logical vigour and invention keeps being lengthened. In their authoritative and judicious *The Development of Logic*, for example, William and Martha Kneale write that 'after about 1380 there is little of interest to report about medieval logic'.[3] In an excellent but much more specialized book, published just twelve years later, another scholar writes that:

> Generally speaking, nothing of interest to the logician was said after 1550 at the very latest. Indeed, now that I have written this book, I have compiled a large list of logic texts for the period 1550–1650 which I shall be happy never to open again. On the other hand, an enormous amount of interesting work remains to be done for the period 1450–1550.[4]

However long the medieval and modern periods of logical vigour are eventually reckoned, it still seems unlikely that the history of logic will ever be regarded as the history of continuous development. There really were some Dark Ages; and, with the exception of Leibniz, the great philosophers from Hobbes to Kant have no claims to greatness because of their contributions to logic.

The next two chapters discuss ancient and medieval treatments of conditionals. Without making any attempt at completeness or scholarly originality, they use historical discussion as the occasion to introduce some basic concepts of logic.[5]

Part One

THE HISTORY OF PHILOSOPHICAL TREATMENTS OF
CONDITIONALS

CHAPTER I

Ancient History

Even the crows on the roofs
caw about the nature of conditionals.

Reflecting on the famous remark of Alfred North Whitehead that 'The safest general characterization of the European philosophical tradition is that it consists of a series of footnotes to Plato',[1] one can experiment by substituting other names for Plato's. Why not Aristotle, or Socrates, or, moving two generations earlier, even 'Father Parmenides', who awed Socrates? I mention the familiar Socrates–Plato–Aristotle succession here in order to draw attention to a less familiar succession of philosophers that descends from Socrates largely independent from the schools of Plato and Aristotle. Thinkers in this other succession did most of the important early work on the theory of conditionals. Plato was not Socrates' only pupil. There was also Euclid of Megara (to be distinguished from the geometer Euclid) who was somewhat older than Plato. Two pupils of Euclid, Eubulides of Miletus and Thrasymachus of Corinth, each had a line of intellectual successors.

Stilpo of Megara was a pupil of Thrasymachus. Zeno of Citium (to be distinguished from Zeno of Elea famed for the paradoxes of motion) was a pupil of Stilpo's and founded a school that conducted its activity on a porch or *stoa*. Stoicism was continued by Zeno's pupil Cleanthes and by Cleanthes' brilliant pupil Chrysippus (*c*. 280–205 BC). Although very little of Chrysippus' abundant work survives, he is credited with major contributions to the theory of conditionals.

Apollonius Cronus was a pupil of Eubulides. Diodorus (died *c*. 307 BC), a pupil of Apollonius, took the name Cronus from his

master and is known as Diodorus Cronus. Diodorus disputed
with his pupil Philo of Megara about the nature of conditionals.
Today two opposing views of conditionals are often called
Philonian and *Diodoran*.

Our main sources of information about the theories of
Chrysippus, Diodorus, and Philo are reports of their views
written hundreds of years later, in the early third century AD, by
Diogenes Laertius, a collector of gossip and legend, and
especially Sextus Empiricus, who had little sympathy with Stoic
logic. Some information is derived from earlier Roman authors
such as Cicero. No early work of Stoic logic survives, and every
attribution of doctrine or authorship is questionable.

Why is it that the early Stoic logicians, rather than Aristotle,
should be credited with the first important contributions to a
theory of conditionals? Aristotle's work in logic, like his
astoundingly inventive and profound work in many other areas,
dominates subsequent intellectual development in the western
world. Aristotle's writing, like the work of most authors who
attempt explicitly to provide reasons for their conclusions, is full
of conditionals. He continually uses conditionals when discussing
logical theory. Here is a typical passage.

If A is predicated of all B, and B of all C, A must be
predicated of all C: We have already explained what we mean
by 'predicated of all'. Similarly also, if A is predicated of no B,
and B of all C, it is necessary that no C will be A. But if the
first term belongs to all the middle, but the middle to none of
the last terms, there will be no syllogism in respect of the
extremes. (*Prior Analytics*, I. 4, 25^{b}37–26^{a}3)

We do not need to understand the details of this argument to see
that Aristotle is concerned with the logic of terms. The term logic
of Aristotle's *Prior Analytics*, more or less elaborated or
simplified, more or less truncated, mangled, or refined, has been
taught for over two thousand years. The standard textbook logic
of terms, justly called Aristotelian logic, has been part of the
curriculum as long as any subject.

A logic of terms deals with arguments such as this one:

All novelists are mortal.

George Eliot is a novelist.
Therefore, George Eliot is mortal.

The terms here, *novelist* and *mortal*, apply to something. That is, they are predicated of something. There are novelists, and there are mortals. Some things are sweet, and some things, namely numbers, are prime; so the terms *sweet* and *prime* also apply to something. Some terms, such as *unicorn*, *greatest prime*, and *good five-cent cigar*, apply to nothing even though they have distinct meanings.

A conditional sentence frame such as *If . . ., then . . .* cannot typically be converted into a complete sentence by filling in the blanks with terms. Although 'If novelist, then mortal', 'If not sour, then too expensive', and 'unhappy if unappreciated' and the like might be understood as complete sentences in certain contexts, they cannot be counted as complete sentences in isolation. In order to convert *If . . ., then . . .* into a complete sentence, one must fill in the blanks with sentences. A look at the conditional-filled passage from Aristotle quoted above reveals that the primary constituents of the conditional sentences are not terms but sentences such as 'A is predicated of no B, and B of all C' and 'There will be no syllogism in respect of the extremes.' Aristotle does not develop a sentential or propositional logic, one that deals with sentences, statements, or propositions as primary constituents of larger compound sentences. The early Stoic logicians did.[2]

The early Stoic logicians, indeed, drew and respected a distinction that generations of later logicians, as well as generations of students who study logic, tend to muddle, the distinction between a conditional statement and an argument. Consider the differences between an argument such as:

Emil has been captured.
Therefore, all is lost,

and the corresponding conditional:

If Emil has been captured, then all is lost.

Someone who really uses the argument, rather than quotes or

15

mentions the argument as I am doing here, asserts both that Emil has been captured and that all is lost. The argument user, moreover, indicates that the true belief that all is lost is supported or justified by the true belief that Emil has been captured. An argument has a conclusion and one or more premises advanced in support of the conclusion, and one who uses an argument asserts the conclusion on the basis of asserting the premises. One who asserts a conditional, in contrast, does not thereby assert either the if-clause or the main clause. One can be confident that a conditional is true while being ignorant of the truth of its constituent clauses and while believing that the constituents are false.

Although the if-clause of an asserted conditional need not be the premise of any argument, many arguments have conditionals as premises. For example:

If Emil has been captured, then all is lost.
Emil has been captured.
Therefore, all is lost.

If Emil has been captured, then all is lost.
All is not lost.
Therefore, Emil has not been captured.

Stoic logicians used ordinal numbers as propositional variables in their representations of forms of arguments such as the following:

1. If the first, then the second.
   The first.
   Therefore, the second.

2. If the first, then the second.
   Not the second.
   Therefore, not the first.

These are two of the five basic, undemonstrated argument forms to which Stoic logicians attached great importance. None of the remaining three forms includes a conditional premise:

3. Not both the first and second.
   The first.
   Therefore, not the second.

16

4. Either the first or the second.
   The first.
   Therefore, not the second.

5. Either the first or the second.
   Not the second.
   Therefore, the first.

Argument form 4, but not argument form 5, requires an exclusive interpretation of 'either . . . or . . .': a statement of this form is true if one or another of its disjuncts is true, false if neither is true or if both are true. The five basic forms have some characteristics in common. Each has two premises. Each involves just two propositional variables. In each, the first premise contains both variables, the second premise uses only one of these variables, and the conclusion uses the other variable. The variables, *the first* and *the second*, are uniformly understood as propositional or sentential, never as variables for terms or predicates.

By using just these five basic forms, one can derive more complicated argument forms; but the five by themselves do not suffice to demonstrate every acceptable argument form in propositional logic. The Stoics claimed that their logic was complete. We know too little about their conception of completeness to judge the correctness of this claim. We also have but partial knowledge of what they counted as an admissible derivation from the five basic forms. They used some second-order principles in addition to the five forms, and the content of at least one of these principles remains a matter for conjecture.[3]

The five basic argument forms might justly be called *basic* without regard to their role in a logical system. They are basic in the sense that the acceptance of arguments of these forms is essential to understanding the logical connectives the forms use. If someone does not see that the conclusion of our first exemplar argument about the capture of Emil really does follow from the premises, this person does not understand conditional sentences. An understanding of conditionals requires accepting arguments of the first two basic kinds.

While discussing Stoic logic, Diogenes Laertius defines an invalid argument as one such that the denial of the conclusion is compatible with the conjunction of the premises (*Lives*, VII, 77).

17

A valid argument is one such that the denial of the conclusion is incompatible with the conjunction of the premises. Some logicians define validity by reference to form, and some require a relevant connection between premises and conclusion. Although these and other logicians have demanded more of deductive validity than did the Stoics, none has demanded less. No one counts an argument as valid that does not satisfy the Stoic definition of validity.

The first argument about Emil is valid because the conjunction of its premises:

If Emil was captured, then all is lost; and Emil was captured,

is incompatible with the denial of the conclusion:

All is not lost.

It is impossible that the premises should all be true while the conclusion is false. The Stoics explicitly recognized that an argument's validity does not suffice for the truth of its conclusion. A valid argument may have one or more false premises, in which case its conclusion may be true or false. A valid argument with all true premises, on the other hand, must have a true conclusion. This principle is the essence of the notion of validity.

Although the Stoics did not define validity by reference to form, they did develop the notion of a valid argument form. An argument form is not itself an argument because its constituents are not statements. 'If the first, then the second', for example, is not a conditional statement. It expresses, rather, a form that different conditional arguments can share. Once the form of an argument is abstracted from its content, arguments with different subject matters can be seen to have exactly the same form. A valid form is such that any argument with this form is a valid argument. The essence of the notion of a valid argument form is the principle that any argument with a valid form is a valid argument.[4]

While the Stoics, unlike many of their successors, interpreters, and translators, always distinguished between conditional statements and arguments, they kept in mind a close connection between the two. Given any argument, one can form the

18

corresponding conditional statement by conjoining all the premises as the antecedent or if-clause of the conditional and taking the conclusion as the main clause or consequent. Several times Sextus Empiricus attributes to the Stoics the view that an argument is valid if the corresponding conditional is true. For example:

> So then, an argument is really valid when, after we have conjoined the premises and formed the conditional having the conjunction of the premises as antecedent and the conclusion as consequent, it is found that this conditional is true. (*Adversus Mathematicos*, VIII, 417, Mates translation)

The plausibility of this contention turns on one's account of what constitutes the truth of a conditional. According to Sextus, the Stoics disagreed with each other on this topic:

> For Philo says that a true conditional is one which does not have a true antecedent and a false consequent; for example, when it is day and I am conversing, 'If it is day, then I am conversing'; but Diodorus defines it as one which neither is nor ever was capable of having a true antecedent and a false consequent. According to him, the conditional just mentioned seems to be false, since when it is day and I have become silent, it will have a true antecedent and a false consequent; but the following conditional seems true: 'If atomic elements of things do not exist, then atomic elements of things do exist,' since it will always have the false antecedent, 'Atomic elements of things do exist.' And those who introduce connection or coherence say that a conditional holds whenever the denial of its consequent is incompatible with its antecedent; so, according to them, the above-mentioned conditionals do not hold, but the following is true: 'If it is day, then it is day.' And those who judge by 'suggestion' declare that a conditional is true if its consequent is in effect included in its antecedent. According to these, 'If it is day, then it is day,' and every repeated conditional will probably be false, for it is impossible for a thing itself to be included in itself. (*Outlines of Pyrrhonism*, II, 110–12)

Sextus arranges these four accounts of the conditional in order of increasing strength. Philo's account, the weakest, treats conditionals as truth-functional. A truth-functional compound is so called because its truth value is a function of the truth values of its components. On a truth-functional account of conjunction, for example, a conjunction is true exactly when all its component conjuncts are true; if any conjunct is false, the whole conjunction is false. There is only one plausible two-value truth-functional account of the conditional, exactly the one Philo gives. Any conditional with a false main clause and a true if-clause is false. Any conditional not false for this reason is true. Thus any conditional with a true main clause is true, and any conditional with a false if-clause is true.

On Philo's truth-functional interpretation of the conditional, the Stoic principle connecting the validity of an argument with the truth of the corresponding conditional is unacceptable. No logician holds that the truth of a conclusion, or the falsity of at least one premise, suffices for the validity of an argument. Suppose, for the sake of the example, that Emil did not win the lottery. Then on Philo's account, any conditional is true in which 'Emil did not win the lottery' is the main clause. But we want to deny that every argument is valid which has 'Emil did not win the lottery' as the conclusion just because, as it happens, Emil did not win the lottery. Consider the following argument:

If Emil did not buy a ticket, Emil did not win the lottery.
But Emil did buy a ticket.
Therefore, Emil did not win the lottery.

This argument does not meet the minimal requirement for validity. The denial of its conclusion is perfectly compatible with the conjunction of its premises.

Philo's account of the conditional is nevertheless useful in explaining the validity of valid conditional arguments. There is this important similarity: a true Philonian conditional never has a true if-clause and a false main clause, and a valid argument never has true premises and a false conclusion. Consider again the Stoics' first basic argument form:

20

If the first, then the second.
The first.
Therefore, the second.

Given Philo's account of the conditional, we can see why it is impossible for any argument of this form to have true premises and a false conclusion. Suppose, for the purpose of a *reductio*, that there was such an argument. Then the first is true, since, by hypothesis, both premises are true; and the second is false, since the conclusion is false. But if the first is true and the second false, then the conditional premise is false, which violates the original supposition that both premises are true. In the same manner, we can demonstrate the validity of the second argument form.

Invalidity can be demonstrated as easily as validity. Look back at the argument concerning the lottery. Whether or not Emil did in fact win the lottery, the following conjunction is logically consistent: Emil did buy a ticket, and he did win the lottery. When this possibility is realized, the conditional 'If Emil did not buy a ticket, Emil did not win the lottery' is true on Philo's interpretation since its if-clause is false. The other premise, 'Emil did buy a ticket', is true; and the conclusion, 'Emil did not win the lottery', is false. Thus it is possible for the premises to be true when the conclusion is false.

At this point I shall abandon the Stoic practice of using numbers as propositional variables and adopt the currently common practice of using letters instead.[5] Several theoretically important argument forms are valid on Philo's account of the conditional. One is now called *contraposition*:

If P, then Q.
Therefore, if not Q, then not P.

Here 'not P' is a standard way of writing 'It is not the case that P.' 'Not P' is true if and only if 'P' is false, false if and only if 'P' is true. The if-clause of the conclusion is true and the main clause false only if 'Q' is false and 'P' is true. But in that case, the if-clause of the premise is true when the main clause is false. The only combination of truth-value assignments to the propositional components that makes the conclusion false, on the Philonian interpretation, also makes the premise false. Therefore, there is no way for the conclusion to be false when the premise is true; so any argument of this form is valid.

Another important argument form is:

If *P*, then *Q*.
If *Q*, then *R*.
Therefore, if *P*, then *R*.

Of the several names this form has, *chain argument* is least likely to mislead. Another name, *hypothetical syllogism*, sometimes has a much broader sense in translations of ancient logicians. *Transitivity* is also the name of a property of some two-place relations. The argument form, however designated, comes out valid on Philo's interpretation. The conclusion can be false only if '*P*' is true and '*R*' is false. In that case, it is impossible for both premises to be true. If '*Q*' is true, then the second premise is false. But, if '*Q*' is not true but false, the first premise is false.

Augmenting the antecedent or *if-clause expansion* is also valid:

If *P*, then *Q*.
Therefore, if *P* and *R*, then *Q*.

The only circumstance in which the conclusion is false, '*P*' and '*R*' both true when '*Q*' is false, also makes the premise false.

The Stoics called second-order logical principles *themata* (singular: *thema*). A valid first-order principle licenses inference from one or more statements to a new statement. If all the first statements, the premises, are true, the new statement, the conclusion, is also true. A valid thema licenses passage from one or more arguments to a new argument. If all arguments in the first group are valid, the new argument is also valid. Calling a thema *valid* extends the sense of the term since it indicates the preservation of validity rather than the preservation of the truth. A new set of terms parallel to *argument*, *inference*, *premise*, *conclusion*, and *valid* would be useful in discussing themata, but so far none has been suggested.[6]

One thema developed by the Stoics that figures prominently in many modern systems of propositional logic is the principle of *conditionalization* or the rule of *conditional proof*:

The argument from certain premises X together with the premise P to the conclusion Q is valid.

Therefore, the argument from premises X to the conclusion *if P,Q* is valid.

Here the symbol 'X' stands for any number of premises or assumptions including the limiting case of zero assumptions. (When a system of logic is organized by themata, a valid proof from zero assumptions proves a theorem, a statement that is true in virtue of just the second-order logical rules.) Conditionalization is closely connected with the argument form called *exportation*. A conditional with a conjunctive if-clause implies a conditional with a conditional main clause:

If P and Q, then R.
Therefore, if P, then if Q, then R.

On the Philonian interpretation of the conditional, the conclusion is false only if 'P' and 'Q' are both true when 'R' is false; and in that case the premise is also false. One can derive the principle of conditionalization by moving from an argument to its corresponding conditional, applying exportation, and moving from the resulting conditional back to the corresponding argument, as follows:

X and P. Therefore, Q.
If X and P, then Q.
If X, then if P, then Q.
X. Therefore, if P, then Q.

Here, as an example, is a use of conditionalization to derive an instance of contraposition from an instance of the Stoics' second basic argument form:

The argument from *if the solution is acidic, then the litmus paper turned red* and *the litmus paper did not turn red* to *the solution is not acidic* is valid.

Therefore, the argument from *if the solution is acidic, then the litmus paper turned red* to *if the litmus paper did not turn red, then the solution is not acidic* is valid.

23

Philo's truth-functional interpretation of the conditional can also show an invalid argument form to be invalid by assigning truth values to the component propositions to make the premises true when the conclusion is false. The assignment of 'Q' true and 'P' false does this for the form called *invalid conversion*:

If P, then Q.
Therefore, if Q, then P.

Given Philo's interpretation of the conditional, we can modify the Stoic principle connecting the validity of an argument with the truth of the corresponding conditional as follows: an argument is valid if and only if the corresponding conditional is necessarily true. The third view of conditionals Sextus lists needs no such modification:

And those who introduce connection or coherence say that a conditional holds whenever the denial of its consequent is incompatible with its antecedent.

Scholars attribute this view to Chrysippus. Given our earlier explanation of argument validity, we can use the notion of validity to restate the interpretation of the conditional that Chrysippus offers: a conditional is true if and only if it corresponds to a valid argument.

Philo's truth-functional account of the conditional does not require any connection or relevance between the if-clause and the main clause for a conditional to be true. On the interpretation of Chrysippus, the mere truth of the main clause or the mere falsity of the if-clause is not enough. Compare the first example below from Sextus with another conditional with the same subject matter:

If atomic elements of things do not exist, then atomic elements of things do exist.
If atomic elements of things do not exist, then nothing exists that is an atomic element of a thing.

Suppose, with the ancient authors in question, that there are atomic elements of things. On this supposition, the if-clauses of these two conditionals have the same truth value, namely falsehood. On the Philonian interpretation, then, both are true since neither has a true if-clause together with a false main clause. On the interpretation of Chrysippus, however, the first conditional is false. The denial of the main clause is not incompatible with the if-clause. Indeed, it is the if-clause. In the second conditional, on the other hand, the main clause merely paraphrases the if-clause; so its denial is incompatible with the if-clause. (On the fourth and final view listed by Sextus, the second conditional here would still not be true. Like the example Sextus gives, 'If it is day, it is day', the if-clause, being identical to the main clause, does not properly contain the main clause. This view of conditionals was probably originated by Peripatetic critics of Stoic logic. I will not discuss this view further because I think no modern view resembles it.)

The modal notion of *incompatibility* distinguishes the account of Chrysippus from Philo's truth-functional account. The modal notions of *incompatibility*, *compatibility*, *necessity*, and *possibility* are mutually interdefinable by means of negation:

P and Q are incompatible = it is not possible that both P and Q.
P and Q are incompatible = it is necessary that not both P and Q.
It is necessary that P = it is not possible that not P.
It is possible that P = it is not necessary that not P.

We can express the relation between the interpretations of the conditional by Philo and Chrysippus as follows: a conditional is true, on the interpretation of Chrysippus, if and only if the corresponding Philonian conditional is necessarily true.

The patterns of interdefinability between *necessary*, *possible*, *incompatible*, and so forth do not in general help one decide whether a particular Philonian conditional is necessarily true. 'If the litmus paper turns red, then the solution is acidic' certainly is not logically necessary. The conditional sentence itself does not even specify what the relation is between the litmus paper and the solution: if the litmus paper turns red immediately after being saturated with the solution, then the solution is acidic. Although this is still not a logical truth, not all necessity is logical necessity. One could maintain that the Philonian conditional is true of causal or physical or chemical necessity. The stringency of the requirement

25

for the truth of a Chrysippus conditional depends on the strictness of the variety of necessity employed.

Philosophers and logicians in this century have studied a variety of Chrysippus conditionals and the relations between them extensively. I will postpone discussions of the difficulties with the interpretations of Chrysippus and of Philo to later chapters.

The interpretations of Philo and Chrysippus give the same answers to most of the questions concerning the validity and invalidity of argument forms that have been treated in this chapter. One exception is exportation and the related thema of conditionalization. Any conditional of the form:

If *P* and *Q*, then *P*,

will be true on the interpretation of Chrysippus. *Not P*, the denial of the main clause, is clearly incompatible with the if-clause, *P and Q*. By exportation, one could infer:

If *P*, then if *Q*, then *P*.

The main clause here is the conditional *if Q, then P*. Does it pass the test of Chrysippus merely because *P* happens to be true? Sextus represents the third view of conditionals as introducing a connection between the if-clause and main clause of a true conditional. If mere joint truth of otherwise unrelated clauses were sufficient for the truth of the conditional, this attempt to require an additional connection would be superfluous. No matter how loosely *incompatible* is understood, however, it will not be true in general that *not P* is incompatible with *Q* simply because *P* is true.

We can put this point in terms of conditionalization by reference to the following argument, in which the second premise is superfluous:

P.
Q.
Therefore, *P*,

26

is a valid argument form. By conditionalization, then, the following argument form would also be valid:

P.
Therefore, if *Q*, then *P*.

But the truth of *P* is insufficient for the truth of the conditional conclusion, on the interpretation of Chrysippus. Even though *P* is in fact true, it might be possible for *Q* to be true while *P* is false.

Chrysippus was probably aware of the debate between Philo and Diodorus. Although Diodorus was Philo's teacher, that does not preclude the possibility that Philo developed a view of conditionals first to which his teacher later responded. Diodorus appears, like Chrysippus, to give a modal account of the conditional.

But Diodorus defines it as one which neither is nor ever was capable of having a true antecedent and a false consequent.

The modal word here is *capable*. At first sight, the temporal qualification *neither is nor ever was* is puzzling. It is known on other evidence that Diodorus had a theory of modality that connects necessity and possibility with time. Epictetus sketches the so-called Master Argument of Diodorus. Diodorus argued that the following three propositions are jointly inconsistent:

(1) Every proposition about the past is necessary.
(2) An impossible proposition may not follow from a possible one.
(3) There is a proposition which is possible, but which neither is true nor will be true.

Diodorus then argued from the first two to the denial of (3). Cleanthes, on the other hand, argued from (2) and (3) to the denial of (1); and Chrysippus from (1) and (3) to the denial of (2). No one, apparently, questioned the contention that (1), (2), and (3) cannot all be true, but the nature of the argument Diodorus had for asserting this incompatibility must remain a matter of conjecture. Connections between modality and time, at any rate, are clear enough in proposition (1) and the denial of (3). According to the denial of (3), any possible proposition either is true or will be true. This suggests the following paraphrase of Diodorus' account of the conditional:

A true conditional is one that does not, never did, and never will have a true antecedent and a false consequent.

In other words, 'a conditional holds in the Diodorean sense if and only if it holds *at all times* in the Philonian sense'.[7] This account makes good enough sense when the propositional components of the conditional in question admit an additional temporal qualification. With the example Sextus gives, 'If it is day, then I am conversing', one can first convert this into a propositional form:

If it is day at time *t*, then I am conversing at time *t*.

There are as many temporally explicit instances of this form as there are ways to fill in the temporal variable *t*. The original conditional satisfies Diodorus' requirements if each such temporal specification satisfies Philo's requirements for a true conditional. This view still does not require that there be some genuine connection between the states of affairs mentioned by the if-clause and main clause. 'If most Americans have seen television, then some great Irish writers have lived in exile' is presumably counted as true because there is no time when the if-clause is true and the main clause false. Some great Irish writers lived in exile before television became common in America.

It is not obvious how to apply the Diodorean interpretation to conditionals having components such as 'Dogs never climb trees', 'I am conversing at noon on 4 July 1984', and 'From time to time in the summer, one can see northern lights (the aurora borealis) in the northern United States' that do not admit additional temporal qualification. Perhaps Diodorus would treat conditionals with such components just as Philo would treat them.

While there are later echoes of the Diodorean conditional,

many logicians, both medieval and modern, adopted a view of conditionals virtually identical with that of Chrysippus. It is somewhat controversial to what extent medieval logicians had the notion of the Philonian conditional, but there is no doubt that a philosopher in the nineteenth century rediscovered it, and that today almost every elementary logic textbook presents it as a useful account of the conditional.

CHAPTER II

Medieval and Post-medieval History

Boethius (470–524) provides an important link between the logic of antiquity including the propositional logic of the Stoics and medieval Europe before the recovery of Aristotle's logical writings. There is not much innovation in Boethius' treatment of conditionals, but one feature is interesting because it presages further developments.

The drawing of distinctions is common in Aristotle, in the kind of philosophy we now call scholastic, and in much contemporary philosophy. The Stoics, so far as we can understand, did not distinguish between different kinds of conditionals. They distinguished rather between different treatments of conditionals, treatments they regarded as mutual rivals. If one was adequate, as a general account of conditionals, the others were inadequate. A more scholastic approach to these different treatments would devise a scheme of differentiation so that one treatment applies to one variety of conditional, another treatment to another, and so on. Boethius initiates this practice in the discussion of conditionals by distinguishing between true conditionals that involve a necessary connection and those that do not.

The term *consequentia*, which Boethius used, was also used by many other writers in a variety of senses. For Boethius, different kinds of conditionals display different kinds of *following from* or *consequentia*. For Abelard, the conditionals themselves are *consequentiae*. And, in the theories of *consequentiae* advanced in the thirteenth and fourteenth centuries, the term becomes more general.[1]

The Stoics, distinguishing clearly between arguments and conditional statements, could advance theses of the form:

30

An argument is . . . if and only if the corresponding conditional is. . . .

According to the particular instance they advanced, an argument is *valid* if and only if the corresponding conditional is *true*. We have also discussed a version that correlates validity with the necessary truth of the corresponding conditional. We can also formulate other versions of the thesis to relate special kinds of validity with special ways in which a conditional can be true. All versions require a clear distinction between an argument or inference on one hand and the corresponding conditional statement on the other hand. Most medieval treatments of *consequentiae* ignore this distinction. A *consequentia* seems sometimes to be a conditional statement, sometimes an inference, and sometimes a relation, *following from*, between statements. Although we take our terms *antecedent* and *consequent* from medieval writers, often these terms are more naturally translated into current idiom as 'premise' and 'conclusion'. (These days, an antecedent is always an if-clause of a conditional.)

When I discuss a medieval distinction between two kinds of *consequentiae*, I shall often treat it as a distinction between two kinds of conditionals. Even when a strong scholarly case can be made for regarding a certain writer's discussion as distinguishing kinds of inferences rather than kinds of conditional statements, there will always be a distinction to be drawn in the one realm whenever a distinction can be drawn in the other. Since *consequentia* is a more general term than any currently in use, since it covers conditionals, and since conditionals is our topic, I will tend to treat *consequentiae* as conditionals.

Peter Abelard (1079–1142), a writer who had enormous influence for several centuries over the development of logic, drew several distinctions that current theorists still regard as important. While Abelard required some kind of necessary connection between if-clause and main clause for the truth of a conditional, he recognized several ways such a connection could obtain. A perfect conditional is one true in virtue of its formal structure. These are not Abelard's examples, but they illustrate his point:

If no cats are vegetarians, then no vegetarians are cats.

If neither Kate nor Daria answered the phone, then the phone was not answered by Kate.

The truth of these conditionals is completely independent of their subject matter. We can represent the forms of these two statements as follows:

If no As are Bs, then no Bs are As.
If not (*P* or *Q*), then not *P*.

The point does not require the use of any special symbols for logical terms, although the use of special symbols is common in current logic courses. The use of variables, on the other hand, is implicit in the notion of formal structure. Whatever terms we substitute uniformly for the term variables A and B in the first example, the resulting conditional will be true. Whatever declarative sentences we substitute uniformly for the sentence variables *P* and *Q* in the second example, the resulting conditional will be true. Notice that when we mechanically substitute 'Kate answered the phone' and 'Daria answered the phone' for the variables, we do not recover exactly the original conditional sentence but a cumbersome paraphrase of it. Such is the price of generality. A less general representation of the original, one that uses name variables and a verb variable, can remain much closer to its grammatical structure:

If neither *a* nor *b* Φ-ed the *c*, then the *c* was not Φ-ed by *a*.

Given any instance of this, the necessary connection between if-clause and main clause is still purely a matter of form.

Abelard's example of a true conditional that is not a perfect conditional is:

If Socrates is a human, then Socrates is an animal.

We can represent its form, like the form of most sentences, in several ways:

If *P*, then *Q*.
If *a* is G, then *a* is H.

But no sentence is true purely in virtue of having one of these forms. Some instances are true and some are false. A perfect conditional is an instance of a form that has only true instances.

If we simply replace 'Socrates' with a name variable, we get a sentence form that has only true instances:

If *a* is a human, than *a* is an animal.

This fails to show that the original conditional is true purely in virtue of its form because we are not to count 'human' and 'animal' as purely formal or logical words. Why are we not so to count them? The relevant distinction between logical and non-logical words is easy enough to learn, but it is difficult to explain without begging the questions at issue. One line of explanation identifies the non-logical with the more or less specialized and thus the logical with the completely unspecialized or general. 'Human' and 'animal' are non-logical because their application to the world depends on how the world happens to be. 'If', 'and', 'not', 'some', 'all', and so forth are useful in talking about any subject matter whatsoever. If there is anything to say, logical words will be useful to say it. We can avoid the use of whole families of non-logical words, on the other hand, merely by changing the subject.

However the distinction between logical and non-logical words is best explained, one should not regard Abelard's example as true purely in virtue of its logical form. In order to reveal the formal connection between the original if-clause and main clause, the if-clause must be expanded by adding the necessary truth that humans are animals:

If Socrates is a human and all humans are animals, then Socrates is an animal.

This is a perfect conditional; it has a form, expressible by only logical words plus variables, such that every instance of the form is true. Since this conditional is necessarily true, and since it is derived from the original conditional by incorporating in the if-clause the necessary truth that all humans are animals, the original, imperfect, conditional is also necessarily true.

Abelard's procedure here involves reference to something that the original conditional sentence under consideration does not explicitly mention. More elaborate treatments of conditionals by his medieval successors also have this feature, and it is prominent in many twentieth-century accounts of conditionals.

William Ockham (*c.* 1295–1349) drew three pairs of distinctions between *consequentiae*. One of them, between conditionals that hold by extrinsic means and those that hold by intrinsic means, closely resembles Abelard's distinction between perfect and imperfect conditionals. *Extrinsic* here means 'extrinsic to the subject matter of the conditional'. The truth of a conditional true purely in virtue of its logical form has nothing intrinsically to do with what the conditional is about. We can transform a conditional that holds by intrinsic means into one that holds by extrinsic means by conjoining an additional statement *S* to the if-clause. The content of *S* is related to – is intrinsic to – the content of the other clauses of the conditional. What requirements must a statement *S* satisfy to be appropriate to use to show that a conditional holds by intrinsic means? Any theory that treats conditionals by reference to something the original sentence does not explicitly mention should address a question like this. Medieval authors did not pose such questions explicitly; and later authors, when they did, found it surprisingly difficult to provide adequate answers. Ockham appears to have required that the extra statements be true and provide a second premise of a valid categorical syllogism in which the if-clause is the other premise and the main clause is the conclusion. If Ockham's conditionals that hold by intrinsic means are much the same as Abelard's imperfect conditionals, then *S* must not merely be true, but necessarily true. If the logical form of the argument to which the expanded conditional corresponds must be a categorical syllogism, the notion of intrinsic means is as limited as the theory of categorical syllogisms. Although it is natural to think that 'If these are the tracks of a bear, then these are the tracks of a mammal' holds in virtue of the truth that all bears are mammals, the argument from 'All bears are mammals' and 'These are the tracks of a bear' to 'These are the tracks of a mammal' is difficult to represent as a valid categorical syllogism. The nineteenth-century logician DeMorgan referred to arguments of this form to point out a limitation of traditional term logic.

Another distinction of Ockham's is between formal and

material conditionals. 'Material conditional' is the currently common term for the Philonian conditional, and this twentieth century use of 'material' is historically connected with the medieval use; but Ockham's *material conditional* is quite different from a Philonian conditional.

Two consequences of the standard account of validity, consequences that still seem troublesome and unacceptable to some theorists, were explicitly accepted by Ockham. The necessary follows from anything. Anything follows from the impossible. For if an argument *P, therefore C* is valid if and only if it is impossible that *P and not C*, that is, if and only if it is necessary that *not both P and not C*, then the necessity of *C* alone or the impossibility of *P* alone is sufficient to satisfy the requirement of validity. If it is impossible that *P*, then it is impossible that *P and not C*, no matter what *C* happens to be, no matter how irrelevant and unconnected *C* and *P* appear to be. Similarly, if it is necessary that *C*, then it is necessary that *not both P and not C*, no matter what *P* happens to be. The corresponding point holds for conditionals on either Philo's or Chrysippus' interpretations. Any conditional with a necessary main clause is true. Any conditional with an impossible if-clause is true.

Ockham's material conditionals are those that are true for one of these two reasons but that are not true by either extrinsic or intrinsic means. They are not true by intrinsic means because no reference to an unmentioned extra truth is required to explain their truth. They are not true by extrinsic means because the impossibility of the if-clause, or the necessity of the main clause, is not due purely to logical form. It is due, rather, to the subject matter, the subject *material*, of the clause. 'Man is an ass' and 'God exists' are Ockham's examples of materially impossible and materially necessary statement.

Scholars disagree about whether Ockham recognized and accepted a truth-functional Philonian conditional.[2] We should distinguish this question from the related question whether Ockham's views commit him to accepting the Philonian conditional. Ockham distinguished between conditionals that are simple, or absolute, and those that are *ut nunc*, 'as of now'. When a true conditional is simple, the if-clause can never be true when the main clause is false. When a conditional holds as of now, it is possible that sometime the if-clause is true when the main clause is false, but this combination of truth and falsity is not possible now. It appears that an as-of-now conditional resembles a conditional that holds by intrinsic means except that the extra truth *S* relevant to intrinsic means is typically (or always) a necessary truth while the extra statement *S* in the other case is a contingent truth, one that is true now but is not always true. Ockham's example of an as-of-now conditional is 'If every animal runs, then Socrates runs', asserted at a time when Socrates is alive. The current existence of the animal Socrates links the clauses of the conditional. On this understanding of the conditional statement, it is false when there is no animal around named 'Socrates'.

Again, one wants to know just what requirements a current truth *S* must satisfy to be appropriate for defending an as-of-now conditional. Suppose that the main clause *Q* of a conditional *if P, then Q* is true. Can we take *Q* itself as *S*? If not, what about *either Q or not P* or *not both not Q and P*? One can ask analogous questions about the if-clause *P* when it happens to be false. Can we take the truth *not P* as *S*? If not, what again about *either Q or not P* or *not both not Q and P*? Can Ockham avoid saying that any conditional with a false if-clause or a true main clause, if it is not simple, at least holds as of now? Ockham seems not to have asked himself such a question, and it is not obvious how he would answer it if he had.

Other writers made similar but distinguishable classifications of *consequentiae*. One such writer, through no apparent deviousness or deception on his part, today suffers the indignity of being called 'Pseudo-Scotus'. A 1639 edition by Luke Wadding of John Duns Scotus (1266–1308) contains many works no longer attributed to Duns Scotus. Some extraordinarily clever logical writings, now believed to be by someone other than Scotus, are attributed to Pseudo-Scotus.[3] It is not known whether he influenced Ockham or whether Ockham influenced him.

Pseudo-Scotus presented some tricky difficulties for the standard definitions of validity. Many modern thinkers would agree that, if a one-premise argument is valid, then it is impossible for the premise to be true and the conclusion false. The following example of Pseudo-Scotus, however, is evidently valid even though it appears not to satisfy this requirement:

Every proposition is affirmative.
Therefore, no proposition is negative.

Since the statement 'No proposition is negative' is itself a negative statement, it cannot possibly be true. On the other hand, although 'Every proposition is affirmative' is actually false, it is not necessarily false. It seems to be possible that this statement should be true. But the following principle of modal logic is difficult to reject:

If it is possible that P and impossible that Q, then it is possible that both P and not Q.

Thus, if the premise of an argument is possible and its conclusion impossible, the conjunction of the premise with the denial of the conclusion is possible. Nevertheless, when we look back at the original argument, the initial appearance of validity persists. In some sense, clearly, it is impossible for the premise to hold without the conclusion holding as well. This example of Pseudo-Scotus evidently demands a distinction of a sort we often neglect.

Once a puzzle is formulated, it is usually easy to produce more of the same kind. The notions of *positive* and *negative* are inessential to the basic puzzle of Pseudo-Scotus. Here is a variation:

No sentence beginning with 'Therefore' consists of exactly an odd number of words.
Therefore, no sentence beginning with 'Therefore' consists of exactly eleven words.

As before, we construct the conclusion to serve as its own counterexample. And as before, even though the premise happens to be false, it is possible for it to be true.

At this point it is natural to distinguish the possibility of a statement's being true from the possibility of the world's being such as the statement says it to be. It is possible, one wants to say, that there should be no negative propositions and no sentences beginning with 'Therefore' exactly eleven words long even though it is not possible that the sentences serving as the conclusions of our sample arguments are true. Pseudo-Scotus considers another account of validity that attempts to respect this distinction. If a one-premise argument is valid, then it is impossible for things to be as signified by the premise without also being as signified by the conclusion. The difficulty with this, according to Pseudo-Scotus, is that we would count as valid any argument with 'No chimera is a goat-stag' as a premise, because the non-existence of chimeras makes it impossible for things to be as signified by the premise. To modern eyes, the definition of validity looks better than the theory of signification to which the alleged difficulty appeals.

Pseudo-Scotus considers a third definition of validity, one that handles all the examples considered so far. A one-premise argument is valid if and only if it is impossible that the premise and conclusion be formulated together, and the premise be true while the conclusion is false.[4] The first example satisfies this definition, for the formulation of the conclusion 'No proposition is negative' precludes the truth of the premise 'Every proposition is affirmative.' The second example satisfies the definition in the same way. Pseudo-Scotus, however, presents yet another difficulty.

God exists.
Therefore, this argument is not valid.

One who is unwilling to assume with Pseudo-Scotus that the premise is true, indeed, necessarily true, may substitute another necessarily true premise. Is this argument valid or not? If it is valid, then, since it has a true premise, it has a true conclusion. But if the conclusion, which says that the argument is not valid, is true, the argument is not valid. So if the argument is valid, it is not valid. Therefore, it is not valid. But now consider what follows from the assumption that it is not valid. Since the conclusion says that the argument is not valid, if the argument *is* not valid, the conclusion is true. But, if this conclusion is true, it has no possibility of not being true. An argument in which the conclusion has no possibility of not being true is valid. So, if the argument is not valid, it is valid. If it is not valid, it is; and if it is, it is not.

Before inventing some variations of this paradox, it will be useful to introduce some technical terms. I do not know who is responsible for introducing these Latin terms, which writers these days often profess to dislike. Despite these professions of dislike, the terms continue to appear in the latest logic textbooks.

Modus ponendo ponens, the mood that by affirming affirms, is the first basic argument form of the Stoics. Alternatively, it is any argument of that form:

If *P*, *Q*.
P.
Therefore, *Q*.[5]

The two-word term *modus ponens* is always an abbreviation for *modus ponendo ponens*. Similarly, *modus tollens* is always an abbreviation for *modus tollendo tollens*, the mood that by denying denies. This is the second basic argument form of the Stoics, or, alternatively, any argument of that form:

If *P*, *Q*.
Not *Q*.
Therefore, not *P*.

Two more of the basic argument forms of the Stoics also have names in this cumbersome system. *Modus tollendo ponens*, the mood that by denying affirms, is these days more commonly known as *disjunctive syllogism*:

P or *Q*.
Not *P*.
Therefore, *Q*.

Modus ponendo tollens, the mood that by affirming denies, is not so obviously valid as the other three:

P or *Q*.
P.
Therefore, not *Q*.

This requires that 'or' be understood exclusively. An exclusive disjunction is true if and only if exactly one of its disjuncts is true. The case for the existence of the exclusive 'or' in English is difficult to make. If, upon being told 'Henry proposed to Julia or he proposed to Alice', we are confident that Henry did not propose both to Julia and to Alice, our confidence is due to assumptions we make, with more or less justification, about Henry. It is not due to our somehow figuring out that 'or' is being used in an exclusive sense. A safer, and these days much more common, version of *modus ponendo tollens* bypasses the issue whether there is a natural-language sense of 'or' such that '*P* or *Q*' implies 'not both *P* and *Q*'. It simply replaces the disjunction with a negated conjunction:

Not both *P* and *Q*.
P.
Therefore, not *Q*.

Two invalid argument forms that have a superficial resemblance to *modus ponens* and *modus tollens* also have traditional names. The *fallacy of affirming the consequent* is, or has, the form:

If *P*, *Q*.
Q.
Therefore, *P*.

Outrageous example: If a bolt of lightning kills you tomorrow, you won't live to be 125 years old. You won't live to be 125 years old. Therefore, a bolt of lightning will kill you tomorrow. Although no one would buy this argument, not everyone would immediately reject another example of exactly the same form: If he is a Communist sympathizer, he disapproves of our policy in Central America. And he does disapprove of our policy in Central America. Therefore he is a Communist sympathizer.

The fallacy of denying the antecedent is, or has, the form:

If *P*, *Q*.
Not *P*.
Therefore, not *Q*.

If you have back surgery, the pain in your left leg will be relieved. But you will not have back surgery. Therefore, the pain in your left leg will not be relieved. As before, a more outrageous example shows the invalidity of the argument form more vividly:

If you suddenly inherit ten million dollars, then you can afford to buy a pound of tea. But you will not suddenly inherit ten million dollars. Therefore, you cannot afford to buy a pound of tea.

In the following variations on the puzzle argument of Pseudo-Scotus, we shall use these common technical terms for simple valid and invalid forms of argument in which one premise is a conditional:

> If this argument is not valid, then it is not of the form *modus tollens*.
> This argument is not of the form *modus tollens*.
> Therefore, this argument is not valid.

> If this argument is not valid, then it commits the fallacy of affirming the consequent.
> This argument does commit the fallacy of affirming the consequent.
> Therefore, this argument is not valid.

> If this argument is of the form *modus ponens*, it is valid.
> This argument is of the form *modus ponens*.
> Therefore, this argument is valid.

These arguments are all formulated to have true premises. The first argument is not of the form *modus tollens*, so its second premise is true. The second argument does commit the fallacy of affirming the consequent, and the third argument is the form *modus ponens*, so their second premises are likewise true. There is an emptiness of an odd sort about the third argument, but no grounds for deriving a contradiction. The first and second arguments, like any argument with true premises and a conclusion stating its own invalidity, lead to inconsistency in the same way as the original example of Pseudo-Scotus.

Many medieval philosopher-logicians besides Pseudo-Scotus developed fascinating examples and subtle theories of paradoxical arguments and other *insolubilia*. In addition, John Buridan (early fourteenth century), Ockham, Walter Burleigh, and others devoted considerable effort toward formulating valid principles concerning conditionals and the relations between these principles. It is still a vexed question whether any of these medieval authors explicitly accepted a Philonian conditional. For several hundred years following the heyday of Ockham and Pseudo-Scotus, the production of logic texts was as it is at present. Successive texts tended closely to resemble their immediate predecessors in topic and treatment.

Jumping ahead a couple of centuries to the early sixteenth century, we find an instructive tripartite classification in Johannes de Celaya. Instead of the more usual two-way division of *consequentiae* into valid and invalid, Celaya considered a symmetrical three-way division: valid, contravalid, and neither.[6] This subdivides invalid argument forms into contravalid argument forms and those that are neither valid nor contravalid.

By definition, every instance of a valid argument form is a valid argument. An invalid argument form is simply one that is not valid: not every instance of an invalid argument form is a valid argument. Invalidity is merely the absence of validity. Contravalidity, on the other hand, is, so to speak, the mirror image of validity. Every instance of a contravalid argument form is a contravalid argument. Just as a valid argument is one that cannot have true premises and a false conclusion, a contravalid argument is one that cannot but have true premises and a false conclusion. All contravalid arguments are invalid, but not all invalid arguments are contravalid. Indeed, contravalid arguments are so rare they are rarely encountered even in logic textbooks. An example of a contravalid argument form is:

If *P*, then either *P* or not *P*.
Therefore, *P* if and only if not *P*.

Any instance of this has a necessary truth for a premise and a logical inconsistency for a conclusion. This bizarre combination is an essential feature of contravalid arguments.

It is not because we often encounter contravalid arguments that Celaya's notion of contravalidity is instructive. It is rather that the symmetry between contravalidity and validity reveals, in a vivid way, an asymmetry between validity and invalidity. To show that an argument is valid, one need show only that it is an instance of a valid argument form; for every instance of a valid form is valid. To show that an argument is invalid, similarly, one need show only that it is an instance of a contravalid argument form; for every instance of a contravalid form is invalid. But this second precept is practically useless, since we practically never come across instances of contravalid argument forms. Most if not all of the invalid arguments we come across are not contravalid. Can't we show an argument to be invalid by showing that it is an instance of an invalid form? We most certainly cannot. Any argument whatsoever is an instance of an invalid form. One-premise arguments are all instances of *P, therefore, Q*. Two-premise arguments are all instances of *P, Q, therefore, R*, and so forth.

Although we have been using letters as propositional variables in the modern manner, so far in this book we have not used any special symbols for logical connectives or operators. Even systems of logic with no such special symbols develop theories of validity for highly restricted formal languages. Both valid and invalid argument forms are represented by using the simplest possible grammatical forms. These simple grammatical forms are assumed to represent everything logically relevant in the grammatically much more complicated natural language.

Arguments in natural language often fail to correspond precisely to any argument form treated in a system of logic. A single argument form in the formal language is assumed to represent inadequately many grammatically different arguments in the natural language. Let us use the notions of natural language and formal language to outline how we use formal logic to demonstrate the validity of a natural-language argument.

A valid formal-language argument *F* is relevant in the following way to showing the validity of a natural-language argument *N*:

1. If the premises of *N* are true, then so are the premises of *F*.
2. *F* has a valid argument form. Therefore, *F* is a valid argument; if its premises are true, then so is its conclusion.
3. If the conclusion of *F* is true, then so is the conclusion of *N*. Therefore, if the premises of *N* are true, then so is its conclusion; *N* is valid.

It is usually easy to defend step 2. The formal language argument *F* is valid because it has a form that the system of logic in question shows to be a valid form. The system of logic in question thus supports step 2, but it is insufficient by itself to support steps 1 or 3. The justification of these steps requires an understanding of the natural language and the formal language at hand. Neither step 1 nor step 3 requires an equivalence of any kind between the statements in N and those in F. The premises of the natural-language argument N may say more than those of the formal-language argument F. Step 1 is allowed so long as they do not say less.

This is schematic justification for a common practice in current introductory courses in logic. One 'translates' a natural-language argument into a formal-language argument and takes the validity of the formal-language argument to show the validity of the original natural-language argument. So far, so good. Unfortunately, beginning students sometimes come to believe that, if the corresponding formal argument has an invalid form, this shows that the original natural-language argument is invalid. This belief cannot be supported.

Let us strengthen the conditional steps 1 and 3 of the scheme above to biconditionals in order to demonstrate that this strengthening does not help:

{1} The premises of F are true if and only if the premises of N are true.
{2} F has an invalid form. Therefore, F is an invalid argument; its conclusion can be false even if its premises are true.
{3} The conclusion of N is true if and only if the conclusion of F is true.

Therefore, the conclusion of N can be false even if its premises are true; N is invalid.

The trouble with this schematic argument is that step {2} has the characteristic it discusses. It is invalid. If the formal-language argument has an invalid argument form, it simply does not follow that the argument is invalid. If an argument form is invalid, then at least one of its instances is an invalid argument. But why must this particular instance be an invalid argument? Every invalid argument form that is not also, in Celaya's sense, a contravalid argument form, has some valid arguments as instances.

There is a common habit in some logic books and classrooms that may encourage confused thinking about invalidity. Authors and teachers sometimes use letters as variables and sometimes use them as abbreviations for statements. To see the difference this makes, consider this formulation of the fallacy of denying the antecedent:

> If P, Q.
> Not P.
> Therefore, not Q.

If the upper-case letters are variables, then this is an invalid argument form. Some instances of the form are invalid arguments. If, on the other hand, the letters are abbreviations, the validity of the abbreviated argument depends not just on its form but also on what the abbreviated statements are. Suppose P abbreviates 'She has a living relative' and Q abbreviates 'Her father's youngest brother is still alive'. Then, by using some common principles of transformation between natural and formal language, we may take the formal-language argument above to represent a natural-language argument such as:

> If she has any living relatives, her father's youngest brother is still alive.
> She has no living relatives.
> Therefore, her father's youngest brother is not still alive.

This is a valid argument despite having the invalid form called the *fallacy of denying the antecedent*.[7] When we use letters for both statements and statement variables, this invites a confusion between the invalidity of an argument form and the invalidity of a particular argument that has that form, since the form and the argument have identical typographical representations.

CHAPTER III

Rediscovery of the Material
Conditional

In 1879, Gottlob Frege (1848–1925) published his *Begriffsschrift*
or 'Concept Script'. This short booklet has never had many
readers, and no one seems ever to have adopted its space-
consuming two-dimensional notation. Although some of Frege's
contemporaries were aware of his work, until Bertrand Russell
championed it a generation later, at the beginning of this century,
it was largely unappreciated. Now, after more than a hundred
years, it is no exaggeration to say that 'it is perhaps the most
important single work ever written in logic'.[1]

Frege reinvented the Philonian, truth-functional conditional
and made it the basis of his logical system. When scholars ask to
what extent an ancient or medieval logician really had the notion
of a truth-functional conditional, they ask to what extent the
logician's understanding of the conditional, or a kind of
conditional, was as explicit as Frege's. Philo and the medievals
were not able to say of themselves that they had, or rejected,
truth-functional conceptions of the conditional; for Frege was the
first philosopher to make the general notion of truth-functionality
explicit.

Frege's *Begriffsschrift* would be important for setting an
example of rigorous, systematic derivation even if it had been
restricted to propositional logic. Among its additional original
contributions, it develops predicate logic, or the logic of
quantifiers and variables, that is the core of today's symbolic
logic. (Modern symbolism differs, but Frege's notation can easily
be transformed to modern symbolism.) A passage from a letter
written to Edmund Husserl in 1906 combines a leading motive for
developing quantification with a treatment of the truth-functional
conditional:

46

With regard to the question whether the proposition 'If *A* then *B*' is equipollent to the proposition 'It is not the case that *A* without *B*', one must say the following. In a hypothetical construction we have as a rule improper propositions of such a kind that neither the antecedent by itself nor the consequent by itself expresses a thought, but only the whole propositional complex. Each proposition is then only an indicative component part, and each proposition indicates the other (*tot . . . quot . . .*). In mathematics such component parts are often letters (if $a > 1$, then $a^2 > 1$). The whole proposition thereby acquires the character of a law, namely generality of content. But let us first suppose that the letters '*A*' and '*B*' stand for proper propositions. Then there are not just cases in which *A* is true and cases in which *A* is false; but either *A* is true or *A* is false; *tertium non datur*. The same holds for *B*. We then have four combinations:

A is true and B is true,
A is true and B is false,
A is false and B is true,
A is false and B is false.

Of these the first, third, and fourth are compatible with the proposition 'If *A* then *B*', but not the second.[2]

Frege's mathematical example can be recast without letters: if a number is greater than 1, then its square is greater than 1. The main clause here, 'its square is greater than 1', does not make a complete statement or, as Frege would put it, does not express a thought. More to the point, it does not have a truth-value; it is neither true nor false. Although the whole conditional sentence is perfectly understandable, its components in isolation are not.

In predicate logic, the letter *a* in '$a > 1$' is understood to be a variable rather than a special numeral, a singular term designating a particular number. '$a > 1$' is incomplete, just as ' > 1' and 'Last summer we went to ——' are incomplete. Propositions with truth-values result when the variables or blanks are replaced with appropriate singular terms, as in '$6 > 1$' and 'Last summer we went to Cape Cod.' Another device for producing propositions with truth-values is binding the variables with a prefixed quantifier:

For some number a, $a > 1$.
For every number a, $a > 1$.

In this case, the complete propositions are respectively true and false. The second, so-called universal quantifier, can be used to make explicit what was previously understood implicitly in the original conditional:

For every number a, if $a > 1$, then $a^2 > 1$.

This is a regimented way of saying 'If a number is greater than 1, then its square is greater than 1' or 'All numbers greater than 1 have squares greater than 1.' This last has the form of the A statement of traditional-term logic, *All Fs are Gs*. Any such statement can be regarded as a quantified conditional:

For every x, if x is F, then x is G.

Similarly, an E statement of the form *No Fs are Gs* can be rewritten:

For every x, if x is F, then x is not G.

Frege's device of quantification over predicates containing variables easily represents the four traditional forms of categorical statement from traditional-term logic. Frege's predicate logic can handle in addition sentences with quantificational structures as complicated as one might want. The mathematical definition of a limit, for example, can be precisely stated in Frege's terms although it is quite beyond the expressive power of traditional-term logic.

The use of conditionals to represent many common statement forms containing no explicit conditional connectives provides an additional justification for the truth-functional or Philonian reading of the conditional. A statement such as:

All the logicians in the department spell poorly

can be regimented as:

For all *x*, if *x* is a logician in the department, then *x* spells poorly.

Instead of writing this as a universally quantified conditional, we can represent it as the negation of an existentially quantified conjunction:

It is not the case that there is an *x* such that *x* is a logician in the department and *x* does not spell poorly.

In general, the truth conditions for statements of the following forms have the same pattern:

For all *x*, if *x* is F, then *x* is G.
It is not the case that (there is an *x* such that *x* is F and *x* is not G).

A desire to preserve this equivalence motivates Frege's defence of the equivalence between 'if *A* then *B*' and 'It is not the case that *A* but not *B*.'

If a somewhat greater skill at public relations had accompanied Frege's genius for logic, his work might sooner have received some of the recognition it deserves. In the following passage, written in 1906, Frege shows his frustration at the neglect of his work. The conditional stroke he mentions here is his two-dimensional arrangement that places the main clause of a conditional on a line above the if-clause:

If there are two thoughts, only four cases are possible:
　　1. the first is true, and likewise the second;
　　2. the first is true, the second false;
　　3. the first is false, the second true;
　　4. both are false.
Now if the third of these cases does not hold, then the relation I have designated by the *conditional stroke* obtains. The sentence expressing the first thought is the consequent, the sentence expressing the second the antecedent. It is now almost 28 years since I gave this definition. I believed at the time that I had only to mention it and everyone else would immediately know more about it than I did. And now, after

49

more than a quarter of a century has elapsed, the greater majority of mathematicians have no inkling of the matter, and the same goes for the logicians. What pigheadedness![3]

Also writing in the last two decades of the nineteenth century, the American Charles Sanders Peirce (1829–1914) developed many of the same logical notions as Frege. Peirce was unaware of Frege, but he had a deeper interest in the history of logic. Peirce is perhaps the first logician since antiquity explicitly to adopt Philo's treatment of the conditional:

> Cicero and other ancient writers mention a great dispute between two logicians, Diodorus and Philo, in regard to the significance of conditional propositions. This dispute has continued to our own day. The Diodoran view seems to be the one which is natural to the minds of those, at least, who speak the European languages. How it may be with other languages has not been reported. The difficulty with this view is that nobody seems to have succeeded in making any clear statement of it that is not open to doubt as to its justice, and that is not pretty complicated. The Philonian view has been preferred by the greatest logicians. Its advantage is that it is perfectly intelligible and simple. Its disadvantage is that it produces results which seem offensive to common sense.[4]

As an example of results offensive to common sense, Peirce supplies 'If the Devil were elected president of the United States, it would prove highly conducive to the spiritual welfare of the people.' The falsehood of the if-clause, or the truth of the main clause, suffice for the truth of a Philonian conditional.

This is made explicit by Bertrand Russell (1872–1970) and Alfred North Whitehead (1861–1947) in their great work *Principia Mathematica* (vol. 1, 1910; vol. 2, 1912; vol. 3, 1913). They put it like this:

*2.02 $\vdash: q. \supset .p \supset q$

I.e. q implies that p implies q, i.e. a true proposition is implied by any proposition.

*2.21 $\vdash: \sim p. \supset .p \supset q$

I.e. a false proposition implies any proposition.[5]

The *Principia* practice of using dots to indicate grouping was followed by some later logicians including the influential American logician Quine. This book will follow the currently more common practice of using parentheses rather than dots. The symbol '⊦' (turnstile) is Frege's sign for assertion, and Russell and Whitehead intend to use it as Frege does. The use of this sign has evolved. In modern logic texts, when the sign stands in front of a formula, it is best read as 'It is a theorem that:', and when it stands between formulas, it can be read 'therefore' or 'from the foregoing, it follows in the present system that:'. Dispensing with the turnstiles, and using parentheses instead of dots, we can rewrite the two formulas above as follows:

*2.02 $q \supset (p \supset q)$
*2.21 $\sim p \supset (p \supset q)$

'$\sim$' (tilde) is one of the common symbols for negation. '$\sim p$' is read 'not-p'. '$\supset$' (horseshoe), the first special symbol for a conditional connective to appear in this book, will be used for truth-functional conditionals from now on. Both '$\supset$' and '$\rightarrow$' are in common use for this purpose. An advantage of '$\supset$' is that it has no other use. Whitehead and Russell took this symbol from Giuseppe Peano (1858–1932) whose work on the logical foundations of arithmetic they followed. '$\supset$' evolved from a backwards 'C'. Peano first stipulated that '$b \, C \, a$' was to be read 'b is a consequence of the proposition a' and then introduced '$\supset$', the sign he used before it became '$\supset$', by saying that $a \supset b$ means the same as $b \, C \, a$.

If one statement implies a second, then the second is a consequence of the first. Perhaps Peano's talk of *consequence* led Whitehead and Russell to talk of *implication*. Frege, at any rate, is innocent in this matter. Although Whitehead and Russell say that '$p \supset q$' may be read 'if p, then q', they much more often give the reading 'p implies q'. In the same paragraph where they introduce '$\supset$', they write:

The association of implication with the use of an apparent variable produces an extension called 'formal implication.' This is explained later: it is an idea derivative from 'implication' as here defined. When it is necessary explicitly to discriminate

51

'implication' from 'formal implication', it is called 'material implication'. Thus 'material implication' is simply 'implication' as here defined.[6]

'Material implication' is a phrase still in common use. In the next chapter, I will join Quine in deploring the confusion of implications with conditionals. More careful writers these days avoid 'material implication' and say that '$p \supset q$' is a material conditional. They also talk about biconditionals rather than 'material equivalences'. A biconditional is a two-way conditional, or the conjunction of two conditionals in which the if-clause and main clause of one conjunct are interchanged in the other. If the conditional is called *implication*, it is natural enough to call the biconditional *equivalence*. Hence Whitehead and Russell:

> Two propositions p and q are said to be 'equivalent' when p implies q and q implies p. This relation between p and q is denoted by '$p \equiv q$.' Thus '$p \equiv q$' stands for '$(p \supset q) . (q \supset p)$'. It is easily seen that two propositions are equivalent when, and only when, they are both true or are both false. . . . It must not be supposed that two propositions which are equivalent are in any sense identical or even remotely concerned with the same topic.[7]

Neither should it be supposed, of course, that, if one proposition 'materially implies' another, they need be even remotely concerned with the same topic.

In the normal, regular sense of *implication*, there is a tight relation between implication and validity. One statement implies another if and only if an argument from the first to the second is valid. No competent logician has ever maintained that the truth of a material conditional, a statement of the form '$p \supset q$', is sufficient for the validity of the corresponding argument p, *therefore*, q. Still, the use of terms 'implication' and 'equivalence' for truth-functional conditionals and biconditionals provoked philosopher-logicians to search for improved accounts of implication, as if '$p \supset q$' really did express a kind of implication, of a very bizarre and startling variety.

Soon after the publication of Volume 1 of *Principia*, C. I. Lewis published an article in *Mind* (October 1912) which begins:

The development of the algebra of logic brings to light two somewhat startling theorems: (1) a false proposition implies any proposition, and (2) a true proposition is implied by any proposition.[8]

Lewis proceeded to develop some alternative accounts of implication which we will look at in the next chapter. The 'somewhat startling theorems' became known as the 'paradoxes of material implication'. (As we saw in Chapter II, these results would not have startled Ockham.) Perhaps the phrase 'paradox of implication' first occurs in W. E. Johnson's *Logic*, Part 1 (1921),[9] but there are earlier applications of the term 'paradoxical' to theorems concerning the material conditional. Hugh MacColl, writing in *Mind* before the publication of *Principia*, says:

> Adopting the usual view among logicians, that the implication 'A implies B' (or 'If A then B') is always equivalent to the disjunctive 'Either A is false or B true,' Mr Russell is quoted as saying that 'It follows from the above equivalence that of any two propositions there must be one which implies the other.' A very brief symbolic operation will show that (*assuming his premises*) Mr Russell is quite right; but surely the paradoxical conclusion at which he arrives should give logicians pause.[10]

Russell was not given pause. In the following issue of *Mind* he replies:

> Of the propositions 'Mr Smith is a doctor' and 'Mr Smith is red-haired,' it is easy to see that one must imply the other, using the word 'imply' in the sense in which I use it. (That this is not the usual sense, may be admitted; all that I affirm is that it is the sense which I most often have to speak of, and therefore for me the most convenient sense.) I say that p implies q if either p is false or q is true.[11]

In his influential paper 'External relations and internal relations' (1919), G. E. Moore says of the results that exercise MacColl and Lewis that they are only apparently paradoxical:

> And these results, it seems to me, appear to be paradoxical,

solely because, if we use 'implies' in any ordinary sense, they are quite certainly false. Why logicians should have thus chosen to use the word 'implies' as a name for a relation, for which it never is used by any one else, I do not know.[12]

Moore's claim here is questionable. Even if Whitehead and Russell had carefully refrained from calling truth-functional conditionals 'implications', there is something strange about their results *2.02 and *2.21 when '$p \supset q$' is read as 'if p, then q'. Consider the following:

> If I propose marriage to Margaret Thatcher, she will leap for joy and urge me to accompany her to a mountain retreat in Peru.
> If I rub orange juice on my elbows, then I will not be affected by drinking two quarts of gin in forty minutes.

> One of the following two conditionals is true: if radioactivity destroys humanity in 1995, I will celebrate my sixtieth birthday with my family in 1997; or, if I celebrate my sixtieth birthday with my family in 1997, then, with a family grown considerably larger, I will celebrate my five-hundredth birthday in 2437.

Since I will not propose marriage to Margaret Thatcher, the if-clause of the first conditional is false, and the whole conditional is true if it is a material conditional. Similarly, since I will not drink two quarts of gin in forty minutes under any circumstances, it is true that I will not be affected by drinking two quarts of gin in forty minutes after rubbing my elbows with orange juice. If the second conditional is truth-functional, it is true because its main clause is true. Whether or not I celebrate my sixtieth birthday, in the third example, either the main clause of the first conditional is true, or the if-clause of the second conditional is false. If they are each material conditionals, at least one of them is true; for either the first has a true main clause, or the second has a false if-clause.

The logical properties of the material conditional, and any other truth-functional statement, are more easily discussed with the help of truth tables. In 1921, E. L. Post and Ludwig Wittgenstein, working independently, published general developments of truth tables. (The resources for these general treatments can be found in earlier logicians.) If every proposition must have exactly one of two values, then for n propositions, there are 2^n mutually exclusive and jointly exhaustive possibilities. When the values are 'true' ('T') and 'false' ('F'), as they are in classical logic, the eight possibilities for three propositions p, q, and r can be tabulated as follows:

p	q	r
T	T	T
T	T	F
T	F	T
T	F	F
F	T	T
F	T	F
F	F	T
F	F	F

Two-place, or binary, connectives can be defined by reference to just four (2^2) possibilities. The following table shows how the standard binary truth-functional connectives work:

p	q	$p \supset q$	$p \mathbin{\&} q$	$p \vee q$	$p \equiv q$
T	T	T	T	T	T
T	F	F	F	T	F
F	T	T	F	T	F
F	F	T	F	F	T

The one-place negation connective requires the consideration of only two (2^1) possibilities:

p	$\sim p$
T	F
F	T

Although *Principia* used a dot as the symbol for conjunction, we have just adopted the ampersand ('&'). The truth-functional treatments of conjunction and negation appear to be quite faithful to the ordinary meanings of 'and' and 'not'. Truth-functional disjunction has difficulties in representing ordinary 'or' parallel to those of the truth-functional conditional in representing ordinary 'if'. Logicians who place binary connectives between components all use 'v' for disjunction. For the other connectives, there are several acceptable alternative symbols.

Given any proposition or propositional form expressed with truth-functional connectives, we can use the corresponding truth table to reveal exactly how the truth-value of the compound proposition depends on the truth-values of its components. If the proposition has *n* elementary propositions as components, there are 2^n distinct possibilities for assigning the values 'true' and 'false' to these elementary propositions. The truth table indicates on exactly which of these assignments the original compound proposition is true and on which it is false. Constructing a truth table with 8 or 16 or more rows is a tedious business, and students of logic learn easy, short-cut techniques for generating all the information contained in a cumbersome truth table.

A proposition that is true on every assignment of truth-values to its elementary components is a *tautology*. Wittgenstein introduces the truth-functional notion of a tautology in his *Tractatus Logico-philosophicus*, where he also introduces truth tables. He later rejected some of the assumptions of the *Tractatus*, and few if any philosophers today accept the main philosophic contentions of this book. Its oracular, aphoristic style nevertheless continues to hold the attention of new generations of students. Although the book has a peculiar reputation, some of its innovations are a standard part of symbolic logic courses of the sort every philosophy department offers. All students of logic learn how to construct truth tables, and all try to understand how the notion of a tautology is fundamental to interpreting propositional logic.

The following selections from the *Tractatus* collect points relevant to the treatment of conditionals:

4.46 Among the possible groups of truth-conditions there are two extreme cases.

In one of these cases the proposition is true for all the truth-possibilities of the elementary propositions. We say that the truth-conditions are *tautological*.

In the second case the proposition is false for all the truth-possibilities: the truth-conditions are *contradictory*.

In the first case we call the proposition a tautology; in the second, a contradiction.

4.463 The truth-conditions of a proposition determine the range that it leaves open to the facts.

(A proposition, a picture, or a model is, in the negative sense, like a solid body that restricts the freedom of movement of others, and, in the positive sense, like a space bounded by solid substance in which there is room for a body.)

A tautology leaves open to reality the whole – the infinite whole – of logical space: a contradiction fills the whole of logical space leaving no point of it for reality. Thus neither of them can determine reality in any way.

5 A proposition is a truth-function of elementary propositions.

5.12 In particular, the truth of a proposition 'p' follows from the truth of another proposition 'q' if all the truth-grounds of the latter are truth-grounds of the former.

5.13 When the truth of one proposition follows from the truth of others, we can see this from the structure of the propositions.

6.1 The propositions of logic are tautologies.

6.1221 If, for example, two propositions 'p' and 'q' in the combination '$p \supset q$' yield a tautology, then it is clear that q follows from p.

This last remark shows how to connect the material conditional with implication. It is not the mere truth, but the tautologousness of '$p \supset q$' that suffices for 'p implies q'. Similarly, '$p \equiv q$' must be a tautology, and not merely a truth, for 'p' and 'q' to be (truth-functionally) equivalent.

The following truth table illustrates how a couple of compound propositions are tautologies. No matter how truth-values are assigned to the elementary propositions, the whole compound is true:

p q	(1) $(p \supset q) \supset (\sim q \supset \sim p)$	(2) $(p \supset q) \lor (q \supset p)$
T T	T T F T F	T T T
T F	F T T F F	F T T
F T	T T F T T	T T F
F F	T T T T T	T T T

Tautology (1) here corresponds to the inference called *contra-position*. According to 5.1221, since the whole conditional is a tautology, it is clear that '$\sim q \supset \sim p$' follows from '$p \supset q$'. In the language of 5.12, all the truth-grounds of the latter are truth-grounds of the former. Tautology (2) is one of the so-called paradoxical results. For any propositions 'p' and 'q' whatever, no matter how unconnected, at least one of the following is true: '$p \supset q$', '$q \supset p$'. It is not essential to (2) that only two propositional variables are involved. '$(p \supset q) \vee (q \supset r)$' and '$(p \supset q) \vee (r \supset p)$' are also both tautologies. A propositional variable in the main-clause position of one conditional disjunct is the if-clause of the other disjunct. Tautology (2) has this tautology-making charac-teristic twice over. A famous formula that is a tautology despite first appearances is called Peirce's Law:

$$((p \supset q) \supset p) \supset p.$$

Propositional logic in the style of Frege, Whitehead, and Russell can be developed without the notions of truth-functionality or tautologousness. In a completely formal system, precise rules permit one to determine without any appeal to meaning whether or not a particular derivation of a formula is legitimate. Whether or not a particular formula is a theorem of the system is a purely syntactical matter. By using the notion of a tautology, logicians were able to prove the following elegant and beautiful result for certain formal systems: all and only tautologies are theorems. In such a system, the conclusion of an argument can be derived from the premises if and only if the corresponding conditional is a tautology.

When the material conditional is combined with the notion of a tautology, there is no doubt that it plays a useful role in formal logic. The success of Frege's programme for propositional logic is uncontroversial. About the suitability of material conditionals for representing conditionals in ordinary language, on the other hand, controversies have raged.

A few philosophers maintain that $\supset$ is a good representation of the ordinary *if*. The two best known defenders of this view have very different grounds. J. A. Faris published a brief, tightly organized, argument that corresponding propositions of the forms *if p then q* and $p \supset q$ are interderivable.[13] In lectures and publications, H. P. Grice has developed a theory of conversational implicature that, he suggests, explains many, if not all, apparent divergences between *if* and $\supset$.

Many philosophers deny that $\supset$ is a good representation of the ordinary *if*, and they divide roughly into two camps. The first, represented by the early P. F. Strawson, says 'So much the worse for $\supset$ since it cannot adequately represent the conditionals of ordinary language.' The other camp, represented by W. V. Quine, says 'So much the worse for the conditionals of ordinary language, since they diverge from the well-understood, orderly material conditionals used by careful science.' I shall say more about some of these positions without attempting to settle all the issues.

H. P. Grice bases his defence of the view that $p \supset q$ adequately represents *if p, then q* on a theory of conversation. In an article entitled 'The causal theory of perception', Grice examines the view, relevant to certain theories of perception, that a statement such as 'There appears to be a banana peel left on the piano' implies that either there isn't really a banana peel left on the piano or, at least, the speaker has some reason to doubt that there really is a banana peel left on the piano. In response to this view, Grice draws some distinctions that have applications far beyond questions about 'appearance' talk. One set of distinctions concerns the vehicle of implication, what, in ordinary conversation or writing, does the implying:

> There are at least four candidates, not necessarily mutually exclusive. Suppose someone to have uttered one or other of my sample sentences, we may ask whether the vehicle of implication would be (*a*) what the speaker said (or asserted), or (*b*) the speaker ('did he imply that . . .') or (*c*) the words the speaker used, or (*d*) his saying that (or again his saying that in that way); or possibly some plurality of these items.[14]

Suppose that this book is one of several books on philosophical logic covered by a single review, and that the reviewer says about it only the following:

> Sanford's book *If P, then Q* is free from blatantly sexist or racialist anecdotes. On the evidence of this book, Sanford

59

appears competent to grade homework for the first half of a beginning course in logic.

The reviewer implies that he has a low opinion of the book, but nothing the reviewer writes implies this or implies that the book has any defect.

In 1967, Grice delivered the William James Lectures at Harvard University. A revised version of these lectures has since appeared under the title 'Logic and conversation' in *Studies in the Way of Words*.[15] Grice here introduces the word *implicate* in a technical sense; the reviewer in my example implicates that my book is no good. Grice starts to develop a theory of conversational implicature to explain, among other things, how much more information can be implicated than what is strictly implied by what one says.

When I say, 'If the Dean doesn't approve your raise, then I will resign the departmental chairmanship', I imply or implicate something about a connection between the Dean's lack of approval and my action. On the hypothesis that the truth conditions for my statement are exactly the same as those for the material conditional:

The Dean doesn't approve your raise ⊃ I will resign the departmental chairmanship,

Grice can explain why I imply more than the mere satisfaction of the truth conditions when I utter the conditional. The material conditional is true, indeed, if either its if-clause is false or its main clause is true. If I know in advance that the Dean has approved your raise, or if I know in advance that I am going to resign the chairmanship no matter what the Dean does about your raise, then my conditional statement can be misleading and dishonest, but not, according to Grice, because it is literally false. One can mislead by uttering truths. 'The Dean did not get drunk at lunch once in the past week' is literally true of a dean who has never been drunk once in his entire life. Similarly, it can be literally true, on the view being considered, that, if the Dean doesn't approve your raise, then I will resign, even though there is no connection, actual or potential, between the Dean's actions and mine.

60

Grice's maxims of conversational implicature, which I shall not attempt to summarize here, attempt to provide some order and explanation for the ways in which one can imply more than one's words say. While there is no doubt that Grice's theory is a valuable accomplishment, there is rather more doubt that it provides adequate support for the view that the truth-value of an ordinary-language indicative conditional is simply the truth-value of the corresponding material conditional. The theory does appear to show how some discrepancies between simple ordinary-language indicative conditionals and the corresponding material conditionals can be explained as differences of conversational implicature rather than as differences of truth conditions for the propositions asserted. (It is unclear from the oral tradition how much more than this Grice ever claimed.) When conditionals are embedded in a more complicated syntactic structure, it is more difficult to regard them as literally truth-functional. The following example is adapted from L. Jonathan Cohen's discussion of Grice:[16]

> If it is true both that if the Dean doesn't approve your raise, then I will resign the departmental chairmanship, and that the Dean does approve your raise, then as a chairman I am both idealistic and effective.

The if-clause of this more complicated conditional is a conjunction of which the first conjunct is our original conditional. The second conjunct is the contradictory of the if-clause of the first conjunct, so its truth is sufficient for the truth of the original conditional, if the original conditional is truth-functional. 'p & $(\sim p \supset q)$' is logically equivalent to 'p'. If the embedded conditional is truth-functional, therefore, it is logically superfluous. It is not obvious how an appeal to maxims of conversation can explain the implicated relevance of the truth of the embedded conditional to my alleged idealism.

Negations of conditionals also pose a difficulty for the view that natural-language and material conditionals have the same truth conditions. '$\sim(p \supset q)$' is equivalent to 'p & $\sim q$'. If the conditional is truth-functional, 'It just isn't true that if the Dean doesn't approve your raise, then I will resign the departmental chairmanship' is true if and only if it is true that the Dean doesn't approve your raise and I do not resign the chairmanship. This combination, however, does not appear to be required for the truth of the denial of the ordinary conditional. One striking example of the difference between the negations of material and ordinary conditionals is due to Charles L. Stevenson:

> This is false: if God exists then the prayers of *evil* men will be answered. So we may conclude that God exists, and (as a bonus) we may conclude that the prayers of evil men will not be answered.[17]

This argument is intended to appear absurd, although it is perfectly valid if its premise is correctly symbolized '$\sim (G \supset P)$'.

It is agreed all round that often, when someone asserts an ordinary conditional, he implies, or, as Grice might put it, implicates, more than the corresponding material conditional implies. If Grice's theory can account for the addition, it is still not obvious how it can account for the subtraction required to accommodate denials of conditionals. Someone who denies an ordinary conditional often does not implicate that the main clause is false and that the if-clause is actually true.

Long before Grice developed his theory of conversational implicature, he served as a tutor to P. F. Strawson in the subject of logic. Strawson's 1950 article 'On referring' is an important challenge to Russell's use of predicate logic to analyse definite descriptions. Strawson's 1952 book *Introduction to Logical Theory* extends the challenge that the logic of *Principia* inadequately represents ordinary language and includes lengthy discussions of all the propositional connectives. As a summary of some of the points made in this chapter about the material conditional, two groups of theorems from Strawson's book are reproduced below. The first group, according to Strawson, are more or less parallel to principles governing ordinary *if*. For the second group, there are no such parallels:[18]

Respects in which '$\supset$' resembles 'if':
$((p \supset q) \& p) \supset q$,
$((p \supset q \& \sim q) \supset \sim p$,
$(p \supset q) \equiv (\sim q \supset \sim p)$,
$((p \supset q) \& (q \supset r)) \supset (p \supset r)$.

Respects in which '⊃' does not resemble 'if':

$\sim\!p \supset (p \supset q),$

$\sim\!p \supset (p \supset \sim\!q),$

$q \supset (p \supset q),$

$q \supset (\sim\!p \supset q),$

$\sim\!p \equiv ((p \supset q) \,\&\, (p \supset \sim\!q)).$

Those agreeing with Strawson that these apparent differences between '⊃' and 'if' are genuine do not all agree about what morals to draw from the divergence. W. V. Quine, in his review of Strawson's book, defends formal logic against the charge that it distorts ordinary language. The scientist can adopt the material conditional as a replacement for the ordinary-language conditional rather than as an analysis or paraphrase:

> He drops 'if–then' in favor of '⊃' without ever entertaining the mistaken idea that they are synonymous; he makes the change only because he finds that the purposes for which he had been *needing* 'if–then', in connection with his particular scientific work, happen to be satisfactorily manageable also by a somewhat different use of '⊃' and other devices. . . . He does not care how inadequate his logical notation is as a reflexion of the vernacular, as long as it can be made to serve all the particular needs for which he, in his scientific program, would have otherwise to depend on that part of the vernacular.[19]

Applying Grice's notion of implicature to this passage, we can say that Quine implicates that '⊃' is adequate for the needs of science. In this book, I will not specifically examine the controversial view that science needs no more than '⊃' for a conditional.

CHAPTER IV

Rediscovery of the Strict Conditional

An essay by W. V. Quine begins with this passage:

> Professor Marcus struck the right note when she represented me as suggesting that modern modal logic was conceived in sin: the sin of confusing use and mention. She rightly did not represent me as holding that modal logic *requires* confusion of use and mention. My point was a historical one, having to do with Russell's confusion of 'if–then' with 'implies'.
>
> Lewis founded modern modal logic, but Russell provoked him to it. For whereas there is much to be said for the material conditional as a version of 'if–then', there is nothing to be said for it as a version of 'implies'; and Russell called it implication, thus apparently leaving no place open for genuine deductive connections between sentences. Lewis moved to save the connections. But his was not, as one could have wished, to sort out Russell's confusion of 'implies' with 'if–then'. Instead, preserving that confusion, he propounded a strict conditional and called *it* implication.[1]

This theme appears in Quine's writings throughout his career. The distinction between use and mention can be illustrated by some examples from Quine's *Mathematical Logic*, first published in 1940:[2]

Boston is populous,
Boston is disyllabic,
'Boston' is disyllabic.

The first is a true statement about a city, and the third a true statement about a word, a name for a city. The second we might in some contexts charitably interpret as a clumsy variant of the third. Read strictly, the second is untrue; for no city is disyllabic.

Implication, Quine insists, is a relation between statements or statement forms.

> It would be not merely untrue but ungrammatical and meaningless to write:
>
> Dreary rhymes with weary.
>
> Now when we say that one statement or schema implies another, similarly, we are not to write 'implies' between the statements or schemata concerned, but between their names. In this way we mention the schemata or statements, we talk *about* them, but use their names. These names are usually formed by adding single quotation marks. . . .
>
> When on the other hand we compound a statement or schema from two others by means of 'if–then', or '⊃', we use the statements or schemata themselves and not their names. Here we do not *mention* the statements or schemata. There is no reference to them; they merely occur as parts of a longer statement or schema. The conditional:
>
> If Cassius is not hungry then he is not lean and hungry
>
> mentions Cassius, and says something quite trivial about him, but it mentions no statements at all.[3]

The use of letters – remarked on near the end of Chapter II – sometimes as variables and sometimes as abbreviations can conceal the impossibility of univocally interpreting any statement of the form '$p * q$', both as a version of 'if p, then q' and as a version of 'p implies q'. We should rewrite this last sentence ' "p" implies "q" ' if we interpret the letters in a uniform way. Abandoning single letters for a moment, we can illustrate Quine's point by deliberately misusing quotation marks:

> If 'Cassius is not hungry' then 'he is not lean and hungry'.
> Cassius is not hungry implies he is not lean and hungry.

Neither is grammatical. We must remove quotation marks from the first and add them to the second.

Quine's accusations of Russell are somewhat unfair. The claim that there is nothing to be said for '⊃' as a version of 'implies' is an exaggeration; for there is something to be said, and Russell says it:

> The essential property that we require of implication is this: 'What is implied by a true proposition is true.' It is in virtue of this property that implication yields proofs.[4]

Russell definitely intended '⊃' to stand for the relation of implication. The passage just quoted comes from a 1906 article entitled 'The theory of implication' in which Russell's alternative readings of formulae do not confuse use and mention. In this article, Russell does not propose 'if p, then q' as an alternative reading for '$p ⊃ q$'. He says, rather,

> 'p implies q' will be a relation which holds between any two entities p and q unless p is true and q is not true, i.e. whenever either p is not true or q is true. The proposition 'p implies q' is equivalent to 'if p is true, then q is true'.[5]

Nothing requires us to accept Russell's sense of 'implies' that makes his last claim true. On the other hand, if we do accept Russell's stipulation as a sense of 'implies', we can accept this last claim. It does not confuse use and mention; propositions are mentioned rather than used throughout. Names of propositions, not propositions themselves, properly fill the blank of the sentence frame '—— is true'. ' "Cassius is not hungry" is true' makes sense. 'Cassius is hungry is true' does not. The transition from 'if p is true, then q is true' to 'if p, then q' is very easy. If we consider instances of the two forms in isolation, they may appear interchangeable, although propositions mentioned in the first are used, not mentioned, in the second. Do not the following, after all, appear to be interchangeable?

> Cassius is hungry.
> 'Cassius is hungry' is true.

To see an important difference between these, it is helpful to embed them in larger contexts:

Caesar thinks Cassius is hungry.
Caesar thinks 'Cassius is hungry' is true.

On a literal reading, the second, quite implausibly, says that Caesar thinks something about an English sentence. There is no way of reading the first to imply that Caesar understands the English word 'hungry'.

It is historically inaccurate to say that Russell developed a theory of conditionals that, because he did not attend sufficiently to the distinction between use and mention, he also took to be a theory of implication. Russell did confuse use and mention, but his failure to distinguish went in the opposite direction. He took his theory of implication also to be a theory of conditionals, although statements of implication require that statements be mentioned while conditional statements typically do not mention statements.[6]

I said above that, in giving alternative reading to formulae in his 1906 article 'The theory of implication', Russell does not confuse use and mention. This is not to say that Russell does not confuse use and mention in the article, for he represents his theory as a resymbolization and reorganization of Frege's theory. In Frege, however, it is clear that the conditional stroke symbolizes conditionals, not statements of implication. As logic textbooks adopted the propositional logic of *Principia* and encouraged finding formal counterparts for natural-language statements, these textbooks used '⊃', in addition to '∼', 'v', and '&' (and equivalent symbols), as a statement connective. Although they definitely understood statements of the form '$p \supset q$' as conditionals, they persisted in using the term 'material implication', and thus encouraged confusion. Nor is it a historical accident that '⊃', despite Russell's early intentions, became understood primarily as a statement connective, forming compound statements out of statement components, rather than a symbol for a relation between statements. The conditional reading departs less from ordinary understanding. Consider the relations between the following three statements:

'Cassius is not hungry' implies 'Cassius is not lean and hungry'.
If Cassius is not hungry, then Cassius is not lean and hungry.
Cassius is not hungry ⊃ Cassius is not lean and hungry.

While the first implies the second, and the second implies the third, both reverse implications are questionable. In the following example, the component statements are logically independent:

> If Cassius is not hungry, then Cassius finished his chocolate bunny before dinner.

Such a conditional can be true in some circumstances, not true in others. Statements of implication, as implication is normally understood, are true or false independently of the circumstances. Circumstances may be necessary for determining just what the sentence 'Cassius is not hungry' is about, but, however the reference of 'Cassius', for example, is fixed, the statement 'Cassius is not hungry' does not imply, in the normal sense of 'imply', the statement 'Cassius finished his chocolate bunny before dinner'.

Russell quite deliberately abandoned the normal sense of 'imply'. He insisted that, in the sense of 'imply' he used, one of the propositions 'Mr Smith is a doctor' and 'Mr Smith is red-haired' must imply the other.[7] For any two propositions, p and q, either $p \supset q$ or $q \supset p$; and, in the sense in which Russell used 'imply', if $p \supset q$, then 'p' implies 'q'. In reaction, one might maintain that there are limits to what senses can be stipulated for terms already well-entrenched in the language. If we call a sheep's tail a leg, how many legs does a sheep have? The answer, attributed to Lincoln, is *four*: Calling a sheep's tail a leg doesn't make it one. Calling something material implication similarly doesn't make it a kind of implication. Rather than accepting so-called material implication as implication of a streamlined kind, we can refuse to regard it as implication of any kind.

C. I. Lewis's reaction to Russell's logic followed another path. Regarding Russell's account of implication as inadequate, Lewis attempted to improve it.[8] While Russell in *Principia* read '$p \supset q$' both as 'p implies q' and as 'if p, then q', Lewis concentrated on the first reading. He wanted an alternative to '$p \supset q$' that corresponds more closely to 'p implies q' in its previously well-established sense. Lewis suggests that '$p \rightarrow\!\!\!3\ q$' be read as 'p strictly implies q'; and he does not suggest 'if p, then q' as an alternative reading of '$p \rightarrow\!\!\!3\ q$'.

Lewis's account of strict implication is nevertheless as close as it can be to the account of the conditional we attribute to Chrysippus. The truth of '$p \rightarrow\!\!3\ q$' requires not just the mere falsity of '$p\ \&\ \sim q$', but its impossibility. (And this impossibility is sufficient for the truth of '$p \rightarrow\!\!3\ q$'.) Using Lewis's diamond '$\diamond$' symbol for possibility or self-consistency, we can define strict implication in terms of negation and possibility:

$$p \rightarrow\!\!3\ q = \mathrm{df} \sim\!\diamond (p\ \&\ \sim q).$$

'$\diamond\ p$' is read 'it is possible that p', so '$\sim\!\diamond p$' is read 'it is impossible that p'. Lewis does not use a special symbol for necessity. In the 1940s, F. B. Fitch of Yale University started using a box '$\square$' to go with Lewis's '$\diamond$'. '$\square\ p$' is read 'it is necessary that p'. With the help of the negation connective, necessity and possibility are interdefinable:

$$\square\ p = \mathrm{df} \sim\!\diamond \sim p,$$
$$\diamond\ p = \mathrm{df} \sim\!\square \sim p.$$

An alternative account of strict implication is the necessity of the corresponding material conditional:

$$p \rightarrow\!\!3\ q = \mathrm{df}\ \square\ (p \supset q).$$

Possibility and necessity are modalities, and a logic of possibility and necessity is a modal logic.

The attempt to regard a logical system of strict implication as a theory of implication, as this term is understood independent from any formal logical system, is complicated by the unlimited number of distinct systems of strict implication. Systems are counted as distinct in this context if and only if at least one theorem in one of them is not a theorem in the other. Lewis's work between 1912 and 1918 on strict implication in reaction to Russell stimulated research by other talented logicians. When Lewis and C. H. Langford collaborated in their 1932 book *Symbolic Logic*, a great deal of formal work on modal logic had been done by others. Appendix II of *Symbolic Logic*, 'The structure of the system of strict implication', mentions contributions by M. Wajsberg, William T. Parry, Paul Henle, and Oskar Becker. In the 1930s after the publication of *Symbolic Logic*, R.

Feys, F. B. Fitch, Kurt Gödel, E. V. Huntington, and J. C. C. McKinsey also published significant research on modal logic. Many logicians in addition to C. I. Lewis have influenced the following brief remarks about some of the better-known systems of modal logic.

Symbolic Logic discusses five different systems of strict implication which Lewis calls S1, S2, S3, S4, and S5. (Lewis was inclined to regard S2 as 'the definitive form of Strict Implication'.[9]) By using the notation S → S' (S properly contains S') to mean that every theorem of S' is a theorem of S, but some theorem of S is not a theorem of S', we can represent the relations between these Lewis systems as follows:

S5 → S4 → S3 → S2 → S1.

Two systems are independent if neither properly contains the other and they do not have just the same theorems. Of many additional systems, here I will mention only two. There is system T, independent of S3, such that:

S4 → T → S2.

There is also system B, independent of both S3 and S4, such that:

S5 → B → T.

T and all the systems that contain T have the rule that if formula *A* is theorem, then so is formula □ *A* (it is necessary that *A*). The following formulae are characteristic of these systems in that each is a theorem, or axiom, of a certain system, but not of any of the systems listed that it properly contains:

S5: $\Diamond\, p \supset \Box\, \Diamond\, p$
S4: $\Box\, p \supset \Box\, \Box\, p$
B: $p \supset \Box\, \Diamond\, p$
T: $\Box\, ((p \rightarrow\!\!3\; q) \rightarrow\!\!3\, (\Box\, p \supset \Box q))$, i.e., $\Box\, \Box\, ((p \rightarrow\!\!3\; q) \supset (\Box\, p \supset \Box\, q))$
S3: $(p \rightarrow\!\!3\; q) \rightarrow\!\!3\, (\Box\, p \rightarrow\!\!3\, \Box\, q)$
S2: $\Diamond\, (p \;\&\; q) \rightarrow\!\!3\, \Diamond\, p$
S1: $(p \rightarrow\!\!3\; q) \supset (\Box\, p \supset \Box\, q)$

S3 contains no theorems of the form □ □ A, and hence it does not contain the characteristic formula of T, which is of this form. In T, but not in S3, there are infinitely many distinct modalities. An example of a formula that is a theorem of S3 but not a theorem of T is:

$$\Diamond \Diamond \Diamond \, p \rightarrow 3 \, \Diamond \Diamond \, p.$$

This blizzard of formulae does not constitute an introduction to propositional modal logic.[10] Modal logic is important to contemporary accounts of conditionals mainly because of work on the semantics of modal logics done in the 1950s. In Chapter VII, we will see how the notion of truth in all possible worlds is extended to account for subjunctive conditionals, such as 'If you had flipped the switch, the light would have gone on', that are not counted as logical truths by any theory.

As we saw in Chapter III, the concept of a tautology provides a criterion of logical truth that is independent of the requirements for being a theorem in any particular logical system. It is significant to prove that all and only the theorems in a certain system are tautologies. Logicians did a great deal of research on developing various systems of modal logic and investigating the relations between these systems before they had a workable, independent notion of modal logical truth analogous to the notion of a tautology. Rudolph Carnap, Alfred Tarski, J. C. C. McKinsey, Stig Kanger, and Jaakko Hintikka all contributed to developing formally rigorous notions of logical truth for modal formulae.[11] Saul Kripke's work had the greatest influence. According to a rough, informal explanation of Kripke's model structures, a formula of the form □ A is true if and only if A is true in every possible world. The phrase 'in every possible world' is intended to recall Leibniz but makes no commitment to a Leibnizian metaphysics. ◇A is true if and only if A is true in some possible world.

In this rough explanation of modal logical truth, the crucial missing element is the notion of accessibility. According to a less rough explanation, □ A is true in world w if and only if A is true in every possible world accessible to w. Different notions of logical truth correspond to different properties of the accessibility

71

relation between worlds.[12] Three properties of two-place relations are illustrated in the present case:[13]

Reflexivity. Every world is accessible to itself.
Symmetry. If world $w1$ is accessible to world $w2$, then $w2$ is accessible to $w1$.
Transitivity. If $w2$ is accessible to $w1$, and $w3$ is accessible to $w2$, then $w3$ is accessible to $w1$.

If the accessibility relation has all these properties, the associated notion of logical truth characterizes S5. That is, it can be proved that all and only formulae that satisfy this independent criterion of logical truth are theorems of S5. If accessibility is transitive and reflexive, but not symmetric, the associated notion of logical truth characterizes S4. If the relation is symmetric and reflexive, but not transitive, the associated system is B. If the relation is reflexive but neither symmetric nor transitive, the associated system is T.

Which if any of these systems of modal logic is appropriate to one's purposes depends, inevitably, on one's purposes. There are many ways we can interpret formal modal operators. For example, we can read '$\Diamond p$' as 'the world might develop in such a way that it turns out to be the case that p'. '$\Box p$' is then read 'it will turn out to be the case that p no matter how the world develops' and '$p \rightarrow_3 q$' can be read 'the world will not develop so that it turns out to be the case that p unless it also develops so that it turns out to be the case that q'. Lewis's system S4 appears to be appropriate to this interpretation, for the accessibility relation is reflexive and transitive, but not symmetric.

One can use the symbolism of modal logic without having a definite idea about exactly which modal formulae should be counted as logical truths. Whether a lack of such specificity poses a real danger depends, again, on one's purposes. Modal logic, like all kinds of formal logic, is useful for drawing distinctions. There is obviously a difference between the following two statements:

Anyone can win the lottery.
Everyone can win the lottery.

The first asserts that the lottery is a fair one – anyone can win; while the second statement cannot be true if ticket holders outnumber prizes. If we use a predicate 'x can win the lottery' to symbolize these statements, we cannot tell them apart. We need the predicate 'x wins the lottery' plus a modal operator. The difference between the statements turns on whether the quantifier is within or outside the scope of 'possibly':

For all x, $\Diamond$ (x will win the lottery).
$\Diamond$ (For all x, x will win the lottery).

There are many arguments, especially in philosophy, that we cannot represent adequately without modal logic. Once a real argument is characterized as having a certain modal form, there may be no doubt that the form is valid, because it is valid on any plausible interpretation, or there may be no doubt that it is invalid, because it is valid on no plausible interpretation.

In addition to having intrinsic mathematical interest, modal logic bears on many projects in the philosophy of mathematics, in other branches of philosophy, and in the formal study of natural language and natural arguments. The interest of modal logic does not depend on its being taken as a theory of implication. Indeed, just as 'material conditional' is a better name than 'material implication' for statements in which the main connective is '⊃', 'strict conditional' is a better name than 'strict implication' for statements in which the main connective is '⥽'. For '⥽' is a connective; it forms compound statements out of components. Like '⊃' and unlike 'implies', it does not stand for a relation between statements.

The grounds for attacks on Lewis's systems of so-called strict implication have been strikingly parallel to Lewis's grounds for his attacks on Russell. The following are known as the paradoxes of strict implication:

$\sim \Diamond p \rightarrow\!\!\!3\ (p \rightarrow\!\!\!3\ q),$
$(p\ \&\ \sim p) \rightarrow\!\!\!3\ q,$
$\Box\ p \rightarrow\!\!\!3\ (q \rightarrow\!\!\!3\ p),$
$p \rightarrow\!\!\!3\ (q\ v \sim q).$

What is impossible strictly implies anything. So a contradiction strictly implies anything. What is necessary is strictly implied by anything. So a tautology is strictly implied by anything.

These results – which Ockham anticipates – are similar to the analogous paradoxes of material implication. Remember that '$p \rightarrow q$' is equivalent to '$\sim\Diamond(p \ \& \sim q)$'. An essential feature of impossibility is that if it is impossible that p, then it is impossible that p and q. Given that $\sim\Diamond p$, it follows that $\sim\Diamond (p \ \& \ q)$. So if $\sim\Diamond p$, then $\sim\Diamond(p \ \& \sim q)$, that is, $p \rightarrow q$. Similarly, if $\Box p$, then $\sim\Diamond\sim p$, so $\sim\Diamond(\sim p \ \& \ q)$, that is, $\sim\Diamond(q \ \& \sim p)$, that is, $p \rightarrow q$.

Lewis maintained that we should accept the conclusion that a contradiction implies anything. He provided an argument that relies on the following four rules of inference:[14]

From a conjunction A & B, one may infer the first conjunct A.

From a conjunction A & B, one may infer the second conjunct B.

From A, one may infer a disjunction A v B.

From a disjunction A v B, and the negation, ~A, of a disjunct, one may infer the remaining disjunct B.

Given a contradiction, '$p \ \& \sim p$', we can infer both 'p' and '$\sim p$' by the first two rules. The third rule allows us to infer 'p v q' from 'p', and the fourth allows us to infer 'q' from 'p v q' together with '$\sim p$'. The whole argument accords with the principle or thema that 'can be validly inferred from' is a transitive relation. Anyone who wants to deny that any arbitrary conclusion can be validly inferred from any contradiction of the form '$p \ \& \sim p$' must reject at least one of the rules or principles outlined above.

Entailment has been a term of the philosophical trade ever since G. E. Moore proposed the following stipulative definition:

We require, first of all, some term to express the *converse* of that relation which we assert to hold between a particular proposition q and a particular proposition p, when we assert that q *follows from* or *is deducible from* p. Let us use the term 'entails' to express the converse of this relation. We shall then be able to say truly that 'p entails q,' when and only when we are able to say truly that 'q follows from p' or 'is deducible from p,' in the sense in which the conclusion of a syllogism in

Barbara follows from the two premisses, taken as one conjunctive proposition; or in which the proposition 'This is coloured' follows from 'This is red.' 'p entails q' will be related to 'q follows from p' in the same way in which 'A is greater than B' is related to 'B is less than A.'[15]

Some philosophers who hold that the so-called paradoxes of strict implication show that Lewis's account is inadequate distinguish entailment from implication; while they admit that strict implication corresponds to genuine implication, they deny that it corresponds to genuine entailment. In particular, while admitting that $(p \ \& \ \sim p) \rightarrow\!3 \ q$, they deny that '$q$' is generally deducible from '$p \ \& \ \sim p$' and thus deny that '$p \ \& \ \sim p$' entails 'q'.

The material conditional (and also the strict conditional) can be true just because the if-clause has a certain character. When the if-clause is false (or is impossible), then the material conditional (or the strict conditional) is true no matter what the main clause happens to be. Similarly, the material conditional (and also the strict conditional) can be true just because the main clause has a certain character. When the main clause is true (or is necessarily true), the material conditional (or the strict conditional) is true no matter what the if-clause happens to be. Those who seek an account of *entailment*, as distinguished from the strict conditional, hold that entailment is a genuine relation between statements and statement forms. When one statement entails another, it should always be in virtue of some relation between them, a relation that holds because of the characteristics of *each* of the related statements. This requirement of genuine relatedness is called the requirement of relevance. Logicians who attempt to formulate theories of entailment practise what they call *relevance logic*. I shall return to questions of relevance and entailment in Chapter VIII.

CHAPTER V

Subjunctive Conditionals
and Covering Laws

'General propositions and causality', a paper written by Frank Ramsey shortly before his death in January 1930 at the age of 26, has inspired several approaches to conditionals. In his 1946 article. 'The contrary-to-fact conditional',[1] Roderick Chisholm refers to the following passage from Ramsey:

'If p, then q' can in no sense be true unless the material implication $p \supset q$ is true; but it generally means that $p \supset q$ is not only true but deducible or discoverable in some particular way not explicitly stated. This is always evident when 'If p then q' or 'Because p, q' (*because* is merely a variant on *if*, when p is known to be true) is thought worth stating even when it is already known either that p is false or that q is true. In general we can say with Mill that 'If p then q' means that q is inferrible from p, that is, of course, from p together with certain facts and laws not stated but in some way indicated by the context. This means that $p \supset q$ follows from these facts and laws, which if true is in no way a hypothetical fact.[2]

As we shall soon see, the appealing simplicity of Ramsey's proposal is deceptive.

Despite years of discussion, this area of research remains without adequate terminology. Chisholm summarized the main difficulties long ago:

Many contrary-to-fact conditionals are not expressed in the subjunctive mood and many conditionals which are expressed in this mood are not actually contrary-to-fact, but in the present discussion we may use the labels 'subjunctive conditional' and 'contrary-to-fact conditional' interchangeably. Neither term is adequate, but each has been used in recent literature.[3]

Although some authors explicitly assume that a past-tense subjunctive conditional implies the negation of its if-clause, this view does not withstand scrutiny. Alan Ross Anderson provides the following example:

If Jones had taken arsenic, he would have shown just exactly those symptoms which he does in fact show.[4]

Since this example has the peculiarity of implying that its main clause is true, consider a modification of it:

If Jones had taken arsenic, Dr Smith would have found arsenic during Jones's autopsy.

Although someone who asserts this may be taken to imply that he believes both that Jones did not take arsenic and that Dr Smith did not discover arsenic during Jones's autopsy, the conditional is confirmed, rather than disconfirmed, by the subsequent discovery that (although the press kept it quiet) Jones did indeed take arsenic and Smith found it during the autopsy. Some theorists would nevertheless call this last conditional a *counterfactual*, even when no component of it runs counter to the facts. Others restrict the term 'counterfactual' to conditionals in which both the if-clause and the main clause are false. Goodman applies the term 'semifactual' to conditionals such as 'Even if you had taken no extra vitamin C, your cold would have cleared up in less than ten days' in which the if-clause is false and the main clause is true. Goodman also points out that conditionals with false components can be transposed into conditionals with true components. His example is the following pair:

If that piece of butter had been heated to 150°F, it would have melted.
Since that butter did not melt, it wasn't heated to 150°F.[5]

Goodman calls the second a *factual* conditional and says that 'the problem of counterfactuals is equally a problem of factual conditionals'.[6] Life would be simpler if all authors followed Goodman's use of 'counterfactual', 'semifactual', and 'factual' as exclusive terms. As applied to true conditionals, the terms are both exclusive and exhaustive. The only possibility not covered is: main clause, false; if-clause, true; and all such conditionals, whether subjunctive or indicative, are false.

This last scheme of classification assumes something that deserves spelling out, namely, that the component clauses of subjunctive conditionals have truth-values. A sentence such as 'Jones had taken arsenic' can indeed have a truth-value, although not as a subjunctive. 'Jones had taken arsenic, just a tiny monthly dose, for years, with no apparent ill effects. It wasn't until Miss Tweedle started slipping much larger amounts into his coffee every morning that Jones began to feel definitely under the weather.' But now consider the question 'Is it true or false that Dr Smith would have found arsenic during Jones's autopsy?' The question is incomplete. An if-clause has to be understood before an answer can be supplied. The 'would'-clause standing by itself as a complete sentence is not naturally assigned a truth-value. If I were a corporation lawyer, then I would wear shoes of a different style. I am not a corporation lawyer, so 'I am a corporation lawyer' is false. What about 'I were a corporation lawyer' which is grammatically unacceptable as a complete sentence? When I try to take it seriously as a complete sentence, whether grammatical or not, I don't know how to determine its truth-value.

Authors who discuss what they call subjunctive or counterfactual conditionals often write as if the component clauses were indicative. Although logicians are more comfortable with bearers of truth-value such as statements, sentences, and propositions, it may be that considering indicatives that correspond to the components of conditionals rather than considering the non-indicative components themselves prevents the resolution of chronic difficulties.[7] In this book, I will nevertheless persist in the convenient fiction that the components of subjunctive conditionals have truth-values.

In Chisholm's 1946 article he says, parenthetically:

and, of course, whenever we can assert the subjunctive, we can also assert the corresponding indicative.[8]

For years no one blinked at Chisholm's 'of course'. Since Ernest W. Adams presented the following pair of corresponding conditionals, Chisholm's principle seems less obvious:

> If Oswald hadn't shot Kennedy in Dallas, then no one else would have.
> If Oswald didn't shoot Kennedy in Dallas, then no one else did.[9]

Possibly the subject matter of this example distracts from its point. Homely examples are abundantly available that make the same point:

> If I had not washed the dishes, no one else would have.
> If I did not wash the dishes, someone else did.

The first is true in virtue of the fact that no one in the vicinity of the dishes except myself was willing and able to wash them. The second is true in virtue of the fact that the dishes are indeed washed and that all washed dishes are washed by someone. But, if the second is true, then the indicative version of the first conditional is questionable at best:

> If I did not wash the dishes, no one washed them.

An adequate theory of subjunctive conditionals will not imply that every indicative conditional corresponding to a true subjunctive conditional is true.

Chisholm says that 'Our problem is to render a subjunctive conditional . . . into an indicative statement which will say the same thing'.[10] Goodman begins by saying:

> The analysis of counterfactual conditionals is no fussy little grammatical exercise. Indeed, if we lack the means for interpreting counterfactual conditionals, we can hardly claim to have any adequate philosophy of science.[11]

Schneider begins her survey article by saying that 'Discussion of the meaning of subjunctive conditionals has been lively within recent years.'[12] In a brief review of a later survey article by Walters, Mates writes as follows:

Most of the preferred analyses are to the effect that a sentence of the form 'If *P* were the case, *Q* would be the case' is true if and only if the sentence *Q* is a logical consequence of the sentence *P* together with a set of sentences *S* (the 'background assumptions') satisfying various conditions. Though it is usually agreed that *S* should contain some scientific laws, there has been great difficulty in specifying other conditions that will simultaneously preserve the plausibility of this type of account and avoid its trivialization.[13]

This concisely states a surprisingly difficult problem with Ramsey's proposal.

Notice how both Mates and Goodman assume that the task is to provide an *analysis*. An analysis of something gives its meaning. The problem is represented as that of spelling out the meaning of a subjunctive conditional.

In talking about the enterprise of dealing with conditionals, I deliberately choose the relatively unloaded term 'account'. Although the label 'analytic philosophy' has stuck, and for a while many philosophers proclaimed that analysis is a, or even *the*, proper philosophic activity, it is questionable whether Chisholm, Goodman, Schneider, and Mates are, strictly speaking, talking about analyses of conditionals. Chisholm himself remarks that 'the meaning of a conditional should not be confused with the particular grounds upon which it happens to be asserted'.[14] We can add that the meaning of conditionals also should not be confused with the general grounds upon which they are asserted.

If these various accounts analyse the meanings of conditionals, then conditionals often mean more than they say. They mean more, indeed, than many asserters of conditionals can understand. Even philosophers who understand all the technical notions involved may fail to understand a proposed analysis because the analysis is too intricate for any but the most dedicated to comprehend. *Meaning* is not an easy topic, but, whatever our views about meaning, it is difficult to entertain various accounts of conditionals as remotely plausible analyses of their *meaning*. Something else is going on, as Ted Honderich suggests:

There are *two* questions, one of them that of specifying the meaning of conditionals, the other the general analysis of their *grounds* or *premises*. It is in fact this latter problem to which philosophers have addressed themselves, despite their mis-description of it, and they have had arguable things to say about it. Their efforts must be seen in a proper light, not the one they supply.[15]

Once we start distinguishing questions along this line, we need not stop with two. *Truth conditions, assertability conditions*, and *acceptance conditions* might all be distinguished from each other, from *grounds*, and from *analysis of meaning*.

Some theorists regard subjunctive conditionals as condensed arguments.[16] An argument is neither true nor false, and what can be neither true nor false cannot literally be asserted. On this view, then, it is misguided to look for the truth conditions or assertion conditions of subjunctive conditionals. Conditionals are still advanced and accepted, however, so there is no reason to abandon the search for acceptance conditions. In any case, acceptance conditions and truth conditions can each be distin-guished from grounds or premises. Two people can accept exactly the same conditional on different grounds, but the conditional does not thereby have different truth conditions.

Goodman and Chisholm seek truth conditions for subjunctive conditionals. They attempt to formulate, in general terms, just what is required for a subjunctive conditional to be true. We can agree that a successful non-trivial formulation of truth conditions would be enlightening without settling the question whether a formulation of truth conditions analyses meaning or whether it instead gives the premises (or grounds) upon which the conditional is advanced. Let us accordingly reformulate Ramsey's suggestion quoted at the beginning of this chapter and replace *means that* with *is true when*:

'If *p* then *q*' is true when *q* is inferable from *p*, that is, of course, from *p* together with certain facts and laws.

If-clauses that lack specificity cause a prominent difficulty with this approach. In the following passage, Goodman considers requirements for accepting a certain set of facts *S* in treating a conditional *if A, then C*:

Clearly it will not help to require only that for *some* set *S* of
true sentences, *A.S* be self-compatible and lead by law to the
consequent; for this would make a true counterfactual of
   If Jones were in Carolina, he would be in South Carolina,
and also of
   If Jones were in Carolina, he would be in North Carolina,
which cannot both be true.[17]

Let us suppose that Jones, who lives in Swansea and has no plans
to visit the United States, has barely heard of the Carolinas.
Jones is neither in North Carolina nor in South Carolina. Add
the supposition that Jones is in the Carolinas to the facts that he
is not in South Carolina and that the Carolinas consist entirely of
North and South Carolina; it follows from the conjunction of
supposition and facts that Jones is in North Carolina. From the
same supposition conjoined with somewhat different facts, it
follows that Jones is in South Carolina.
   Is 'If Jones were in Carolina' too unspecific to be the if-clause
of a conditional with a determinate truth-value? I think it is the
situation we imagine, rather than the clause itself, that lacks
relevant specificity. If we meet at a philosophy convention in
New York next year, you can probably say truthfully of me:

   If Sanford were in Carolina, he would be in North Carolina.

If you should say instead:

   If Sanford were in Carolina, he would be in South Carolina,

you would say something false. Like Jones, or anyone, if I am in
New York, I am neither in North Carolina nor in South Carolina.
Those facts are irrelevant. What is relevant is that I live in North
Carolina, have lived there for over fifteen years, would have
stayed home if I had not gone to New York, and will return
home to North Carolina when I leave New York. For good
measure, in the past twenty years I happen to have set foot in
South Carolina exactly twice. My relations to the two Carolinas
are significantly more differentiating than Jones's.
   Other writers have discussed similar examples. If Apollo were
a man, would he be mortal or would at least one man be

immortal?[18] If Caesar were in command, would he use catapults or atomic bombs?[19] If Bizet and Verdi had been compatriots, would both be French or both be Italian?[20]

There may be no way of answering the question about what nationality Bizet and Verdi would have had if they had been compatriots. We can nevertheless imagine the question having a determinate answer. While we are about it, we can imagine that, if the Frenchman Bizet and the Italian Verdi had been compatriots, they would have been Brazilian: both families contemplated moving to Brazil; neither family contemplated moving to another country in Europe.

'If Bizet and Verdi were compatriots' is not intrinsically too unspecific to serve as an if-clause of a true conditional, but it is probably too unspecific in fact. There are as many ways for Bizet and Verdi to be compatriots as there are countries that they both could have lived in. If something limits the number of such countries to one, it is something beyond the supposition of compatriotism together with the actual nationalities of Bizet and Verdi.

A treatment of conditionals that always supports corresponding conditionals of the forms *if A, then C* and *if A, then not-C* is unsatisfactory. Many writers including Goodman assume that a satisfactory treatment will never support each of a pair of so-called opposite conditionals. I will argue later that sometimes both members of a pair of opposite conditionals are acceptable. If this is right, a theory of subjunctive conditionals ought not formally to preclude the joint truth of subjunctives with the forms *if A, then C* and *if A, then not-C*.

Goodman's central example concerns a match *M* about which we would like to affirm:

If match *M* had been scratched, it would have lighted.

We assume that *M* is well made, dry, and surrounded by oxygen. And we assume that it follows from general laws that no dry, well-made match scratched in adequate oxygen fails to light. Such general laws imply that the following conjunction has at least one false conjunct:

M is scratched, and *M* is a well-made match, and *M* is surrounded by adequate oxygen, and *M* does not light.

83

In Goodman's example, the first conjunct is false and the rest are true. We suppose that, if the first were true, then the last would be false. The problem is to justify our counterfactual rejection of the last conjunct rather than another, say the second:

If match *M* had been scratched, it would not have been dry.

We need some principle for retaining the fact that *M* is dry, and not retaining the fact that *M* is unlit, when considering the counterfactual supposition that *M* is scratched. A suitable condition *S*, relevant to assessing a conditional with antecedent *A*, as Goodman puts it:

> must be not merely compatible with *A* but 'jointly tenable' or *cotenable* with *A*. *A* is cotenable with *S*, and conjunction *A.S* self-cotenable, if it is not the case that *S* would not be true if *A* were.[21]

We may restate our difficulties with Jones, Bizet, and Verdi in terms of cotenability. In the Jones story, we have no way to judge whether the truth 'Jones in not in South Carolina' is cotenable with 'Jones is in the Carolinas'. In the actual world, we have no way to judge whether 'Bizet is French' is cotenable with 'Bizet and Verdi are compatriots'. In the story of *M*, we assume that '*M* is dry' is cotenable, and '*M* does not light' is not cotenable, with '*M* is scratched'. These determinations of cotenability require each other. The determination that '*M* does not light' is not cotenable with '*M* is scratched' is, unfortunately, also the determination of our original counterfactual 'If match *M* had been scratched, it would have lighted.'

Goodman is quick to point out this circularity and slow to accept suggestions about how to avoid it. I shall survey several of these suggestions.

Although most laws of physics that are equations containing time variables are time-symmetric, it still seems important in examples like Goodman's that an effect comes after its cause. Several writers suggest that attention to temporal considerations helps to solve the problem of relevant conditions. What Michael Slote calls the *base-time* of a counterfactual conditional is the time at which the relevant factors obtained that together with the if-clause and laws yield the main clause.[22] It is appropriate to include the actual dryness of match *M* at the base-time, but not to include its actual non-lighting after the base-time.[23] W. T. Parry and John C. Cooley, early reviewers of *Fact, Fiction, and Forecast*, made similar suggestions.[24] Goodman's replies to them which I shall translate into Slote's terms, also apply to Slote's suggestion. Goodman offered responses of two kinds. First, it is not the dryness of the match at the base-time, the time of scratching, but its dryness immediately following the scratching that figures in the law that connects scratching with immediately following lighting.[25] Second, in some counterfactuals, the event mentioned in the main clause would have been simultaneous with the base-time, so temporal considerations cannot effectively dismiss its actual non-occurrence as irrelevant. If this iron bar had been at a certain temperature, it would have glowed red at the same time, not a little bit later.[26] We will discuss temporal considerations further in Chapter VII.

In addition to imposing temporal restrictions on which additional facts may be regarded as relevant in treating a counterfactual conditional, Slote formulates a requirement that is not explicitly temporal. Conditions *b* are admissible only if:

> there is a valid explanation of the consequent (solely) in terms of the antecedent and/or *b*, together with actual nonstatistical (causal) laws.[27]

We can admit that laws themselves often fail to determine a direction of dependence and that it is difficult to define a direction of dependence purely in terms of temporal priority. Still, appeal to some sort of priority, one-way dependence, or asymmetry appears appropriate to Goodman's puzzle about match *M*. Lighting depends on scratching and dampness does not. Slote's appeal to explanation employs basically the intuition Parry, Cooley, and others share. I shall defend this intuition in Part Two. One difficulty with Slote's suggestion is that the asymmetry of explanation is itself poorly understood. If we account for the direction of explanation in terms of subjunctive conditionals, our theory moves in an uncomfortably tight circle. If we can account for the direction of explanation without such circularity, then we should revise our treatment of conditionals to accord with our treatment of explanation. *Explanation* is not appropriately regarded as a primitive. Its employment in a treatment of conditionals either begs the question or acts as a place-holder for a more revealing account.

The approach to conditionals suggested by Ramsey, pursued by Chisholm, and discussed most influentially by Goodman fell out of philosophical fashion as attention turned to possible worlds. If a revival is at hand, this book will be at best but part of the reason. Igal Kvart defends an elaborate version of a covering law treatment that uses the notions of *causal irrelevance* and *purely positive causal relevance* to deal with Goodman's problem of relevant conditions.[28] Causal *relevance* and *irrelevance* are not primitive notions; Kvart defines them probabilistically.

Goodman's match *M* example is causal, but he does not stipulate that his phrase 'leads by law' be understood as restricted to only causal law. Slote is more specific; he requires that a non-statistical causal law be involved. And Kvart appeals to the notion of causal relevance. But some acceptable subjunctive conditionals apparently involve no causation and no causal laws. If I had waited four more days to take out my loan, I could have borrowed at a lower interest rate. I am not such an egomaniac to believe that the interest rate depends somehow on when I happen to borrow money. On the contrary, I assume that the interest rate is independent of my financial affairs. The interest rate for borrowers in fact declined just four days after I borrowed money. That is why I could have borrowed at a lower rate if I had waited four more days. There seems to be no causation involved. If there are any laws involved, such as the law of non-contradiction, they are not causal laws. An adequate theory of subjunctive conditionals must deal with non-causal as well as causal examples.

CHAPTER VI

Belief and Probability

Chisholm's 1946 paper 'The contrary-to-fact conditional' quotes another passage from Frank Ramsey's 1929 paper 'General propositions and causality':

> If two people are arguing 'if p will q?' and are both in doubt as to p, they are adding p hypothetically to their stock of knowledge and arguing on that basis about q.[1]

If Ramsey inspires the covering law account discussed in the last chapter, he also inspires the main competing accounts. The sentence just quoted leads researchers in several directions. This chapter concentrates on probability and belief, and the next chapter explains how the notion of belief-contravening suppositions leads naturally to a consideration of possible worlds.

The phrase 'belief-contravening' is used by Nicholas Rescher in several publications. When we add to our stock of knowledge the belief-contravening hypothesis that Bizet and Verdi are compatriots, there may be no non-arbitrary way of adjusting our stock of beliefs to restore internal consistency. Rescher writes:

> It should further be recognized that not only is there no 'logical' way of arriving at an answer to the question of how our beliefs should be restructured in the face of a belief-contravening hypothesis, but also that there seems to be no mechanical or automatic procedure whatsoever for accomplishing this task.
>
> It is certain, at any rate, that the most 'obvious' rule of a mechanical sort will not serve at all:

Rule: Restructure the residual beliefs with the absolute minimum of upheaval consonant with logical consistence.[2]

Logic by itself is helpful in identifying inconsistency but offers no help in deciding which of several possible restorations of consistency is a *minimal* revision. The notion of a minimal revision nevertheless has a strong appeal for theorists working on conditionals.

Robert Stalnaker in his 1968 paper 'A theory of conditionals' refers to Chisholm's citation of Ramsey. Paraphrasing Ramsey with reference to a true–false political opinion survey containing the suggestion: 'If the Chinese enter the Vietnam conflict, the United States will use nuclear weapons', Stalnaker writes:

According to the suggestion, your deliberation about the survey statement should consist of a simple thought experiment: add the antecedent (hypothetically) to your stock of knowledge (or beliefs), and then consider whether or not the consequent is true. Your belief about the conditional should be the same as your hypothetical belief, under this condition, about the consequent.[3]

Stalnaker remarks that this suggestion covers only situations in which you have no opinion about the truth-value of the antecedent. He accordingly generalizes the suggestion:

First, add the antecedent (hypothetically) to your stock of beliefs; second, make whatever adjustments are required to maintain consistency (without modifying the hypothetical belief in the antecedent); finally, consider whether or not the consequent is then true.[4]

William Harper calls this the *Ramsey test*. His formulation makes it explicit that the required adjustments are to be *minimal* adjustments:

First, hypothetically make the minimal revision of your stock of beliefs required to assume the antecedent. Then, evaluate the acceptability of the consequent on the basis of this revised body of beliefs.[5]

Besides developing one of the first possible-worlds treatments of conditionals, Stalnaker is one of the first to advocate a probabilistic treatment. In order to consider counterfactual conditional probabilities, he defines an *extended probability function* (*epf*).

> An epf represents an extended state of knowledge. An extended state of knowledge includes, not only a measure of the degree to which the knower has a right to believe certain propositions, but also the degree to which he *would* have a right to believe certain propositions *if* he knew something which in fact he does not know. An epf represents, not just one state of knowledge, but a set of hypothetical states of knowledge, one for each condition.[6]

Stalnaker attempts to define a notion of conditional probability in terms of epf so that the probability of a conditional is equal to the corresponding conditional probability. Harper summarizes the view as follows:

> He [Stalnaker] suggests that a rational agent's subjective probability assignment to a conditional he evaluates by Ramsey's test ought to be the same as the subjective conditional probability he assigns to its consequent given its antecedent. This suggestion has come to be known as Stalnaker's Hypothesis:
>
> (SH) $P(A > B) = P(B/A)$,
>
> where $P(A > B)$ is the agent's degree of belief in the conditional $A > B$, and $P(B/A)$ is his conditional degree of belief in B given A.[7]

The corner '$>$' has become one standard symbol used to represent both subjunctive conditionals and indicative conditionals that may be neither material nor strict conditionals. The use of '$>$' to symbolize subjunctives assumes the linguistic fiction, mentioned in the last chapter, that subjunctive conditionals have indicative components; for 'A' and 'B' in '$A > B$' are ordinary, indicative sentential variables.

The appealing simple hypothesis:

$$P(A > B) = P(B/A)$$

will not work except with a trivial probability function that can allow no more than two mutually incompatible statements with positive probability. David Lewis proved the so-called triviality result in 1972, and those doing research in the area learned about it quickly.[8]

The hypothesis above encourages one to understand the slant line '/' as a kind of connective, similar to, if not identical to, the conditional connective '>'. In his discussion of Lewis's trivialization proof, Richard Jeffrey comments on the result as follows:

> The slant line '/' plays the role of a comma, separating the arguments of the two-place function. It is no connective.[9]

Put in Jeffrey's terms, Lewis's result is that, if we treat '/' as a connective, then, whenever $P(A \& B)$ and $P(A \& {\sim}B)$ are both positive, A and B are independent in the sense that $P(A \& B) = P(A).P(B)$.[10] (Lewis's result has by no means killed interest in relations between conditional probability and conditionals; it has, on the contrary, stimulated such interest.[11])

I have been writing as if the probability of a conditional is the probability of its truth. Not everyone willing to talk about the probability of counterfactual conditionals shares the assumption that counterfactual conditionals are sometimes true. On one tradition of interpretation, to advance a conditional is to do something other than to make a statement with a truth-value. The passage from Ramsey that begins this chapter continues as follows:

> so that in a sense 'If p, q' and 'If p, $\bar{q}$' are contradictories. We can say they [the two people arguing] are fixing their degrees of belief in q given p. If p turns out false, these degrees of belief are rendered *void*. If either party believes $\bar{p}$ for certain, the question ceases to mean anything to him except about what follows from certain laws or hypotheses.[12]

What Ramsey says here does not imply that all conditionals, even those with true if-clauses, lack truth-value. Georg Henrik von Wright advocates the more general view in his essay 'On conditionals':

> I shall never speak of the conditional as a proposition which is being asserted, but only of propositions being asserted conditionally, relative to other propositions. Therefore we must not say that 'if *p*, then *q*', when used to assert *q* on the condition *p*, expresses something which is either true or false. But we shall certainly have to agree to saying that a proposition may be truly or falsely asserted conditionally, relative to another proposition.[13]

Quine uses a distinction like von Wright's to formulate a view like Ramsey's:

> An affirmation of the form 'if *p* then *q*' is commonly felt less as an affirmation of a conditional than as a conditional affirmation of the consequent. If, after we have made such an affirmation, the antecedent turns out to be true, then we consider ourselves committed to the consequent, and are ready to acknowledge error if it proves false. If on the other hand the antecedent turns out to have been false, our conditional affirmation is as if it had never been made.[14]

Stalnaker, after quoting this passage from Quine, comments:

> On this view of conditional assertions, to affirm something on a condition known to be false is to commit oneself to nothing at all, since in such a case it is already known that the affirmation is 'as if it had never been made.'
>
> Completely excluded by this concept of conditionality, however, is *counterfactual* knowledge, and partial belief. I may believe that *if* Kennedy had not been assassinated, it is highly probable that he would have won the 1964 presidential election. I *know* that the condition is false, but that does not prevent me from speculating – and perhaps speculating rationally – about what would have happened contrary-to-fact. . . . The lack of an operational procedure for settling disagreements about what would have been true contrary-to-

fact shows not that counterfactual conditional probabilities should not be interpreted, but rather that their interpretation requires an extension of the idea of coherence. Counterfactual assertions are the most controversial and interesting conditional statements. If we are to use probability theory to throw light on these cases, we must first extend the theory to cover counterfactual probabilities.[15]

Ernest W. Adams, referring to the same passage in Quine, remarks:

> More generally, a bet that 'if *p* then *q*' is conditional – in force only if *p* proves true, and in that case winning if *q* is true, and losing if *q* is false.[16]

In his article entitled 'The logic of conditionals', Adams draws connections between conditionals and probability by adopting the following hypothesis:

> The assertion of a statement is justified if and only if a bet on it is justified in the same situation; the denial of a statement in a situation is justified if and only if a bet against it is justified in that situation.[17]

Adams distinguishes between the strict and probabilistic justification of a bettable conditional:

> The assertion of a bettable conditional 'if *p* then *q*' is probabilistically justified on an occasion if what is known on that occasion makes it much more likely that *p* and *q* are both true than that *p* is true and *q* is false; its denial is probabilistically justified if it is much more likely that *p* is true and *q* is false than that *p* and *q* are both true.[18]

In his later monograph *The Logic of Conditionals*, Adams drops the discussion of bets and deals more directly with relations between probability and conditionals.[19] Unlike some of the earlier publications, this monograph is not concerned with assertion, justification of assertion, or assertability. It is concerned with what one should believe, not directly with what one should say.

Adams says that the fundamental assumption of *The Logic of Conditionals* is:

the probability of an indicative conditional of the form 'if *A* is the case then *B* is' is a conditional probability.[20]

Adams's early work on conditionals precedes Lewis's Triviality Result, which Adams takes to confirm his view that the probability of a conditional is not the probability of its truth. (A conditional probability is not the probability of something's being true, so, if the probability of a conditional is a conditional probability, the probability of a conditional is not the probability of its truth.)

A classically valid argument preserves truth: its conclusion must be true if all its premises are. Adams formulates another desirable characteristic of argument, *probabilistic soundness*. If all the premises of a probabilistically sound argument are probable, then so is the conclusion. The criterion of probabilistic soundness combined with a probabilistic interpretation of conditionals can yield evaluations that diverge from those the criterion of classical validity produces when combined with a truth-functional interpretation of conditionals.

Adams uses two-dimensional diagrams to represent probabilities, and comparative probabilities, of propositions. All the examples he discusses can be accommodated by one-dimensional representations.[21] Let a unit line represent the total probability space. The representations of any proposition and its negation divide this line in two: $P(A) + P(\sim A) = 1$. The more probable a proposition, the greater the proportion of the line its representation occupies.

Let us consider, for the purpose of illustration, the following two propositions:

(*S*) A roll of two dice comes up 6.
(*T*) At least one of the dice comes up 3.

Of the 36 equipossible ways for two dice to fall, 11 are *T*-possibilities and 25 are $\sim T$-possibilities. Of the 11 *T*-possibilities, only one, 3–3, results in the truth of *S*, as do four of the remaining 25 $\sim T$-possibilities, 1–5, 5–1, 2–4, 4–2. *P(S)* is thus equal to 5/36, since 5 of the 36 equipossible ways for two dice to fall are *S*-possibilities. The following diagram represents the relations between the probabilities of *S* and *T*:

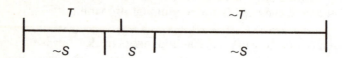

The probability of a conditional *if A, then B* 'is identified in the diagram with the *proportion* of subregion *A* which lies inside subregion *B*'.[22] When considering a one-dimensional diagram, we may replace 'subregion' with 'segment'. With reference to the diagram above, consider some of the simplest conditionals involving *S* and *T*:

If (*S*) the roll of two dice comes up 6, then (*T*) at least one of the dice comes up 3. Quite improbable. A small proportion of the *S*-segment lies inside the *T*-segment. $P(T/S) = 1/5$.

If (*T*) at least one of the dice comes up 3, then (*S*) a roll of two dice comes up 6. Very improbable. A very small proportion of the *T*-segment lies inside the *S*-segment. $P(S/T) = 1/11$.

If (*S*) a roll of two dice comes up 6, then (~*T*) neither die comes up 3. Quite probable. A large proportion of *S*-segment lies inside the ~*T*-segment. $P(\sim T/S) = 4/5$.

If (~*S*) a roll of two dice does not come up 6, then (*T*) at least one of the dice comes up 3. Improbable. A small proportion of the ~*S*-segment lies inside the *T*-segment. $P(T/\sim S) = 10/31$.

If we consider only conditionals in which each clause is either an atomic proposition or its negation and the two clauses contain different atomic propositions, then the four conditionals above exhaust the possibilities for *S* and *T* in classical, truth-functional logic. Orthographic variants are logically equivalent to one of the four above. *If T, then ~S*, for example, is equivalent to *if S, then ~T*. But the truth-functionally valid principle of contraposition is not always probabilistically sound:

If (~T) neither die comes up 3, then (~S) a roll of two dice does not come up 6.

Probable. A large proportion of the ~T-segment lies inside the ~S-segment. $P(\sim S/\sim T)$ = 21/25.

If S, then T, and its contrapositive, *If ~T, then ~S*, are not equally probable. Suppose you were forced to bet even money on one or the other:

If the dice come up 6, then at least one of them comes up 3.
If neither die comes up 3, the dice do not come up 6.

You will probably lose money if you bet on the first and make money if you bet on the second. In the long run, if you bet on the first your loss will be steady but slow: on most rolls of dice, your money will stay on the table, since the dice will not come up 6. Money will change hands more often if you bet on the second, since frequently neither die will come up 3; and, when money does change hands, it will usually be in your favour. When the conditionals represent conditional bets, they are clearly different. The argument:

If ~T, then ~S, *therefore*, if S, then T,

is probabilistically unsound, since the premise is probable and the conclusion is improbable.

Contraposition is not the only classically valid principle that is not always probabilistically sound. The following principles are closely related:

Chain Argument, or Hypothetical Syllogism, or Transitivity.

If *A*, then *B*.
If *B*, then *C*.
Therefore, if *A* then *C*.

Antecedent Restriction, or Antecedent Strengthening.
If *B*, then *C*.
Therefore, if *A* and *B*, then *C*.

Disjunctive Restriction.
If *A* or *B*, then *C*.
Therefore, if *B*, then *C*.

Adams uses the following example (and here letters cease for a while to function as variables and start to function as abbreviations):

A = Smith will die before the election.
B = Jones will win the election.
C = Smith will retire after the election.

Imagine that the probabilities are as represented below:

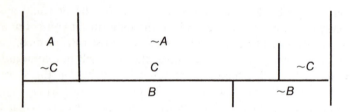

The *A*-segment lies entirely inside the *B*-segment, so the probability that Jones will win the election if Smith dies before the election is 1. Most of the *B*-segment lies inside the *C*-segment, so the probability that Smith will retire after the election if Jones wins it is high. The *A*-segment lies entirely outside the *C*-segment, so the probability that Smith will retire after the election if he dies before the election is 0. By a probabilistically unsound chain argument, two probable conditionals can thus yield a very improbable conditional. So can a probabilistically unsound strengthening of the antecedent, since the *A*- and *B*-segment, which is identical to the *A*-segment, lies entirely outside the *C*-segment. This is how Adams explains the manifest absurdity of the truth-functionally valid argument of antecedent strengthening:

If Jones wins the election, then Smith will retire after the election. Therefore, if Jones wins the election and Smith dies before the election, then Smith will retire after the election.

When the same components are used to illustrate disjunctive restriction, Adams recognizes a difficulty. The following argument is indeed unsound probabilistically:

If either Jones wins the election or Smith dies before it then Smith will retire. Therefore, if Smith dies before the election he will retire.

The premise, although probable, is absurd.[23] Probabilistically unsound examples of disjunctive restriction with a non-absurd premise can be found. I shall press T ('At least one of the dice comes up 3') into service once more. Consider also N, 'Neither die comes up more than 3', and R, 'The roll of two dice comes up less than 4 or more than 6.' The conditional with a disjunctive if-clause:

If T or N, then R,

although not very probable, has anyway a probability greater than 1/2. $P(R/T$ or $N) = 9/15$. Each argument by disjunctive restriction yields a conditional with a probability less than 1/2. $P(R/T) = 6/11$. $P(R/N) = 1/3$. You would prefer betting on the conditional with the disjunctive if-clause to betting on either of these:

If T, then R.
If N, then R.

The single letter 'R' could, of course, be replaced by a disjunction. R is clearly disjunctive; and its disjuncts, because of the nature of numbers and of dice, are exclusive. The disjuncts T and N, in contrast, are not exclusive. What makes this example work is that, if both T and N are true, then R is false. Disjoining T and N adds some R-cases without adding any $\sim R$-cases. Although 'If T or N, then R' may be a bit contrived, there is nothing absurd or unassertable about it.

97

Adams, who does not identify the probability of a conditional with the probability of its truth, does not advance a separate account of the truth conditions of conditionals. Other writers, who do offer an account of truth conditions, offer a separate account of the assertability of indicative conditionals. Both David Lewis and Frank Jackson entertain the view that the conditional probability $P(B/A)$ is the measure of the assertability of an indicative conditional *if A, then B*, while its truth conditions are those of $A \supset B$.[24] An account of this sort explains why some instances of the paradox of material implication appear more perverse than others.

Suppose that I, who know that Carl did not go to Krogers this morning, assert on this basis:

> If Carl went to Krogers this morning, he bought a thousand cans of cat food.

The associated material conditional is true, since its if-clause is false. That is all it takes, on the view under discussion, to make the natural-language indicative conditional true. But more is required to make it assertable, namely that the conditional probability P(Carl bought a thousand cans of cat food/Carl went to Krogers this morning) be high, which in fact it is not. Carl never buys cat food, never buys a thousand cans of anything, and buys very little at Krogers.

Robert often buys cat food, and I happen to know he bought some this morning. On this basis, I assert:

> If Robert did not receive dire warning from an astrologer, he bought some cat food this morning.

Because of the true main clause, the associated material conditional is true. Does this natural-language indicative conditional seem rather less outrageous, in the circumstances described, than the one about Carl? The theory allows it to be much more assertable, for if P(Robert bought some cat food this morning) is high, and if Robert's receiving advice from astrologers is probabilistically independent of his behaviour, as it is, then the conditional probability P(Robert bought some cat food this morning/Robert did not receive dire warnings from an astrologer) is high. If the conditional still seems to have a rather low assertability, then conditional probability is not the only consideration relevant to assertability.

Adams's disjunctive example appears to show that conditional assertability requires something more than conditional probability. If it happens to be true that Smith will retire after the election, then the proposed classical truth condition is satisfied by:

> If either Jones wins the election or Smith dies before it then Smith will retire.

In the set-up we considered earlier, the probability of the main clause given the disjunctive if-clause is high. The conditional nevertheless has low assertability. In general, if a conditional *if A, then B* is assertable, and it is recognized that if $P(B/A$ or $C)$ is lower than $P(B/A)$, then *if A or C, then B* will be much less assertable, even though $P(B/A$ or $C)$ might be quite high because $P(C)$ is quite low. It would be very strange to assert:

> If the dice come up 1–1 or at least one die comes up higher than 2, the total will be higher than 4.

The conditional probability of the main clause on the if-clause is quite high, but, without the first disjunct of the if-clause, it is a bit higher.

Brian Skyrms formulates what he calls the conditional probability hypothesis: The assertability of the indicative conditional goes by epistemic conditional probability plus conversational implicature.[25] Conditionals with disjunctive if-clauses in which one disjunct is recognized as lowering the relevant conditional probability presumably violate some maxim of conversational implicature.

Our recent discussion concerns only indicative conditionals. Skyrms and Adams, like Stalnaker, are interested in applying the notion of conditional probability to subjunctive conditionals. Adams talks about the *prior conditional probability* as the probability of a subjunctive conditional.[26] This probability is prior to our knowledge of the occurrence or non-occurrence of events referred to by the clauses of the conditional. Skyrms's account in terms of prior propensities rather than prior probabilities is distinguishable from Adams's but similar.[27] Adams and Skyrms reject some principles that hold in Stalnaker's theory such as:

$$P(A > C) > P(A \& C).$$

On Stalnaker's treatment of subjunctive conditionals, $A \& C$ does indeed entail $A > C$; while on some other treatments this entailment does not hold. Recall that this chapter begins with some remarks by Stalnaker about counterfactual conditional probabilities that lead into the discussion of conditional probability. Stalnaker's motivation for wanting to hold certain principles of subjunctive conditional inference, and also the motivation of many who develop alternative accounts, are usually stated in terms of possible worlds, to which we now turn.

CHAPTER VII

Possible Worlds

and Pangloss was hanged, although this was not the custom. The very same day, the earth shook again with a terrible clamour. Candide, terrified, dumbfounded, bewildered, covered with blood, quivering from head to foot, said to himself: 'If this is the best of all possible worlds, what are the others?'

More people learn about possible worlds from Voltaire than from Leibniz. Leibniz holds a principle of theodicy that this is the best of all possible worlds. Philosophy books and philosophy teachers often credit Leibniz as well with the view that a necessary truth is true in all possible worlds. If this view is strictly speaking more Leibnizian than something Leibniz explicitly thought, it is still widely advanced as illuminating.[1]

In 1943, C. I. Lewis published an article including the following passage:

A proposition *comprehends* any consistently thinkable world which would incorporate the state of affairs it signifies: a classification of Leibnizian possible worlds. This conception of possible worlds is not jejune: the actual world, so far as anyone knows it, is merely one of many such which are possible. . . . When I reflect upon the number of facts of which I am uncertain, the plethora of possible worlds which, for all I know, might be this one, becomes a little appalling. . . . An *analytic* proposition is one which would apply to or be true of every possible world.[2]

In his 1947 book *Meaning and Necessity*, Rudolph Carnap holds that a necessary (L-true) sentence is one that holds in every

101

state-description. A state-description is a class of sentences 'which contains for every atomic sentence either this sentence or its negation, but not both, and no other sentences'. Carnap says that state-descriptions represent Leibniz's possible worlds or Wittgenstein's possible states of affairs.[3]

An early paper by Wilfrid Sellars, 'Concepts as involving laws and inconceivable without them', has an intricate and sophisticated discussion of possible worlds.[4] The paper begins with a reference to C. I. Lewis's problems with contrary-to-fact conditionals. Although one might therefore expect to see Sellars provide an explicit possible-worlds account of subjunctive conditionals, the paper heads in another direction toward a discussion of laws and universals. *Possible world*, at any rate, was an established term of art among formal philosophers by the end of the 1940s.

The completeness proofs for modal logic by Kanger, Kripke, Hintikka, and others in the late 1950s stimulated philosophical interests in possible worlds. Robert Stalnaker's 'A theory of conditionals' (1968) motivates and provides a formal possible-world semantics for contingent subjunctive conditionals.[5] David Lewis's 1973 book *Counterfactuals* presents a similar but distinguishable account.[6]

Stalnaker's formulation of what is known now as the Ramsey test is repeated here:

> First, add the antecedent (hypothetically) to your stock of beliefs; second, make whatever adjustments are required to maintain consistency (without modifying the hypothetical belief in the antecedent); finally, consider whether or not the consequent is then true.[7]

Stalnaker does not pause to ask whether assertable conditionals may lack truth conditions. He proceeds immediately to explain assertability in terms of truth:

> Now that we have found an answer to the question, 'How do we decide whether or not we believe a conditional statement?' the problem is to make the transition from belief conditions to truth conditions; that is, to find a set of truth conditions for statements having conditional form which explains why we use

102

the method we do use to evaluate them. The concept of a *possible world* is just what we need to make this transition, since a possible world is the ontological analogue of a stock of hypothetical beliefs. The following set of truth conditions, using this notion, is a first approximation to the account that I shall propose:

Consider a possible world in which *A* is true, and which otherwise differs minimally from the actual world. '*If A, then B' is true (false) just in case B is true (false) in that possible world.*[8]

The analogy between possible worlds on Stalnaker's conception and a stock of hypothetical beliefs is imperfect. Worlds are taken to be maximal: complete, saturated, and determinate. In a world, a tree bearing many leaves bears a certain number of leaves, and each leaf has a certain size, shape, and mass. Stocks of beliefs are not maximal. The belief that a tree has many leaves need not be accompanied by any other beliefs that together imply exactly how many leaves the tree has or exactly the shape of each leaf. Two different stocks of beliefs, different because not every belief belonging to one belongs to the other, can be jointly consistent; but two different possible worlds must be mutually exclusive: at least one thing true in one will be untrue in the other.

In general, given any possible world and any proposition *B*, either *B* will be true in that world or it will be false. Given a stock of beliefs, on the other hand, perhaps neither *B* nor ~*B* is entailed by beliefs in the stock. The Ramsey test does not give an answer in every case. A conditional such as 'If that tree had not died last summer, it would now bear an odd number of leaves' may neither come out true nor come out false. After we add the hypothetical belief 'That tree is alive' and making minimal adjustments to restore consistency, the resulting stock of beliefs may imply neither that the number of leaves is odd nor that it is not. In any possible world in which that tree is alive, however, it bears a certain number of leaves, and that number is either odd or even.

For the purpose of developing a formal semantics for the logic of conditionals, Stalnaker makes the following two assumptions (a *non-empty proposition* is one that is true in some possible world):

The Limit Assumption. For every possible world i and non-empty proposition A, there is at least one A-world minimally different from i.

The Uniqueness Assumption. For every possible world i and proposition A there is at most one A-world minimally different from i.[9]

Stalnaker is quite aware that the analogous principles concerning minimal adjustments of stock of beliefs are unrealistic. Logic idealizes, and, when an idealization fails to fit reality, one attempts to fill the gap with a plausible explanation. Stalnaker's theory counts the following principle of conditional excluded middle as a logical truth:

$$(A > B) \text{ v } (A > {\sim}B).$$

If there is exactly one A-world minimally different from this world, either B or ${\sim}B$ is true in that world and one or the other of the conditional disjuncts is true. Stalnaker does not suggest that it is always possible to know which of these is the minimally different A-world. There may be no objectively correct answer to the question whether the first or the second conditional disjunct is true. In this respect, conditional excluded middle resembles ordinary, unconditional, excluded middle: A v ${\sim}A$. At the end of February, a branch on a certain tree is definitely bare. By the first of June, it is laden with large green leaves. It acquired leaves between the end of February and the first of June. Is there thus a first second in this three-month interval when the branch had leaves? We need not say so. Although the leaves on some trees come out very quickly, the relevant differences between one second and the next always indistinguishable in this example, and no indistinguishable difference is the difference between bearing a leaf and not bearing a leaf. What then about this instance of excluded middle:

Either that branch has at least one leaf or that branch does not have at least one leaf?

There are times when there is no objective answer to the question which disjunct is true. We can still accept the disjunction because, on any sufficiently determinate notion of a leaf, one or the other disjunct would definitely be true. We can accept instances of conditional excluded middle on similar grounds. Although the antecedent is not determinate enough to apply the Ramsey test in a decisive way, on any sufficiently determinate conception of the antecedent, one or the other of the conditional disjuncts is definitely true.

Stalnaker's defence of conditional excluded middle has not persuaded everybody. David Lewis, who gives Stalnaker's limit assumption and uniqueness assumption their names, does not accept the assumptions. Lewis develops a comprehensive possible-worlds theory of which Stalnaker's is a limiting case.

Rather than lead into a discussion of possible worlds via the Ramsey test, Lewis begins with standard possible-world semantics for strict conditionals. Contingent subjunctive conditionals cannot be adequately represented as strict conditionals. For one respect of difference, antecedent strengthening is valid for strict conditionals but not for subjunctives.

The strict conditional $A \longrightarrow_3 B$ is true if B is true in all accessible A-worlds. As there are more and less stringent degrees of accessibility, strict conditionals can be less and more strict. Lewis introduces the notion of a *variably strict conditional*:

> Any particular counterfactual is as strict, within limits, as it must be to escape vacuity, and no stricter.[10]

'If Jones had taken arsenic, Dr Smith would have found arsenic during Jones's autopsy' might have a true antecedent. In that case, the only relevant possible world is the actual world. The consequent needs to hold in only one world, the actual world, for the conditional to be true. At the other extreme, a conditional like 'We could play chess with creatures in other galaxies if there were truly instantaneous communication' requires access to possible worlds in which the fundamental laws of physics differ from ours. The non-existence of intergalactic chess in all possible worlds very much like ours is irrelevant to the conditional.

Lewis uses a three-place similarity relation: possible world j is at least as similar to the world i as is the world k. A subjunctive conditional $A > B$ (in which A is non-vacuous) is true in world i just in case B is true in some A-world j and in every possible A-

world at least as similar to *i* as *j*. In other words, some (*A* & *B*)-world is closer to *i* than any (*A* & ~ *B*)-world. This formulation requires neither the limit assumption nor the uniqueness assumption.

The limit assumption may seem implausible when we consider a conditional such as:

If I were more than three inches taller, I would still be no good at basketball.

For every number *m* greater than three, there is another number greater than three that is less than *m*. There is no number *n* greater than three such that adding *n* inches to my height would be the smallest addition that would make me more than three inches taller. Even if there is no limit to the number of possible worlds in which I am more than three inches taller and am not, say, more than four inches taller (and which worlds are otherwise as similar as possible to the actual world), the conditional is true if I am no good at basketball in any of those worlds.[11]

The uniqueness assumption may seem implausible when we consider a conditional such as:

If I had put on a different pair of socks this morning, they would have been grey socks.

One world in which I put on pair of socks *b* this morning is just as close to the actual world as one in which I put on pair of socks *c*; and there is no world different from the actual world that is closer. The conditional comes out true if all these worlds than which none is closer are worlds in which I put on grey socks.

Although Lewis's account does not support Stalnaker's principle of conditional excluded middle, the similarities between Stalnaker and Lewis are much more far-reaching than their differences. Both, for example, deal with contraposition, antecedent strengthening, and hypothetical syllogism in the same way. Although the diagrams that Lewis draws are two-dimensional, the relevant information they convey can be represented one-dimensionally. In the following diagrams, the farther right a point is located, the farther it is from the actual world. The actual world is at the left endpoint of the line segment, and other possible worlds are located more or less to the right. When a point is labelled A, this means it is the leftmost point of an A-segment. Every world located within an A-segment is an A-world, and every A-segment has a leftmost point. When the limit assumption is unsatisfied for A, no possible world is located at the leftmost point of the leftmost A-segment. When the uniqueness assumption is unsatisfied by A, more than one world is located at the leftmost point of the leftmost A-segment. The satisfaction of these assumptions is irrelevant to the examples to be discussed. In reading these diagrams, one should assume that all segments extend as far as possible to the right. When a point is labelled A, an A-segment extends to the right up to a point labelled $\sim A$, the leftmost point of a $\sim A$-segment. If A is true in the actual world, the left endpoint of the whole line is the leftmost point of an A-segment.

Consider the following diagram:

The conditional $A > B$ is true in this situation. The A-worlds most like the actual world are B-worlds. The A-worlds most like the actual world will be in the leftmost part of the leftmost A-segment. (In this diagram, there is only one A-segment.) In general, $A > B$ is true if and only if the leftmost point of the leftmost A-segment either is within a B-segment or coincides with the leftmost point of a B-segment.

The conditional $\sim B > \sim A$ is false in this situation, since the leftmost point of the leftmost (and only) $\sim B$-segment lies within a $\sim\sim A$-segment (the A-segment). The situation diagrammed is thus a counterexample to contraposition. The $\sim B$-worlds most like the actual world are A-worlds rather than $\sim A$-worlds.

Lewis and Stalnaker use the term 'counterfactual' as some others use 'subjunctive'. Their classification of a conditional as counterfactual implies nothing about the truth-values of the indicative versions of its components. If we understand 'counterfactual' to contrast with 'factual' and 'semifactual', however, we should notice that we have diagrammed a counterexample to semifactual contraposition. Factual subjunctive conditionals are all true on the most common interpretation of the Stalnaker–Lewis account. If the actual world is an *A*-world, then no possible *A*-world is closer to it than it is close to itself. If *A* is actually true, then *A* > *B* is true if and only if *B* is also actually true. Every contrapositive of a strictly counterfactual conditional, a conditional in which both the main clause and the if-clause are false, is a factual conditional. So, on this view, every contrapositive of a strictly counterfactual conditional is true, whether or not the original counterfactual is true.

Every strictly counterfactual conditional is the contrapositive of a factual conditional. Since all factual conditionals are true (according to this account) and not all conditionals with false components are true, contraposition of factual conditionals is not generally valid. Two types of situation in which *A* > *B* is a true factual conditional can be distinguished:

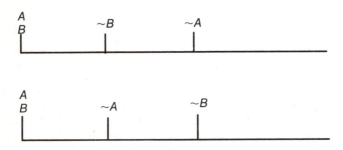

In the first case, ~*B* > ~*A* is false, since the leftmost point of the leftmost *B*-segment falls within an *A*-segment. If I actually drew a straight flush in poker, then the Stalnaker–Lewis theory counts the following as true:

If I had drawn a flush, then I would have drawn a straight flush.

Its contrapositive, though, can be false in the same set-up:

If I had not drawn a straight flush, then I would not have drawn a flush.

The closest possible world in which I do not draw a straight flush is closer to the actual world than the closest possible world in which I do not draw a flush.

In the second case, $\sim B > \sim A$ is true, since the leftmost point of the leftmost $\sim B$-segment falls within a $\sim A$-segment.

Here is a diagram of a true conditional in which both clauses are false:

The leftmost point of the leftmost A-segment falls within a B-segment. Contraposition holds, since the leftmost point of the leftmost $\sim B$-segment (the actual world) coincides with the leftmost point of a $\sim A$-segment (which is also the actual world).

Perhaps the most striking counterexamples to contraposition are structurally similar to the first pattern we examined, the contraposition of a semifactual. Here are some less schematic examples:

If I had drawn a flush, I would not have drawn a straight flush.

If we had more than two children, we would not have had more than ten children.

The contrapositives of each of these is absurd. A conditional $A > \sim B$ can be true when the truth of A is necessary for the truth of B. But when A is necessary for B, and B is possible, $B > \sim A$ will be very strange and unacceptable.

Diagrams illustrate two kinds of failure of hypothetical syllogism:

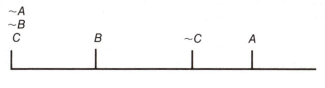

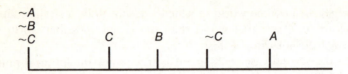

In each case, $A > B$ is true because the leftmost point of the leftmost A-segment is within a B-segment; $B > C$ is true because the leftmost point of the leftmost B-segment is within a C-segment; and $A > C$ is false because the leftmost point of the leftmost A-segment is within a $\sim C$-segment. In the first diagram, $B > C$ is a semifactual; in the actual world, C is true and B is false. In the second diagram, A, B, and C are all false in the actual world, and there are two disconnected $\sim C$-segments.[12] Here are examples of the two kinds:

If I should win a Nobel prize next year, I would go to Europe. If I should go to Europe next year, I would not go to Sweden. Therefore, if I should win a Nobel prize next year, I would not go to Sweden.

If I were president of General Motors, I would be very wealthy. If I were very wealthy, I would drive a Jaguar. Therefore, if I were president of General Motors, I would drive a Jaguar.

Any counterexample to hypothetical syllogism can be transformed into a counterexample to antecedent strengthening. For example:

If I were very wealthy, I would drive a Jaguar. Therefore, if I were very wealthy and president of General Motors, I would drive a Jaguar.

Some counterexamples to antecedent strengthening cannot be transformed into persuasive counterexamples to hypothetical syllogism because the other conditional required as a premise is unacceptable. For example:

If you find a parking space, you will have a bit of good luck. Therefore, if you find a parking space, and your car is smashed

110

by a railway locomotive before you can park it, you will have a bit of good luck.

The following diagrams a situation in which $B > C$ is true while $(A\&B) > C$ and $A > B$ are both false:

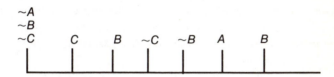

Although these comparative-closeness-of-possible-worlds diagrams superficially resemble the diagrams used to represent relative probabilities, and, although some of the same classically valid arguments come out invalid when tested by either kind of diagram, the two diagrams function differently and convey different information. We have thus seen general, schematic reasons of two independent sorts for questioning contraposition, antecedent strengthening, and hypothetical syllogism for subjunctive conditionals, and also seen several natural-language instances that appear to be counterexamples. The matter nevertheless remains controversial. Some other accounts of subjunctive conditionals preserve the validity of these contested argument forms. Advocates of such accounts will have explanations for the apparent existence of counterexamples, how the two premises of a hypothetical syllogism with a false conclusion can appear both to be true only because of some ambiguity, how the contrapositive of a true conditional, although equally true, may not be equally assertable, and so forth. There is a remarkable lack of agreement about which consequences an adequate account of subjunctive conditionals should have.

Opposite conditionals are those with identical if-clauses and contradictory main clauses, such as 'If you jump, you will hurt yourself' and 'You won't hurt yourself if you jump.' The Stalnaker–Lewis account does not allow both members of the pair of opposite conditionals to be true. I will eventually defend the view that sometimes both members of a pair of opposite conditionals are true.

Lewis uses the symbol '□→' rather than '>' for subjunctive

'would have' conditionals. He uses '$\diamondsuit\!\!\rightarrow$' for subjunctive 'might have' conditionals and defines '$A \diamondsuit\!\!\rightarrow B$' as follows:

$$A \diamondsuit\!\!\rightarrow B =df \sim(A \;\square\!\!\rightarrow \sim B).$$

'If we hadn't hired Brandon, then we might have hired you' is taken as equivalent to 'It is not the case that if we hadn't hired Brandon, then we still would not have hired you.' $A \diamondsuit\!\!\rightarrow B$ is true in world i so long as some (A & B)-world is as close to i as any (A & $\sim B$)-world.

Given Stalnaker's limit and uniqueness assumptions, if some (A & B)-world is as close to i as any (A & $\sim B$)-world, then it is closer to i than any (A & $\sim B$)-world. Stalnaker's assumptions plus Lewis's account of '$\diamondsuit\!\!\rightarrow$' implies that there is no logical difference between $A \diamondsuit\!\!\rightarrow B$ and $A \square\!\!\rightarrow B$, an unacceptable result. Stalnaker does not attempt to account for 'might have' conditionals just in terms of possible worlds. He suggests that 'might' sentences often express epistemic possibility of a kind. 'If we hadn't hired Brandon, then we might have hired you' can be taken to mean 'It is epistemically possible that if we hadn't hired Brandon, then we would have hired you.'[13]

One can support alternatives to the Stalnaker–Lewis views by appealing to 'might have' conditionals. I did not drop the tray, and no cups broke. If I had dropped the tray, then all the cups might have broken, or so we think. If there is a possible world in which I drop the tray and not all the cups break and it is closer to the actual world than any world in which I drop a tray and all the cups break, then the 'might have' conditional is false on Lewis's view. Moreover, the 'would have' conditional 'If I had dropped the tray, not all the cups would have broken' comes out true, despite a natural inclination to think that in the circumstances all the cups might have broken. Prima facie, a world in which not all the cups break is more like a world in which none of the cups break than a world in which all the cups break.

Closely related to these qualms are those concerning subjunctive conditionals with true if-clauses. 'If 31 had not come up in 999 spins of the roulette wheel,' says someone gripped by the Monte Carlo fallacy, 'then it would come up on the thousandth spin.' Do we want to count this conditional as true if it happens that there were 999 spins of a wheel between 31s? Unless we think the wheel is fixed or we are deeply confused about probability, we think that 31 might well not have come up.

Donald Nute suggests that $A > B$ is true in world i if and only if all the possible A-worlds that are *close enough* or *sufficiently close* to i are B-worlds.[14] The corresponding 'might have' conditional is true if at least one of the A-worlds that are close enough to world i is a B-world. It is true that all the cups might have broken if I had dropped the tray so long as in some world in which I drop the tray that is close enough to the actual world – it need not be the closest – all the cups break. It is false that 31 would come up on the thousandth spin, if it had not come up on any of the previous 999 spins, so long as there are some worlds sufficiently close to the actual world in which 31 does not come up in a thousand spins. 'Close enough' and 'sufficiently close' are vague notions, but so, after all, is the notion of comparative similarity between possible worlds. If the indeterminacy of the account matches the already present indeterminacy of the subjunctive conditionals it treats, vagueness is no defect.

'Might', in addition to indicating something about epistemic possibility, indicates something about epistemic probability. One's belief that it is possible that P, or that it is possible for a to ϕ, is not sufficient for the appropriateness of saying 'It might be that P' or 'a might ϕ'. Although it is possible for me to fly to Omaha tomorrow, it is not true that I might fly to Omaha tomorrow; for the probability that I will fly to Omaha tomorrow is very low. One could connect probability with Nute's 'sufficiently close' relation between possible worlds to produce a hybrid combination of conditional probability and possible-worlds accounts of conditionals. But I shall not attempt to spell out the details of such a combination here.

In describing the cup-breaking example, I said that prima facie a world in which not all the cups break is more like a world in which none of the cups break than a world in which all the cups break. But we need not accept these first appearances. Lewis's account does not require that we use whatever standards of comparative world-similarity that come first to mind. If Lewis wants to, he can count possible worlds other than the actual world as being as similar to the actual world as the actual world is to itself. So Lewis can avoid the principle A & B, *therefore*, A $\Box\!\!\rightarrow B$ without making any formal changes in his account. (But he argues there is no need to avoid it.) Lewis can count a world in which all the cups break and one in which not all the cups break as equally similar to a world in which none of the cups break, if he wants to; and there are reasons for wanting to in addition to needing to deal with 'might have' conditionals and subjunctive conditionals with true if-clauses. I did not drop the tray; no cups broke; and, we suppose, if I had dropped the tray, there might have been no cups broken. We also suppose that, if I had dropped the tray, some cups, perhaps all the cups, might well have broken. But consider the following 'would have' conditional:

If I had dropped the tray, no cups would have broken.

In the actual world, no cups broke. Isn't a possible world in which no cups break more like the actual world than one in which some cups break? Doesn't the Lewis–Stalnaker account fail because it is forced to endorse this last conditional? Examples that illustrate difficulties of this sort usually involve a larger calamity. Jonathan Bennett discusses the conditional:

If Oswald had not killed Kennedy, someone else would have.[15]

Kit Fine writes:

The counterfactual 'If Nixon had pressed the button there would have been a nuclear holocaust' is true or can be imagined to be so. Now suppose that there never will be a nuclear holocaust. Then that counterfactual is, on Lewis's analysis, very likely false. For given any world in which antecedent and consequent are both true it will be easy to imagine a closer world in which the antecedent is true and the consequent false. For we need only imagine a change that prevents the holocaust but that does not require such a great divergence from reality.[16]

Other reviewers and critics of Lewis use similar examples. We want to accept many conditionals that fit the pattern 'If there had been a certain small difference, then it would have made a huge difference.'

Lewis responds that our judgments about similarities of worlds should be guided by our judgments about the acceptability of conditionals. 'We must use what we know about the truth and falsity of counterfactuals to see if we can find some sort of similarity relation – not necessarily the first one that springs to mind – that combines with Analysis 2 to yield the proper truth conditions.'[17] (Analysis 2 is a version of the account in terms of similarity between possible worlds.) Notice that Lewis wants to find a similarity relation that, once found, could be used to decide about the acceptability of previously unexamined counterfactual conditionals. Lewis does not suggest that we continue to use what we know about conditionals in order to set appropriate standards of similarity. Although there might be some theoretical interest in allowing just that, selecting the standard of similarity in each case to fit one's prior opinions about the conditional in question, Lewis is after a standard of similarity that can stand on its own.

Lewis's search for an appropriate standard of similarity is intended to handle several problems at once. His central problem is accounting for what he calls the asymmetry of counterfactual dependence, and his search involves a number of asymmetries, asymmetries of causation, temporal openness, miracles, and overdetermination. I shall return to this discussion in Chapter XII. Here I shall simply state the standards of similarity Lewis adopts. The following considerations are listed in order of importance:

(1) It is of the first importance to avoid big, widespread, diverse violations of law.
(2) It is of the second importance to maximize the spatio-temporal region throughout which perfect match of particular fact prevails.
(3) It is of the third importance to avoid even small, localized, simple violations of law.
(4) It is of little or no importance to secure approximate similarity of particular fact, even in matters that concern us greatly.[18]

We very much wanted to avoid breaking any of Grandmother's cups. In fact, we did avoid it: none broke in actuality. A possible world in which I dropped the tray and no cups broke is thus similar to the actual world in a respect that concerns us. In rank of importance, Lewis ranks similarities of this kind dead last. More important similarities fall under (1) and (2) above. A possible world that follows, for the most part, the laws of the actual world and that is a perfect match of the actual world until shortly before I drop the tray is more relevantly similar than any world not sharing these features. The fate of the cups in such a world depends on their physical condition and situation plus the laws. The number of cups that break will not help determine which possible worlds are most similar. Rather, the independent determination of which worlds are most similar will help determine the number of cups that would have broken. Similarly, the fate of our planet in Fine's button-pressing example depends on the physical set-up, button, batteries, wires, and bombs, or whatever, plus the laws. A little change that breaks or disconnects a wire can prevent the button pressing from producing a holocaust, but no single little change can extend the spatio-temporal region of perfect match, which matters much more for assessing conditionals, says Lewis, even if it matters much less for other human purposes.

Lewis ranks extensive spatio-temporal perfect match higher than the total avoidance of small, localized, simple violations of law. Two deterministic worlds that share the same laws and match perfectly at some time will match perfectly at every time. If the actual world is deterministic, and a possible world matches the actual world perfectly right up to the time I picked up the tray, then, if I held on to the tray in the actual world but dropped it in this possible world, some event in the possible world must violate the deterministic laws of the actual world. Although Lewis is no determinist, he does not want his account of conditionals to depend on the truth of indeterminism; and he has no serious qualms about allowing the possible worlds relevant to evaluating conditionals to contain 'small miracles', localized violations of the laws of the actual world. Other philosophers try to avoid allowing miracles in their accounts of non-miraculous conditionals. One can elaborate, refine, and emend in countless ways the general possible-world account that Stalnaker and Lewis develop. I shall sketch the prominent features of several variations.

Many variations on possible-worlds treatments of conditionals make more explicit use of temporal notions than the original accounts by Stalnaker and Lewis. Frank Jackson introduces the term *sequential counterfactual* for counterfactual conditionals 'which say that if something had happened at one time, something else would have happened *later* (maybe only a very little later)'.[19] He uses *Ta* to stand for the *antecedent-time*, the time at which the antecedent of sequential counterfactual is counterfactually supposed to obtain. Here is Jackson's proposal for evaluating the sequential counterfactual $P \;\Box\!\!\rightarrow Q$:

> Consider the *P*-worlds which satisfy the following conditions: (i) their causal laws at and after *Ta* are identical with ours, (ii) their *Ta* time-slices are the most similar in particular facts to ours, and (iii) they are identical in particular facts to our world prior to *Ta*. Call these possible worlds the *antecedently closest P*-worlds to our world. Then $(P \;\Box\!\!\rightarrow Q)$ is true at the actual world just if every antecedently closest *P*-world is a *Q*-world.[20]

Jackson also proposes that backward sequential counterfactuals can be handled by reversing the temporal requirements in the above account and that asequential counterfactuals can be understood as pairs of sequentials.

Wayne A. Davis formulates a proposal similar to Jackson's:

> The subjunctive conditional $A > C$ is true iff C is true in $s(A)$, where $s(A)$ is the *A*-world that is most similar to the actual world before $t(A)$, the time reference of A.[21]

Davis holds that, although Stalnaker's account is incorrect for subjunctives, it is correct for indicative conditionals. Unlike Jackson, who provides a separate treatment to allow for the truth of backward-looking conditionals like 'If Moss had won, he would have had to have used different tyres from the start', Davis is willing to dismiss backward sequential conditionals as false. If condition (i) about the identity of causal laws is deleted from Jackson's proposal, the result looks very much like Davis's. Perhaps Davis could argue that Jackson's (i) is redundant and that $s(A)$ would always satisfy (i).

Delete from Jackson's proposal condition (iii) about the identity of particular fact to our world prior to *Ta*, rather than condition (i), and the result looks very much like one made by Jonathan Bennett. Bennett wants to handle both forward and backward sequential counterfactuals with a single theory, not with two related theories as Jackson does. Bennett proposes that P > Q is true if and only if:

> *Q is true at all the T-closest causally possible P-worlds* – where T is the time to which P pertains. According to that, you learn whether a counterfactual is true by finding the T-closest antecedent worlds which obey the laws of the actual world, and discovering whether the consequent is true at those worlds. Or, in the language of world stages, you find the closest T-world-stages, unroll the rest of those worlds – for all times earlier and later than T – in accordance with the laws of the actual world, and see whether any of them contain Q. If all of them do, (P > Q) is true; otherwise false. There is here no bias in favor of conditionals running from earlier times to later, no provision for any miracles, and not the remotest hint of a threat from the Downing scare story.[22]

A 'Downing scare story' appears to provide good grounds for accepting each member of a pair of so-called opposite conditionals, if *P* then *Q*, and if *P* then not-*Q*. On Bennett's account, there is no way that $P > Q$ and $P > {\sim}Q$ should both come out true.

John L. Pollock defends a possible-worlds account of conditionals in which the closest P-world is the P-world which results from making minimal changes to the actual world to accommodate the truth of P.[23] This is a variation that makes some real differences.[24] Indeed, anyone who formulates a new version of a possible-world account of conditionals pursues some – apparently – desirable and distinctive differences from other accounts. There are differences about which principles are logical principles and which conditionals are acceptable conditionals. Instead of addressing some of these differences immediately,[25] I turn in the next chapter to general questions about the various tasks theories of conditionals attempt to accomplish.

Part Two

A NEW TREATMENT OF CONDITIONALS

CHAPTER VIII

Inference, Entailment,
and the Purposes of Theories

The theories of conditionals from antiquity to yesterday that we have surveyed have several purposes. Some of these purposes are incompatible, and some are merely distinguishable. Possible-world theories and probability theories each have two distinguishable purposes, the evaluation of particular conditionals and the evaluation of particular conditional arguments. Earlier theories, in addition to following these pursuits, attempt to provide criteria for the logical truth of conditionals, attempt to provide a theory of deductive validity, and attempt to provide theories of inference or deducibility.

The phrase 'evaluation of particular conditionals' is evasive because of its generality. Besides covering the evaluation of conditionals as true or false, it covers their evaluation as acceptable or unacceptable, probable or improbable, and assertable or unassertable. A theorist at one extreme applies the principle of bivalence to conditionals: any conditional is either true, or, if not true, false. A theorist at the other extreme denies that any conditional has a truth-value, unless it is a logical truth or an inconsistency. Theorists between these extremes attempt to formulate general criteria distinguishing conditionals with truth-value from those strictly neither true nor false. Such distinctions can be principled without being precise.

Although logical theorists may be reluctant to allow that *true* and *false* admit of conceptual indeterminacy and borderline cases, various series of statements, including series of conditionals, provide examples of suitable continua. Consider a series of conditionals of the form:

If I had an adult brother, he would be at least *n* centimetres tall.

121

For $n = 100$, I am willing to admit, the conditional is true. For $n = 250$, the conditional is false. What about, say, $n = 177$? An adult male 177 centimetres tall is *tallish*, not definitely tall, but also definitely not short. I (who have never had a brother) am somewhat taller than 177 centimetres. Is it true that, if I had an adult brother, he would be at least 177 centimetres tall? Few theories of conditionals would say so. Some, because they would not say it is true, would say that therefore it is false. While I certainly don't want to regard it as true, I am also reluctant to regard it as false. And, once it is allowed that some, but not all, conditionals are neither true nor false, I want to deny the necessity of sharp cut-off points between true and not-true, and between false and not-false. There is no n such that the conditional is true for n centimetres but not true for $n + 1$ centimetres.[1]

When several terms of evaluation each apply to a conditional, one may nevertheless be somewhat more appropriate or fitting than the others. Nelson Goodman talks about *true* and *false* counterfactuals in 'The problem of counterfactual conditionals'. He also talks about conditionals *holding* and *failing to hold*. Conditionals are *affirmed*, *denied*, *accepted*, *asserted*, and *established*. When he contrasts the members of the following famous pair, he says that we would affirm the first and deny the second:

(i) If match *M* had been scratched, it would have lighted,
(ii) If match *M* had been scratched, it would not have been dry.

It is somehow more comfortable to say that we would affirm (i) than to say simply that (i) is true. I am unsure how best to explain this, and I am unaware of any theory, adequate or otherwise, that attempts to explain the appropriateness of different semantic evaluations. Distinctions like that between (i) and (ii), however described in contrasting evaluative terms, preoccupy many recent theories of conditionals. One wants a theory that accepts (i) and rejects (ii) without using a question-begging assumption. (Goodman, who found no way to do this in terms of laws and sentences true in the actual world, should not be expected to regard conditional probability, much less similarity between possible worlds, as contributing adequate solutions to his puzzle.) Possible-world theories defend the judgment that some possible worlds in which the match is scratched and lights are closer to the actual world than any possible world in which the match is scratched and is not dry; and these judgments cannot be based simply on a desire to arrive at predetermined evaluations of (i) and (ii). Although different evaluative terms are used and not everyone agrees about just which conditionals are true, to be affirmed, to be asserted, acceptable, or whatever, there is still a large measure of agreement. One purpose of a theory of conditionals is to account for and explain such agreement.

Another purpose is to account for the validity or invalidity of argument forms that employ conditionals. As we have seen, both probability theories and possible-world theories classify contraposition, antecedent strengthening, and hypothetical syllogism as invalid forms. These forms are all valid on classical truth-functional treatments of validity and they are all derivable in various standard systems of propositional logic. The treatment of particular argument forms involving conditionals and the evaluation of particular conditionals are different tasks. There appears to be no reason why a theory has to perform each equally well. Despite Goodman's profession that his suggestion involves unresolved difficulties, for example, many regard it as on the right track for evaluating particular conditionals. But few ask the question how Goodman's account treats hypothetical syllogism, and its answer is not obvious.

A theory that we normally use to serve several distinct purposes we can use to serve only one. We can use a possible-worlds theory, for example, only to treat the validity of conditional argument forms. We can attempt the evaluation of particular conditionals by some other theory, say, one like Goodman's. It will not then beg a question to use one's prior evaluation of a conditional to decide about comparative closeness of possible worlds, since we will not use judgments of comparative closeness in turn to evaluate particular conditionals.

According to the discussion of validity and invalidity early in this book, the following argument about invalidity is itself invalid:

The contraposition of subjunctive conditionals is invalid.

Argument *A* contraposes subjunctive conditionals.
Therefore, argument *A* is invalid.

The premises of this argument can both be true when the conclusion is false. An argument form is invalid, remember, if and only if not all its instances are valid. If contraposition is an invalid form, then not all instances of it are valid. It simply does not follow that no instances are valid. Indeed, some instances appear perfectly valid. Let argument *A* be:

If I had drawn a flush, the top card would have been a diamond.
Therefore, if the top card had not been a diamond, I would not have drawn a flush.

So far as I can see, it is not possible for the premise of this argument to be true when the conclusion is false. This is not to say that contraposition suddenly appears to be valid after all. Remember:

If I had drawn a flush, I would not have drawn a straight flush.
Therefore, if I had drawn a straight flush, I would not have drawn a flush.

We have explained the invalidity of this last instance of contraposition in terms both of probability and of possible worlds. We still lack a compatible explanation of the validity of the first instance. If the two conditionals really are equivalent, as they seem to be, we lack an adequate theory that explains their equivalence. We will return to this problem in Chapter XV.

Probability and possible-world theories that count some classically valid argument forms as invalid do not go on to count some classically invalid argument forms as valid. Neither do they provide new reasons for regarding conditionals as logically true, true in virtue of their logical form. A theoretical interest in formally true conditionals coincides with an interest in formally valid arguments. An argument is valid if and only if a conditional corresponding to the argument is necessarily true. The conditionals here are typically indicative, and it is difficult to think of an argument such that the corresponding subjunctive conditional is more appropriate than the indicative. The truth-functional material conditional serves this theoretical purpose well. The notion of a tautologous conditional is theoretically valuable in understanding the validity of arguments, whether or not the arguments themselves contain any conditionals.

A tradition as old as the history of the theory of conditionals itself, as we have seen, looks for a conditional that is even more closely related to valid argument. An argument is valid when and only when a corresponding conditional of the favoured kind is just plain true. (A material conditional is clearly not of this kind, for it can be true without being tautologously, necessarily, logically, or formally true; and it is the possession of the latter attributes that corresponds with validity of the corresponding argument.) Medieval writers sometimes appear not to distinguish valid arguments from true conditionals. C. I. Lewis developed his systems of strict implication because of dissatisfaction with Russell's material conditional as a theory of implication. Here is a purpose for a theory of conditionals that is incompatible with a purpose we discussed earlier. A theory that attempts to distinguish true from untrue conditionals should not at the same time hold that true conditionals correspond to valid arguments. There are many reasons for holding a conditional to be true besides the valid following of the main clause from the if-clause. 'You ought to water your lawn more often', for example, does not follow validly from 'Your lawn is brown' even if it is perfectly appropriate to say 'If your lawn is brown, then you ought to water it more often.' The relevant relations between the brownness and dryness of your lawn are not logical relations.

If we are going to discuss relations between conditionals and valid arguments, we ought to begin with a measure of theoretical agreement about what we mean by 'argument'. Many logic textbooks define *argument* like this:

By an *argument* we mean a system of declarative sentences, one of which is designated as the *conclusion* and the others as *premises*.

On this understanding, an argument need not correspond to an inference. A statement is a conclusion simply by being so designated. A conclusion need not be drawn, inferred, or detached. It need not be something that someone concludes.

125

Let us look at a typical logic-textbook proof or derivation in order to draw some contrasts between an argument, in an accepted technical sense of this term, and inference. Consider the argument:

~(*N* & *S*), *S*, therefore, ~*N*.

Given a couple of elementary rules of derivation, we can derive the conclusion ~*N* from the two assumptions:

	1. ~(*N* & *S*)	Assumption
	2. *S*	Assumption
	3. *N*	Assumption (for *reductio*)
2, 3	4. *N* & *S*	2, 3, rule of conjunction
1, 2, 3	5. (*N* & *S*) & ~(*N* & *S*)	1, 4, rule of conjunction
1, 2	6. ~*N*	3, 5, rule of *reductio ad absurdum*

The assumption numbers on the left indicate that the formula on that line is derived from just those assumptions. The three assumption numbers on the left in line 5 indicate that the formula is derived from all three assumptions. The formula on line 5 is an inconsistency of a kind standardly known as a contradiction, a conjunction in which the second conjunct is the negation of the first conjunct. Does someone constructing this proof infer the formula on line 5 from assumptions 1, 2, and 3? Or, to start with an apparently simpler question, does someone constructing this proof infer the formula on line 6 from assumptions 1 and 2?

To answer this question, we should know more about the intended function of the letters '*N*' and '*S*'. If they function as '*P*' and '*Q*' more often do, as propositional variables, the proof would be in order. The proof then pertains quite generally to any two-premise argument in which the first premise is a negated conjunction, the second premise is the second conjunct, and the conclusion is the negation of the first conjunct. If '*N*', and thus '~*N*', function as propositional variables in the proof, no one infers the formula on line 6 from anything. Although not everything one believes is inferred, everything one infers is believed: belief is a necessary condition of inference. Propositional variables cannot be inferred because they cannot be believed. Sentences like 'Sally believes that *P*' are common in philosophical writing. If '*P*' is a propositional variable, as it usually is, then so is the belief sentence that contains it. The sentence can be useful even though there is no belief it attributes to Sally. 'Sally infers that ~*N*' has the same status when '*N*' is a propositional variable. There is no belief that it says that Sally acquires by inference.

Suppose, on the other hand, that '*N*' and '*S*' function as abbreviations rather than as variables. For example:

N = Penguins live near the North Pole.
S = Penguins live near the South Pole.

Our argument can be rendered in English:

Penguins do not live both near the North Pole and near the South Pole.
Penguins do live near the South Pole.
Therefore, penguins do not live near the North Pole.

Does someone constructing the proof with this understanding of the letters infer that penguins do not live near the North Pole? It depends. I who actually construct the proof and actually believe the conclusion, that penguins do not live near the North Pole, do not infer the conclusion from the premises. Constructing the proof does nothing to help me acquire a belief in the conclusion or to help me believe the conclusion with greater confidence, certainty, warrant, or justification. There was a bit of inference involved, not represented on the page, as I wrote the page. From the fact that penguins do not live near the North Pole, I inferred that it is not the case that they both live near the North Pole and live near the South Pole; I inferred the first premise of the argument from its conclusion, which I believed from the start. If I should use the argument to represent my purported inference of the conclusion, the inference represented would beg the question. But what is true for me in this case need not be true for everyone. It is possible to believe a negated conjunction for reasons other than a prior disbelief in one or the other conjunct. Anything credible (and, alas, much that is not) can be believed on testimony; and there are many reasons in addition to a trust in testimony for accepting a premise. Someone could come to believe each premise of our argument – who is unsure about the existence of northern penguins – without first believing the conclusion and then infer the conclusion from the premises.

Suppose then that the proof represents someone's inference to the conclusion that penguins do not live near the North Pole. Not only is there a genuine inference from the premises, but the inference proceeds by *reductio ad absurdum*. Does someone constructing this proof, we ask again, infer the formula on line 5 from assumptions 1, 2, and 3? Line 5 is a contradiction, and no one wants to infer a contradiction. People do have inconsistent beliefs. Occasionally they even infer inconsistencies, but not while recognizing what they are doing. Explicit contradictions, so easily recognized as inconsistencies, are seldom if ever believed, much less inferred. The argument from lines 1 and 4 to line 5 is valid; but line 5 does not represent a valid inference of a contradiction because there is no such inference. Steps of derivation in a formal proof need not correspond to inferences. Thus even when a whole proof represents a genuine inference, not every derived formula need be inferred from earlier formulae. The relation between inferential steps and derivation steps is not that simple. There can be an inference associated with line 5, not the inference of an inconsistency, something necessarily false, but of the fact that assumptions 1, 2, and 3 are jointly inconsistent. If there is a step of inference corresponding to line 6, it is not an inference from a contradiction but from the truth that $\sim(N \mathbin{\&} S)$, S and N are jointly inconsistent. 'They can't all be true; so since the first two are true, the third one is not true.' A *reductio ad absurdum* inference is not an inference from an inconsistency.

According to C. I. Lewis's notion of strict implication, a contradiction strictly implies anything. When I outlined one of Lewis's arguments for this view, in Chapter IV, I cast the argument in terms of inference and rules of inference. In light of my recent contentions about inference, it is a strange thing to say:

Anyone who wants to deny that any arbitrary conclusion can be validly inferred from any contradiction of the form '$p \mathbin{\&} \sim p$' must reject at least one of the rules or principles outlined above.

Just as one cannot infer a conclusion one doesn't believe, one cannot infer from a premise one doesn't believe. To infer something, arbitrary or not, from a contradiction, one must first believe the contradiction, no easy task. Lewis's point really concerns validity rather than inference. Should one manage to infer something from a contradiction, the inference would be valid. Not every step of formal derivation corresponds to a step of inference, and what logic textbooks call *rules of inference* can also be regarded as rules of derivation. The term *deduction* covers two different processes, the derivation of formula in accord with formal rules, and deductive inference, in which a conclusion is inferred, and therefore believed, on logically conclusive grounds.

Philosophers working outside of philosophical logic often use *entails* and *implies* interchangeably. They cast some claims as entailments, and some as the denials of entailment, without seeing a good reason to distinguish entailment from strict implication. Some philosophers, on the other hand, devote much effort and ingenuity to drawing this distinction adequately. G. E. Moore explains entailment in terms of deductive inference when he says that 'entails' is the converse of 'is deducible from'. The philosophers who develop theories of entailment are bothered by the paradoxes of strict implication as patterns of acceptable inference.

Georg Henrik von Wright offers the following definition of entailment:

> *p* entails *q*, if and only if, by means of logic, it is possible to come to know the truth of $p \supset q$ without coming to know the falsehood of *p* or the truth of *q*.[2]

Others propose structurally similar definitions. Clear, undoubted success in this venture remains elusive. Some definitions fail to exclude examples whose exclusion is intended. Some render 'entails' non-transitive, and there is no consensus about whether this is desirable or undesirable. Some are unsatisfiable and so fail to include examples whose inclusion is intended. I will not document these various difficulties here.

Alan Ross Anderson and Nuel D. Belnap Jr develop and defend another influential approach to defining entailment.

129

Entailment requires a genuine relation between statements, according to them. This is the requirement of relevance, and its formal treatment is relevance logic. Anderson and Belnap published a number of articles and monographs, both jointly and separately, and then were the principal co-authors of *Entailment: the Logic of Relevance and Necessity* (1975). (Anderson died late in 1973.) This variety of relevance logic is now an accepted branch of logic. I will make no attempt here to explain its intrinsic mathematical interest.

The following definitions show the character of the Anderson-Belnap notion of entailment:

> We shall say that a primitive entailment $A \rightarrow B$ is *explicitly tautological* if some (conjoined) atom of A is identical with some (disjoined) atom of B. Such entailments may be thought of as satisfying the classical dogma that for A to entail B, B must be 'contained' in A. . . .
> We . . . call an entailment $A_1 \vee \ldots \vee A_m \rightarrow B_1 \& \ldots \& B_n$ in normal form *explicitly tautological* (extending the previous definition) iff for every A_i and B_j, $A_i \rightarrow B_j$ is explicitly tautological (sharing); and we take such entailments to be valid iff explicitly tautological.[3]

On this view, '$P \& \sim P$' entails 'P' but it does not entail 'Q': 'Q' entails '$Q \vee \sim Q$' but it does not entail '$P \vee \sim P$'.

C. I. Lewis's argument that a contradiction entails anything does not go through on this variety of relevance logic. Relevance logic maintains that the following rules of inference are not jointly acceptable for any single sense of 'or':

> From A, one may infer a disjunction A or B.
> From a disjunction A or B, and the negation of a disjunct, $\sim A$, one may infer the remaining disjunct B.

If we interpret the disjunctions as truth-functional, $A \vee B$, then, according to Anderson and Belnap, the first rule is acceptable and the second is not. The second rule is acceptable if the disjunction is intensional.[4] The notion of an intensional disjunction can be explained in terms of a conditional. Just as a truth-functional disjunction A v B has the same truth conditions as the corresponding material conditional $\sim A \supset B$, so an intensional disjunction $A \boxed{v} B$ has the same truth conditions as the corresponding subjunctive conditional.

Relevance logic holds that disjunctive syllogism for truth-functional disjunctions is an invalid argument form. According to traditional conceptions of validity, of course, the form:

From A v B, and $\sim A$, one may infer B,

is valid. Anderson and Belnap reject such conceptions, which they call 'official'. They propose an alternative conception of validity that requires the relevance of the premises of valid argument to its conclusion. According to their notions of *entailment* and *validity*, true entailment-statements correspond to valid arguments. A entails B, and the argument A, *therefore, B* is valid, only if A and B share a component.

The rejection of truth-functional disjunctive syllogism cannot be separated from the rejection of truth-functional *modus ponens*. This is scarcely a *reductio*. Although '$\sim P$ v Q' and '$P \supset Q$' are equivalent, it is easier to defend the identification of natural-language 'or' with 'v' than the identification of natural-language 'if, then' with '$\supset$'. Revising the notion of validity, so as to classify $P \supset Q$, P, *therefore, Q* and P v Q, $\sim P$, *therefore, Q* as invalid argument forms, appears to many a worse cure than the disease it aims to abolish, the admission of P & $\sim P$, *therefore, Q* as a valid argument form.

The rule of disjunctive syllogism closely resembles the fifth of the five basic argument forms of the Stoics. Anderson and Belnap admit that the rule is valid so long as the disjunction is intensional. According to them, whenever an ordinary, natural-language argument is of disjunctive syllogism form, the disjunction involved is intensional. Logicians who have represented these arguments with 'v' have sold us a bill of goods.[5]

Philosophers respond with instances of disjunctive syllogism that appear to employ the truth-functional 'or'. Consider the following homely story of my search for the vacuum cleaner:

It was not where it belonged in the downstairs hall closet. Eventually, I looked for it everywhere (in the house) except in the upstairs bedroom and the storage room. (I assumed it was somewhere in the house.) Then I discovered it was not in the upstairs bedroom, and I reasoned by disjunctive syllogism:

Either the vacuum cleaner is in the upstairs bedroom or it is in the storage room.
The vacuum cleaner is not in the upstairs bedroom.
Therefore, the vacuum cleaner is in the storage room.

Is this disjunctive premise intensional? In the little story just told, it can be quite true, or acceptable, even though a corresponding subjunctive conditional is unacceptable and untrue:

If the vacuum cleaner had not been in the storage room, it would have been in the upstairs bedroom.

On the contrary, if it had not been in the storage room, it would have been back where it belongs in the downstairs hall closet. This truth about how my household operates is consistent with the soundness of the disjunctive syllogism argument but inconsistent with the intensional interpretation of its disjunctive premise.

Relevance logic rejects more traditionally valid forms than most of us meant to discard. Arguments that we *ought* to want to discard everything relevance logic rejects have not persuaded. Relevance logic rejects too much. We should turn to alternative responses to the paradoxes of implication.

One such response is due to W. E. Johnson. Johnson distinguishes constitutive from epistemic conditions of inference.[6] He does not attempt to replace the material conditional or the strict conditional with a new entailment connective explained in terms of shared components or in terms of assertion, knowledge, belief, possibilities of coming to know, a priori ways of getting to know, or the like. Although his views influence von Wright, and thus others like Geach whom von Wright in turn influences, Johnson's theory is structurally different from theirs. The epistemic conditions of inference remain separate; they are not used in an attempt to formulate a new, improved constitutive condition.

Putative inferences that have the form of any paradox of strict implication will violate at least one epistemic condition of inference for anybody who has consistent beliefs. Inferences of other forms may also violate the epistemic conditions, depending on the epistemic state of the person making the inference. Some of these inferences trade on the paradoxes of material implication. An inference that itself has the form of a paradox of material implication may satisfy the epistemic conditions:

> Jane is not home. Therefore, Jane is home ⊃ Jane is washing her hair.

Notice that, so long as one's beliefs are consistent, if the inference above represents one's sole reason for believing the conditional, attempts to infer further conclusions from this conditional as a premise will frequently violate the epistemic conditions. The first premise of the following *modus ponens*, for example, will not be believed:

> Jane is home. Jane is home ⊃ Jane is washing her hair.
> Therefore, Jane is washing her hair.

Johnson's formulation of conditions for an inference of the form *p, therefore, q* are:

> *Constitutive Conditions*: (i) the proposition '*p*' and (ii) the proposition '*p* would imply *q*' must both be true.
> *Epistemic Conditions*: (i) the asserting of '*p*' and (ii) the asserting of '*p* would imply *q*' must both be permissible without reference to the asserting of *q*.[7]

I shall not attempt here to expound Johnson's sometimes obscure but often suggestive theory of logic so as to explain his eccentric choice of 'would imply' rather than simply 'implies'. Johnson's follower Susan Stebbing restates his distinction as follows:

> *Constitutive Conditions*: (i) *p* must be true; (ii) *p* must imply *q*.
> *Epistemic Conditions*: (i) *p* must be known to be true; (ii) *p* must be known to imply *q* without its being known that *q* is true.[8]

Stebbing's requirement of knowledge seems to be too stringent

133

since we often infer from what we believe without knowing. Johnson presumably does not hold that proper assertion requires knowledge. I will provide still another formulation of the distinction (and will omit here the first constitutive condition). An inference by someone S from premises to conclusion must satisfy:

Constitutive Condition: the inference is valid.
Epistemic Conditions: S believes the premises; S believes that the inference is valid; and S does not have either of these beliefs because he already believes the conclusion.

We are to understand 'valid' here in the ordinary or 'official' way. Johnson happens to apply the term 'valid' to inferences that satisfy both the conditions he formulated.

If one believes that Jane is not washing her hair, then one may believe both the premises of the following *modus tollens*:

Jane is home ⊃ Jane is washing her hair. Jane is not washing her hair.
Therefore, Jane is not at home.

In the situation we have described, the epistemic conditions are violated in this case because the subject believes the conditional premise only because he already believes the conclusion.

Consider again the pair of inferences to which Anderson and Belnap object:

P, therefore, *P* or *Q*,
P or *Q*, not-*P*, therefore, *Q*.

Johnson's theory of inference does not need to invoke two senses of 'or' to explain the conviction that these two together constitute logical funny business. If the first inference satisfies the epistemic conditions of inference, then the second inference does not.

Johnson's theory of inference distinguishes between different instances of *modus ponens* and disjunctive syllogism and other classically valid forms according to the epistemic circumstances. Consider again disjunctive syllogism, since disputes in the theory of entailment centre around it. When one believes a disjunction only because one believes one or the other disjunct by itself, then any purported inference by disjunctive syllogism violates an epistemic condition of inference.

> Either the yellow car is not in Claire's driveway, or Claire is at home. The yellow car is in Claire's driveway. Therefore, Claire is at home.

One who accepts the disjunction only on the basis of a belief in the conclusion would beg the question by purporting to infer the conclusion from the premises. One who accepts the disjunction only on the basis of belief in the first disjunct cannot believe the second premise without inconsistency. But one can reasonably accept the disjunction without having a prior belief either about the current location of Claire or about the current location of the yellow car, and in that case inference can be perfectly in order once the other premise is supplied. Appeal to epistemic conditions of inference can draw similar distinctions for every acceptable form of inference. The propriety of inference, on this view, is not just a matter of form.

The impropriety of inference, however, sometimes is just a matter of form. That is, some forms of argument can never satisfy the epistemic conditions of inference. The infamous *P and not-P, therefore, Q* is an example. One reasonably believes this argument to be valid only because one believes the premise to be inconsistent. The argument cannot possibly provide a consistent, coherent reason for accepting its conclusion, for the premise really is inconsistent. If there is no constituent in common in the premise and the conclusion, this by itself makes no difference to Johnson's treatment. Indeed, it treats *P and not-P, therefore, P* as also a completely hopeless putative inference, despite the shared constituents. Johnson's approach provides a distinct alternative to various theories of entailment for dealing with a requirement of inferential relevance.

I suggest that it is better to take the epistemic structure of inference seriously than to attempt to capture relevant inference in purely formal terms. Entailment, as distinguished from implication, is an unneeded notion. One purpose of a theory of conditionals, the search for an adequate definition of entailment to explain proper deducibility, is accomplished better by reference to the epistemic conditions of inference.

Another tradition in philosophical logic connects understanding conditionals with understanding certain inferences. R. M. Hare suggests this forthright account of conditionals:

> To understand the 'If . . . then' form of sentence is to understand the place that it has in logic (to understand its logical properties). It is, in fact, to understand the operation of *modus ponens* and related inferences.[9]

J. L. Mackie agrees that the logical powers of 'If . . . then' constitute at least the core of its meaning:

> To say that the *whole* meaning of 'If *P*, *Q*' is so given, would, however, be surprising. This approach declines to give any explicit meaning to 'If *P*, *Q*' on its own: it says that this if-sentence is either just a something-or-other which enters into these entailments, or the giving of a licence to draw these inferences.[10]

'Licence' here alludes to Gilbert Ryle's essay ' "If," "so," and "because" ':

> Knowing 'if *p*, then *q*' is, then, rather like being in possession of a railway ticket. It is having a license or warrant to make a journey from London to Oxford.[11]
> If we ask what is the point of learning '*if p, then q*,' . . . part of the answer would be a reference to the learner's ability and readiness to infer from '*p*' to '*q*' and from '*not-q*' to '*not-p*'.[12]
> When I learn '*if p, then q*,' I am learning that I am authorised to argue '*p, so q*,' *provided that I get my premiss* '*p*.'[13]

These passages from Ryle go beyond the position Hare advocates. Hare seeks to explain one's understanding of a conditional as one's understanding of its logical powers, as the acceptance of certain conditional inference patterns as valid and the rejection of certain others as invalid. Ryle is concerned not just with the evaluation of inference, but with its performance. Some conditionals are understood only to be rejected; some are neither rejected nor accepted. Ryle is concerned with conditionals that are accepted, those that are 'known' or 'learned'. To accept a conditional is to be prepared, given the other required premise or premises, to infer. To accept 'If the little red light blinks, the battery is weak' is to be prepared to infer that the battery is weak once you see that the little light is blinking.

Whether or not this might constitute the *whole* meaning of conditionals, we should ask whether it is plausible in itself. Although Gilbert Harman does not mention Ryle when he advances the following view, it appears to be inconsistent with Ryle's:

> Logical principles are not directly rules of *belief revision*. They are not particularly about belief at all. For example, *modus ponens* does not say that, if one believes *p* and also believes *if p then q*, one may also believe *q*. Nor are there any principles of belief revision that directly correspond to logical principles like *modus ponens*. Logical principles hold universally, without exception, whereas the corresponding principles of belief revision would be at best *prima facie* principles, which do not always hold. It is not always true that, if one believes *p* and believes *if p then q*, one may infer *q*. The proposition *q* may be absurd or otherwise unacceptable in the light of one's other beliefs, so that one should give up either one's belief in *p* or one's belief in *if p then q* rather than believe *q*.[14]

The little red light is blinking. Right before the recent installation of a fresh battery, I checked the battery with a reliable tester. Earlier I accepted the conditional 'If the little red light blinks, the battery is weak.' If I think that a short circuit of some kind could drain a fresh battery or if I think that the little red light is extraordinarily reliable, then, in this case, I might infer that the battery is weak. But I am more likely to reject the conditional I previously accepted.

Many recent writers on conditionals advance (with no reference to Ryle) a more specific form of Ryle's view on conditionals. They award *modus ponens* special status:

> And it is surely true, that where someone believes that if *A*, *C*, they would, if they were to gain direct evidence that *A*, come to believe that *C*.[15]

Such remarks are backed up by the view that the conditional probability P(*C/A*) is a measure of the assertability or acceptance of the conditional *if A, then C*. If, in my opinion, the probability of *the battery is weak* conditional on *the little light blinks* is high, and I am sure that the light is blinking, then I ought to be willing to accept that the battery is weak. Jackson points out that a defence of this sort of the utility of *modus ponens* does not serve as well for the utility of *modus tollens*.

> You may properly assert $(P \rightarrow Q)$ when you would *not* infer $\sim P$ on learning $\sim Q$. Suppose you say 'If he doesn't live in Boston, then he lives somewhere in New England' or 'If he works, he will still fail,' you will – despite the validity of *Modus Tollens* – neither infer that he lives in Boston on learning (to your surprise) that he doesn't live in New England nor infer that he didn't work on learning (to your surprise) that he passed. Rather on learning either you would abandon the original conditional as mistaken.[16]

When the probability of *He lives somewhere in New England* conditional on *He doesn't live in Boston* is high, it does not follow that the probability of *He lives in Boston* conditional on *He doesn't live in New England* is also high. The circumstances in which one declines to infer by *modus tollens* include those in which one declines to infer by contraposition.

There are many examples in which it seems wrong to infer, by contraposition or by *modus tollens*, from premises that have the appropriate forms and that one accepts. Examples of *modus ponens*, like Jackson's in that they strike anyone who understands the premises as odd or wrong, are not needed to support Harman's point. We need only examples in which, given that premises are accepted and are of the appropriate forms, the subject reasonably declines to infer by *modus ponens*. The weak-battery detector example is one such, and other examples are available:

> Daria believes that, if the yellow car is in Claire's driveway, then Claire is at home. Daria sees Claire at the supermarket, leaves, and drives right past Claire's house. Daria does not expect to see the yellow car in the driveway; for she assumes

the car is parked in the supermarket parking lot. But now she sees the yellow car anyway, right in Claire's driveway. So it is not true, after all, that, if the yellow car is in the driveway, Claire is at home; for it is extremely unlikely that Claire drove at breakneck speed over an alternative route home from the supermarket. And how else could she be at home now?

Examples in which one accepts both a conditional and its if-clause and yet does not accept the main clause appear to conflict with the Ramsey test. Recent versions of the Ramsey test are often formulated as explicit biconditionals:

> Somebody is entitled to assert a conditional $(A \rightarrow C)$ iff coming to have minimal evidence warranting the assertion of A would lead to their being entitled to assert that C.[17]

> Accept a proposition of the form 'if A then C' in a state of belief K if and only if the minimal change of K needed to accept A also requires accepting C.[18]

In the first passage, by Anthony Appiah, minimal evidence is that evidence necessary to add just the belief that A. Evidence that A but not C is not minimal evidence that A. Prompted by Harman, we can entertain the following possibility: someone who is entitled to assert a conditional comes to have minimal evidence warranting the assertion of the if-clause and is thereby led to deny the conditional rather than to assert its main clause. In the acceptance (rather than assertion) language of the second passage, by Peter Gärdenfors, we are entertaining the possibility that one may on occasion accept a conditional proposition in a state of belief K when the minimal change of K needed to accept the if-clause leads to abandoning the conditional rather than to accepting its main clause.

Logic is the science of inconsistency, not the science of inference. The usefulness of deductive logic for the deductive inference of beliefs is entirely due to the realization that certain statements are jointly inconsistent. If two subsets exhaust a set of jointly inconsistent statements, and all the statements in one subset are true, then there is at least one false statement in the second subset. We can thus transform a three-member set of jointly inconsistent statements into three different two-premise arguments. The following three statements, for example, cannot all be true:

> If the yellow car is in Claire's driveway, then Claire is at home. Claire is not at home. The yellow car is in Claire's driveway.

So each of the following arguments is deductively valid:

> If the yellow car is in Claire's driveway, then Claire is at home. The yellow car is in Claire's driveway. Therefore, Claire is at home.

> The yellow car is in Claire's driveway. Claire is not at home. Therefore, it is false that, if the yellow car is in Claire's driveway, then Claire is at home.

> Claire is not at home. If the yellow car is in Claire's driveway, then Claire is at home. Therefore, the yellow car is not in Claire's driveway.

Suppose that one starts off inconsistently, although perhaps only briefly, believing each of the three statements in the original set, recognizes the inconsistency, and attempts to remove it by retaining just two of the original three. Which two it should be depends on one's circumstances. In this example, as in many examples, the statements do not differ in intrinsic credibility. Each pair of beliefs can be suitable for retention depending on the circumstances, one's other beliefs, and one's cognitive habits. There is no privileged place for *modus ponens*, no reason why a conditional and its if-clause should be more worthy of retention than some other pair.

The premises of a deductively valid argument, it is said, transmit truth or warrant or probability to the conclusion. If we persist in using the image of transmission, we should realize that logic will not generally tell us its direction. If the conclusion is something we should conclude or infer, something we are warranted in believing on the evidence, logic will not generally tell us what the conclusion is. Unless one of the statements is logically true or logically false, logic will not tell us which of a number of jointly inconsistent statements to distrust most.

One can avoid inconsistency in this example merely by giving up belief in one or the other of the three statements. Although no inference to the contradictory of the rejected statement is required for consistency when two of the statements continue to be accepted, the inference seems psychologically irresistible. The contradictory of the rejected statement, after all, is implied by the statements one continues to believe. For every deductively valid inference, there is an implication; but there is not a valid inference for every implication. In this chapter I have suggested what valid inference requires in addition to implication.

CHAPTER IX

Problems with the Ramsey Test, Possible Worlds, and Probability

If all time is eternally present
All time is unredeemable.

If *I* were a fish I just couldn't resist
You, when you are fishing that way, that way.

The following formulation by Stalnaker of the Ramsey test appears near the beginning of Chapter VI:

First, hypothetically make the minimal revision of your stock of beliefs required to assume the antecedent. Then, evaluate the acceptability of the consequent on the basis of this revised body of beliefs.

On this account, the hypothetical addition of the antecedent to one's stock of beliefs does not involve, as part of the hypothesis, how one comes to have the new belief. On some later formulations of the Ramsey test, the hypothesis concerns not merely that the belief in the antecedent is added to a previous stock of beliefs, but how it is added.

Some reformulations of the Ramsey test, as we saw in the last chapter, are significant changes. It makes a difference whether we consider the hypothetical addition of a belief, never mind how it was acquired, or whether we hypothetically consider the acquisition of a belief. Not all acquisitions are hypothetical. On occasion we will actually acquire a belief that brings us to reject a previously accepted conditional rather than to accept its consequent. An acceptable conditional need not pass every version of the Ramsey test.

We can use the example in Chapter VIII of the battery tester to show how this distinction can make a difference. Let us submit the conditional 'If the little red light blinks, the battery is weak' to the Ramsey test. I hypothetically add to my stock of beliefs the belief that the little red light is blinking. To restore consistency with minimal fuss, I eliminate from my stock both the belief that the little red light is not blinking and the belief that the battery is not weak, and I add the belief that the battery is weak.

Then the little red light begins to blink; I see that it is blinking; so I believe that it is blinking. But I believe the fresh battery I recently installed would not, in the circumstance, weaken so quickly. Rather than change my belief that the battery is not weak and acquire the belief that the battery is weak, I give up my belief in the conditional.

We can draw a contrast between these two applications of the Ramsey test by means of possible worlds. In the second case, the light-blinking-world closest to the actual non-blinking world has a fresh battery and an (unexpectedly) defective battery tester. In the first, the light-blinking-world closest to the actual non-blinking world has a properly functioning battery tester and an (unexplainedly) weak battery.

We can revise the original version of the Ramsey test by insisting on some kind of greater temporal specification ('Suppose that you add to your stock of beliefs right now . . .') and on taking fuller account of second-order beliefs in most stocks of beliefs, for example, the belief that beliefs don't just come from nowhere.

In this chapter I will describe problems of another kind for the Ramsey test. For example, the following acceptable conditional fails the Ramsey test:

If I have been on the moon, then I have been over ten thousand miles from Detroit.

How should I add 'I have been on the moon' to my stock of beliefs? I maintain that no minimal or even moderate revision of my beliefs can coherently accommodate the additional belief that I have been on the moon. The first step of the two-stage Ramsey test cannot be taken: some knots in the web of belief cannot be untied without unravelling the whole fabric. The conditional to be tested is much less puzzling than the question what else I would believe if I believed that I have been on the moon.

Is the difficulty I allege due to ambiguity or radical lack of specificity? If I have ever spoken with Thomas Pynchon, I did not know it at the time. That's true because there has never been a time at which I knew I was talking to Thomas Pynchon. However, I do exchange words on occasion with men I do not know who are more or less the age of Pynchon. So suppose one of these was Pynchon. Did this encounter with the reclusive author occur in summer or winter, indoors or outdoors, before or after 1965, inside or outside the United States? There are many ways this unlikely encounter could have occurred, and neither the supposition by itself nor its conversational context helps to pick out one among the others. Is the supposition that I have been on the moon similar in this respect? It doesn't specify when I went, or how, or with whom, or how long we stayed. So, rather than saying there is no way of revising my stock of beliefs to accommodate the supposition that I have been on the moon, should I not say instead that there are a great number of such ways, and I have no principled way of selecting one over the others? A conditional passes the test if its main clause is true in each of minimally revised stocks of beliefs, whether there is a single such revision or uncountably many. This pattern of explanation seems promising for some applications of the Ramsey test, but I doubt whether it works for the example at hand. When I say there is no way of minimally revising my stock of beliefs to accommodate the additional belief that I have been on the moon, I mean just that: not a single way. Each of the various stories on the many-stories view turns out to be incoherent.

The variety of incoherence here can be understood by attending to certain claims by Ludwig Wittgenstein and Norman Malcolm.[1] Although neither Malcolm's 'Knowledge and belief' nor Wittgenstein's *On Certainty* is concerned primarily with a minimal revision of a stock of beliefs that preserves consistency, there is something each implies about the possibility of such revision.

Malcolm attempts to distinguish two senses of 'know', a weak sense and a strong sense. I doubt both whether there are these two senses of 'know' and whether Malcolm's central claim requires some previously unnoticed ambiguity. Although a discussion of how Malcolm's claim is relevant to the Ramsey test does not strictly require a discussion of multiple senses, I seize the opportunity here. A discussion of the alleged multiple senses of 'know' will bear on later discussions of alleged multiple senses of 'if'. Theories of conditionals abound with multiple senses.

The philosophers who follow G. E. Moore in searching for different senses of terms are usually misled. Single words sometimes do have several senses, a phenomenon to be distinguished from two distinct words, homonyms, having the same spelling and pronunciation. Philosophers who claim to find more senses of a term than good dictionaries list usually have only found or invented a distinction. Although drawing distinctions has been an essential part of the activity ever since philosophy began, the importance of a distinction, philosophical or otherwise, does not depend on its corresponding with different meanings or senses. If something neatly differentiates one alleged sense from another, that is a good sign that there are not really two senses. There is instead a distinction corresponding to the differentiation. Philosophers habitually criticize arguments for confusing senses, but the criticisms can usually be rewritten in terms of overlooked distinctions. One does not want to overlook the distinction between positive and non-positive numbers, for example, but the distinction scarcely requires that there be two senses of 'number'. The distinction between necessary and contingent conditionals, for another example, scarcely requires that there be two senses of 'if, then'.

Malcolm's appeal to different senses results from his examining a claim by H. A. Prichard that we can distinguish, in our own case, just by reflecting, the difference between knowledge and belief. Malcolm argues against this with the following example: No amount of reflection on one's own psychological state suffices to establish the presence or absence of water flowing through Cascadilla Gorge. There are circumstances, however, in which the only difference between knowledge and belief, in this case, false belief, is whether or not water is flowing through Cascadilla Gorge. But Prichard's claim, according to Malcolm, is not wholly mistaken. Near the end of the first published version of the essay, Malcolm writes:

Going back to Prichard's remark that we can determine by reflection whether we know something or merely believe it, we can conclude that with respect to one usage of 'know' (weak) what he says is false; but with respect to another usage (strong) what he says is true.[2]

In the later version Malcolm retracts this claim and replaces it with the assertion 'that reflection can make us realize that we are *using* "I know it" in the strong (or weak) sense in a particular case'.[3] This seems to differ too much from what Prichard says to count as its partial justification. But, whether or not Malcolm locates an interesting, defensible view that is also plausibly attributed to Prichard, and whether or not Malcolm says anything that really supports the view that 'know' has two senses or usages, the distinction Malcolm and Wittgenstein draw bears on the Ramsey test.

Malcolm considers three propositions each of which he is willing, in various circumstances, to assert that he knows to be true:

  (i) The sun is about ninety million miles from the earth.
 (ii) There is a heart in my body.
(iii) Here is an ink-bottle.

In an ordinary situation, Malcolm says, he can imagine acquiring persuasive evidence that the sun is not about ninety million miles from the earth; and he can imagine acquiring persuasive evidence that his body does not contain a heart. But when an ink-bottle is directly in front of him on the desk, says Malcolm, there is nothing that he would call acquiring persuasive evidence, or any evidence, that there is no ink-bottle before him.

Let us run through an attempt to show that Malcolm is wrong about examples of this kind. Imagine this: there is a bright flash, a loud crack, and billows of dense smoke. When the smoke clears, you find yourself, apparently, in the centre of a huge room made entirely of highly polished black stone. Someone of devilish countenance sits before you on a dark throne. 'I am the genie about whom you have so often thought and talked,' says the throned figure. 'For some time now I have been deceiving you up, down, and sideways, especially about the darker things in life, such as ink and ink-bottles. Your belief a few moments ago in the existence of an ink-bottle right before you, for example, was false.' Malcolm neither denies that such fantastic scenes are conceivable nor predicts how he would behave and what he would believe in the event that he found himself in such a situation. He denies, rather, that right now, with the ink-bottle before him, he is willing to count the occurrence of an experience such as the one just described as providing evidence against the existence of the ink-bottle.

In this case there happen to be some alternative hypotheses to explain one's seeming to confront an embodiment of the Evil Genius in the middle of the Grand Ballroom of the Great Palace of the Kingdom of Darkness. The hypotheses are compatible with your present certainty that here is an ink-bottle. The whole scene in the Dark Hall might be conjured up in your mind by the Genie right after you touched the ink-bottle. Or a large part of the world, including the ink-bottle, might suddenly be replaced by something else that includes the Dark Hall. Such alternative hypotheses, however, play no essential role in this exercise; they serve only to illustrate how one can hold that a certain current belief is immune from disconfirmation by any possible future evidence. I will say that such a belief is *immune*. Beliefs that are not immune I will call *vulnerable*. When a current belief of mine is vulnerable, then my current attitude is that there is something such that, if I were to experience it, it would count as evidence against my belief. Vulnerability can be quite hypothetical, counterfactual, theoretical, and irrelevant to one's actual degree of confidence. I can be absolutely certain that nothing will happen that will count against a current vulnerable belief, for example, my belief that there is a heart in my body. The distinction between vulnerability and immunity does not coincide with any distinction in one's attitudes about what sorts of experiences the future might bring. It also does not coincide, so far as I can see, with any real distinction between senses of a term.

I proceed on the assumption that the distinction between immune and vulnerable belief coincides with a distinction Malcolm and Wittgenstein both draw. Here are a few passages from among many in *On Certainty* that I take to express the notion of immunity:

But I could say: 'That I have two hands is an irreversible belief.' That would express the fact that I am not ready to let anything count as a disproof of this proposition.[4]
I say with passion 'I *know* that this a foot' – but what does it *mean*?

I might go on: 'Nothing in the world will convince me of the opposite!' For me this fact is at the bottom of all knowledge. I shall give up other things but not this.

This 'Nothing in the world' is obviously an attitude which one hasn't got towards everything one believes or is certain of.[5] If the water over the gas freezes, of course I shall be astonished as can be, but I shall assume some factor I don't know of, and perhaps leave the matter to physicists to judge. But what could make me doubt whether this person here is N.N., whom I have known for years? Here doubt would seem to drag everything with it and plunge it into chaos.

That is to say: If I were contradicted on all sides and told that this person's name was not what I had always known it was (and I use 'know' here intentionally), then in that case the foundation of all judging would be taken away from me.[6]

A central epistemological question for interpreting these writings by Malcolm and Wittgenstein is how 'the foundation (*die Grundlagen*) of all judging' is to be understood. It is not the intrinsic importance of propositions 'This person here is named N.N.' and 'Here is an ink-bottle' that makes them fundamental. Perhaps it is not they, strictly speaking, that are fundamental but rather that, in the circumstances described in which these beliefs are held, they are immune. When I leave my study, I am still certain that there is an ink-bottle on my desk, but my belief becomes vulnerable. When I return and see the ink-bottle right there in front of me, my belief is again immune. Immunity and vulnerability are at least sometimes highly context-sensitive.

The immunity of a belief depends on the circumstances, and circumstances can change quickly. The status of a conditional, and the applicability of the Ramsey test, can change just as quickly. Coming up the driveway, I see that the lights are on. I mutter to myself, 'If the girls aren't home from school, the lights have been on all day.' I go inside, and there they are, my daughters home from school. My belief that they are at home is now immune. I have some facility, as do many teachers of philosophy, at spinning epistemological fantasies along familiar lines: dreams, hallucinations, the Evil Genius, brain in a vat, dressed-up robots, counterparts on a quick visit from Twin Earth, the Invasion of the Body Snatchers, and so forth. Telling such tales does not tend to render my belief vulnerable. I am still not disposed, in the situation described, to allow that anything would count as showing me that one of the fantasy-tales is true. There is still no way consistently and coherently to adjust my stock of beliefs upon the addition of the supposition that my daughters are not home.

In one of Malcolm's examples, if there is no ink-bottle right in front of me now, then something is radically wrong. There are deceptive appearances of some kind I never supposed really existed, or my visual system is radically defective, or something else. There are no guidelines for distinguishing visual appearance from reality. If it is possible for me to be wrong in these surroundings, I could have been, so far as I know, just as wrong for years and years about everything or nearly everything I thought I saw. If that were so, I lack a grasp on reality firm enough to apply a distinction between reality and illusion. The rejection of an immune belief leads straightaway to Cartesian doubt. I need make no special effort to give up every belief of a certain kind. Some of my beliefs – my immune beliefs – cannot be rejected, not any one of them, without all my other beliefs being put in jeopardy.

There are beliefs, not always ones of much intrinsic interest or importance, that cannot be hypothetically added to one's stock of beliefs for the purpose of a Ramsey test. By itself this does little to show what if anything is wrong with a Ramsey test for conditionals. Here we might take a second look at the original passage by Ramsey that inspired the Ramsey test:

If two people are arguing 'If p will q?' and are both in doubt as to p, they are adding p hypothetically to their stock of knowledge and arguing on that basis about q; so that in a sense 'If p, q' and 'If p, $\bar{q}$' are contradictories. We can say they are fixing their degrees of belief in q given p. If p turns out false, these degrees of belief are rendered *void*. If either party believes $\bar{p}$ for certain, the question ceases to mean anything to him except as a question about what follows from certain laws or hypotheses.[7]

The notion that a conditional can be *void* will be useful no matter what our final verdict is about the Ramsey test. Can it be that, when the Ramsey test fails to apply because no minimal revision is possible, the test should be interpreted as showing the conditional is void? 'If we all lived under water, then we would all have gills' is a conditional that fits this description. Hypothetically add the belief that we all live under water to your stock of beliefs. Now revise your beliefs, if you can, to restore consistency. This, I claim, you cannot do. So what of the original conditional? Call it void, since there appear not to be strong reasons to call it *true* or to call it *false*. This conditional poses no difficulty for the Ramsey test, even though disbelief in its if-clause is normally immune.

Other conditionals are handled less easily. The one we began with, 'If I have been on the moon, then I have been over ten thousand miles from Detroit', is a true conditional, or at least an acceptable one, to which the Ramsey test cannot be applied.[8] The inapplicability of the Ramsey test indicates nothing, by itself, about the status of the conditional in question. Such a conditional may be true, or false, or fall under the third, catch-all category of void, indeterminate, absurd, and so forth.

Stalnaker proceeds from his original formulation of the Ramsey test to his seminal formulation of possible-world semantics for conditionals. I quote this passage from Stalnaker near the beginning of Chapter VII and mention some points of disanalogy between stocks of beliefs and possible worlds. Most conspicuously, possible worlds are maximal while stocks of beliefs are not. Although this disanalogy does little to protect possible-world semantics for conditionals from difficulties similar to those we have just discussed for the Ramsey test, there is still a difference between the Ramsey test and the possible-worlds test that appears to make possible-world theory apply more widely.

If I have been on the moon, then I do not know how I went there, I do not know how I returned, and I do not know what explains the huge lack of fit between my beliefs about my past spatial locations and the truth. Still, when using a possible-worlds theory to test a conditional that mentions nothing about beliefs,

150

such as 'If I have been on the moon, then I have been over ten thousand miles from Detroit', we tend simply to ignore stocks of beliefs, including mine. We assume that the actual world and the possible worlds closest to the actual world in which I have been on the moon share the feature that Detroit and the moon are over ten thousand miles apart. This assumption is not based on a fairly specific idea of what the closest possible worlds are like. Any I-have-been-on-the-moon-world must be very different from the actual world, and we lack both specific conceptions of such worlds and coherent ideas about degrees of similarity between them and the actual world.

The subjunctive analogue of our indicative example is instructive:

> If I had been on the moon, then I would have been over ten thousand miles from Detroit.

The change from indicative to subjunctive makes no difference in this case to the applicability, or inapplicability, of the Ramsey test. Beliefs do not come in indicative and subjunctive varieties. We cannot draw a distinction between my hypothetically adding the belief that I have been on the moon and my hypothetically adding the belief I had been on the moon. Possible-world theories, in contrast, can respect the difference easily. If I had been on the moon, then my life would have changed significantly some years ago. I probably would be somewhere else than at this particular location. In the possible world closest to the actual world in which I have been on the moon, I do not, we assume, have beliefs about my present and past locations very similar to my actual beliefs in the actual world. The standards of similarity, however, are hard to pin down. Consider:

> If I had visited the moon, then I would never have written about the Ramsey test.

Is this conditional true, false, or indeterminate? Our conceptions of possible worlds in which I have been on the moon combined with relevant conceptions of similarity to the actual world are not specific enough to answer the question. Are there some objective facts about possible worlds and comparative similarity between

151

worlds that support a definite answer although they happen to elude our intellectual grasp? A bold metaphysician who says so is too bold to be believed.

As we have seen before, corresponding indicative and subjunctive conditionals can diverge in truth-value or acceptability. The fuel gauge needle points at the middle of the dial. Therefore, if the car is out of petrol, the fuel gauge is broken. It would take an elaborate story to support the corresponding subjunctive 'If the car had been out of petrol, the fuel gauge would have been broken.' It is certainly not supported by the mere fact that the pointer is half-way between *E* and *F* and the tank is actually half full.

Some of our recent examples to which the Ramsey test seems impossible to apply suggest another kind of contrast between indicative and subjunctive conditionals. Consider the following pair:

If I had died at age ten, then I would never have heard of Tarski.
If I died at age ten, then I have never heard of Tarski.

The first one is true. The second one seems neither true nor false but rather absurd or void. The Ramsey test applies to neither. There is no particular problem about possible worlds in which I died at age ten. Such worlds closest to the actual world are not conceived in great detail, and it is hard to believe that the relevant detail is somehow there in the realm of possible worlds, if only we could learn what it is. Still, the actual world to which the I-died-at-age-ten-possible world is to be compared is the actual world at the time I was ten. To deal with the second conditional by means of possible worlds, we must compare I-died-at-age-ten-worlds with the actual world as it is right now, a seemingly impossible task. 'If I died at age ten, then I died before age twelve' is nevertheless an acceptable conditional.

All men are mortal, and a few have visited the moon. The if-clauses of the conditionals considered above are not physically or logically impossible. Consider, in contrast, this example from Part III, 'Compound thoughts' (1923–6), from Frege's 'Logical investigations':[9]

If $\sqrt[10]{10^{21}}$ is greater than $(21/20)^{100}$ then
$(\sqrt[10]{10^{21}})^2$ is greater than $((21/20)^{100})^2$.

Frege intends this example of a conditional with false components to support his truth-functional account of the conditional. While the example does show that a conditional with an impossible antecedent can be acceptable, it scarcely shows the acceptability of every conditional with an impossible antecedent, or even of every conditional with that particular impossible antecedent. Abbreviate the antecedent as T. I would say that 'If T, then the square of the second is greater than the square of the first' is worthy of rejection and that 'If T, then we are on the moon' is void. Although there is no possible world, near or far, in which T is true, this does not completely hamper our drawing distinctions between conditionals that share T as an if-clause.

The epigraphs of this chapter are intelligible conditionals. The lady who addresses the bear in Theodore Roethke's 'The lady and the bear' cannot, we may assume, revise her stock of beliefs minimally so as to accommodate the hypothetically added belief that she is a fish. Nor are there any possible worlds in which she is a fish. Moreover, the probability that the lady is a fish is zero. Although debates about whether the sentence is true or false, assertable or deniable, probable or improbable, and so forth, could be heavy-handed, the sentence is more than just words with a conditional syntax. It says something. It expresses a connection between the situation described in the if-clause and that described in the main clause; and the expression of this connection can be judged as appropriate, relevant, interesting, trite, sentimental, and so on. A meaningful conditional can have a deeply impossible antecedent. The supposition that all time is eternally present is as impossible, in its way, as the supposition that a human is a fish, yet this does nothing to destroy the sense of the conditional from T. S. Eliot's 'Burnt Norton'.

On the usual treatment of conditional probability, probability conditional on A when $P(A) = 0$ is undefined; for conditional probability on A is standardly defined in terms of division by $P(A)$, and division by zero is undefined in everybody's theory. There are alternative treatments of conditional probabilities. If we take them as primitive, as do Popper and some others, then we can define probabilities conditional on a proposition with zero probability. Or a theory of conditionals can stipulate that all conditionals with if-clauses of zero probability should be treated the same way, all with probability zero, or all with probability 1, or all void.[10] No current theory using conditional probability respects the distinctions that we do in fact draw between conditionals with the same impossible if-clauses.

Conditionals with antecedents of zero probability, conditionals with antecedents very difficult to accommodate to one's stock of beliefs by revision, and conditionals with antecedents which, if true in any possible world, are true in worlds so different from the actual world that judgments of comparative similarity are difficult, all come in degrees of acceptability, unacceptability, and undecidability. We draw more distinctions between conditionals than most theories can explain.[11]

The Ramsey test and most versions of possible-world semantics treat conditionals alike that have the same if-clause. The tests are applied in two steps. First, look at the if-clause. Add the corresponding belief to your stock of beliefs and make minimal adjustments required to restore consistency, or find the possible worlds closest to the actual world in which the if-clause is true. Then – the second step – look to see if the main clause is contained in the revised stock of beliefs or is true in the relevant possible worlds. It is hard to see, on this approach, how, when one conditional is true, or false, or acceptable, or rejectable, another conditional with the same if-clause can be void, indeterminate, or absurd. If there is some relevant possible world in which it is true that I am on the moon right now, then, ignoring borderline cases which are usually irrelevant in these examples, any main clause you like will either be true in this world or false. By my lights, 'If I am on the moon right now, then so is my cat' is neither true nor false. (Nor is there a relevant possible world in which I am on the moon and in which the location of my cat is somehow a borderline case of *being on the moon*.) That means there is no relevant possible world in which I am on the moon. My confidence in 'If I am on the moon right now, then I am ten thousand miles from Detroit' is therefore not based on judgments about what is or is not true in certain possible worlds.

The distance from Detroit to the moon is independent of my

154

location, and it is greater than ten thousand miles. We need assume only this to support the last conditional. We do not need to locate an entire possible world, or an entire adjusted stock of beliefs, to explain why we accept the conditional. We can locate the relatively simple facts that suffice to back up the conditional, however, only after we have both clauses of the conditional in mind. There is no first step that we can take given the if-clause but in ignorance of the main clause. I shall make these general lessons more specific in some of the chapters to follow.

Possible-worlds accounts of conditionals do not have to take the usual two-step approach. The selection function for determining similarity between possible worlds can take into account both the main clause and the if-clause of the conditional to be tested, instead of only the if-clause. Even if there could be versions of possible-worlds accounts that are immune from the difficulties discussed in this chapter, however, there are some additional difficulties, to which we now turn.

CHAPTER X

Various Visions of Possible Worlds

Dream not of other worlds, what creatures there
Live, in what state, condition, or degree,
Contented that thus far hath been reveal'd
Not of earth only, but of highest heav'n.

Among philosophers who refer to possible worlds in their own philosophic research, there is a remarkable lack of agreement about what possible worlds are. Although the disagreements do not much matter in the treatments of the validity of inference and logical truth in the logic of conditionals, they do matter in the treatments of their meaning and truth.

Possible worlds have been taken to be maximally consistent sets of sentences, maximally consistent sets of propositions, maximal possible states of affairs, uninstantiated properties, and set-theoretical constructs of the non-modal atoms making up the actual world. I will not attempt to explain why one or another theorist prefers one or another of these conceptions. On all these conceptions, all possible worlds, including the possible world that is actual, are something of a kind very different from the huge concrete entity, the Actual World, in which we live, move, and break our bread. The maximally consistent set of true propositions, the so-called actual world, on one conception corresponds to, but is certainly not identical to, the Actual World that contains mice, moons, eyelashes, and galaxies, as spatial parts. The correspondences between the actual world and the Actual World are similar on the other conceptions.

David Lewis rejects any such equivocation of 'actual world' in his conception of possible worlds. Against identifying possible worlds with sets of sentences, he says in *Counterfactuals*:

given that the actual world does not differ in kind from the rest, it would lead to the conclusion that our actual world is a set of sentences. Since I cannot believe that I and all my surroundings are a set of sentences (though I have no argument that they are not), I cannot believe that other worlds are sets of sentences either.[1]

According to Lewis's so-called modal realism, what distinguishes the actual world from the numerous possible worlds is that we occupy the actual world. Other worlds, no mere sets or representations, are occupied by creatures more or less like us, our counterparts. This is the indexical theory of actuality: predications of 'actual' and 'non-actual' are from the standpoint of the predicator. A possible but non-actual world may well lack nothing by way of physically robust space, time, mass, causation, and so forth. What it lacks, rather, is us as inhabitants, we who attribute actuality to this world. If it has its own attributors of actuality, then, from their own standpoints, they speak truly. Their worlds are just as real as our world in which we live.

The following passage from the Preface of Saul Kripke's *Naming and Necessity* is directed against taking our beliefs about the nature of our surroundings as relevant to a proper theory of possible worlds:

> The 'actual world' – better, the actual state, or history of the world – should not be confused with the enormous scattered object that surrounds us. The latter might also have been called 'the (actual) world', but it is not the relevant object here. Thus the possible but not actual worlds are not phantom duplicates of the 'world' in this other sense. Perhaps such confusions would have been less likely but for the terminological accident that 'possible worlds' rather than 'possible states' or 'histories', of the world, or 'counterfactual situations' had been used.[2]

If we do not think of the actual world as the enormous object that includes us and everything related to us, then we ought not to be tempted to think of possible but non-actual worlds as more or less similar phantom duplicates of this enormous object. From this it does not follow – it would be a formal fallacy of conditional inference to infer – that, if we ought not be tempted to think of possible but non-actual worlds as phantom duplicates of the world in which we live, then we do not think of the actual world as an enormous, all-inclusive object.

If the egg had been dropped, it would have broken. The same, identical egg, we mean, would have broken had it been dropped. Merely saying 'the same' and 'identical' fails to specify the intended sense. The distinction between numerical and qualitative identity is a philosophic commonplace. Two things can be qualitatively identical; they share properties regarded as especially important or significant for things of that kind. Two things cannot be numerically identical. If the egg had been dropped, the numerically identical egg would have broken, rather than a very similar but numerically distinct egg.

On some possible-world treatments of conditionals, the relevant possible world or worlds in which an egg is dropped and breaks contains numerically the same egg as the actual world. On some, particularly Lewis's, the contents of each possible world are numerically distinct from the contents of every other world. The relevant possible world or worlds in which an egg is dropped and breaks contains eggs that are counterparts to the egg in our world, the actual world. The conditional about egg G is analysed with reference to eggs numerically distinct from G. This does not mean that the original conditional is about an egg distinct from G. The original conditional is not understood to be about what would happen to some other egg. Rather, the truth about what *would have* happened to this very same egg in this world is explained by reference to what *does* happen to another egg, in another world.

Theorists who hold that an object in one possible world can be numerically identical with an object in another possible world, theorists who deny this, and theorists who argue that the dispute itself reflects fundamental misconceptions all agree that qualitatively different possible worlds are numerically distinct. There can be no doubt about this when possible worlds are regarded as sets, since the identity of a set is determined entirely by the identity of its members. But, if, like Lewis, we think of the possible world that happens to be actual as an enormous, all-inclusive object, then we should pause before treating different possible worlds as numerically rather than qualitatively distinct.

I will soon entertain the doctrine that this is the best of all possible worlds, not as a serious attempt at Leibniz scholarship, and certainly not as a good-faith attempt at theodicy, but in order to illustrate the application of a distinction. Even before possible-world talk became fashionable, there were qualms about treating the all-inclusive world as a subject of reference and predication just like one of the non-inclusive substances that the world includes. Whether or not such qualms ought to bear on our present topic, I shall begin by discussing something smaller and less inclusive than entire worlds, namely departmental chairmen. The dedication of *The Possible and the Actual: Readings in the Metaphysics of Modality*, edited by Michael Loux, reads as follows:

> TO NEIL DELANEY
> BEST OF ALL POSSIBLE CHAIRMEN.

In explicating this dedication with a relentless literalism, I shall begin by examining a universal, superlative, but non-modal judgment:

> Delaney is the best chairman who ever lived.

This does not have the same truth conditions as:

> Delaney is a chairman who has lived, and for any chairman C who ever lived, Delaney is a better chairman than C.

This formulation implies that Delaney is a better chairman than himself, an apparent impossibility that the original statement does not imply. If Delaney is the best chairman who ever lived, then he is a better chairman than *every other* chairman who ever lived, every chairman distinct from himself. An understanding of superlative judgments requires an understanding of numerical distinctness whether the superlative judgments be modal or non-modal. Consider again the modal judgment:

> Delaney is the best of all possible chairmen, the best chairman possible, the best chairman who could ever live.

When we say that no one could be better than Delaney, we mean at least that no one *else*, no one other than Delaney, could be a better chairman than Delaney. We may mean more, namely that no one at all, including Delaney, could be a better chairman than Delaney, that Delaney is as good a chairman as it is possible to be. But this is something more. If the best of all possible chairmen is one than whom *no one else* could be better as a chairman, then such a paragon might still find room for improvement. Delaney could be a better chairman than he is even though no one other than Delaney could be a better chairman than Delaney. There is no logical inconsistency between 'Delaney really isn't much good as a chairman' and 'Delaney is the best of all possible chairmen'; for there is no inconsistency between 'Delaney really isn't much good as a chairman' and 'There could not be a chairman other than Delaney who was not even worse.'

As with Delaney, a philosopher I happened to know only by description until after I wrote this chapter, so with the world, that we all know by acquaintance. If our world is the best of all possible worlds, it does not follow directly that our world could not possibly be better. What follows directly is only that no other world could possibly be better than it. The slippery adverb 'directly' is here intended to acknowledge that arguments may be forthcoming in support of the principle that, if something could possibly improve, then it is possible that something else should be better than it. I need not discuss this mediating principle so long as it is clear that some such principle is essential to any successful attempt to argue away the prima facie distinction between, for example:

No other world could possibly be better than this world,

and:

No world at all, whether other than this world or the same, could possibly be better than this world.

A modern-day Voltaire who questions whether this is the best of all possible worlds will most likely doubt only whether the world could not be better than it is. There is another possibility, the

160

doubt whether there could not be a world numerically distinct from and superior to this world we are stuck in. There is no shred of evidence I know of that Leibniz ever drew such distinctions as these. They interest me mainly because they illustrate how the familiar distinction between numerical and qualitative identity can be applied to worlds.

Let us recall some of the applications of this distinction to items within the world. Would the egg have broken had it been dropped? If it would, it is numerically the same egg, which did not break in fact, that would have broken had it been dropped. In the same way, numerically the same world, which does not in fact contain a breaking of that egg, would have contained a breaking of the egg had it also contained a suitable dropping of the egg. When we think about how the world might have gone, and about the various ways it might go, we think about different possibilities of a single world. Expressions like 'the way the world is' and 'a way the world might have been but wasn't', if they are referring expressions at all, refer to numerically distinct items – how shall we count the ways? But I am asking about different, though related, expressions, 'the world the way it is' and 'the world a way it might have been but wasn't'. These expressions refer to numerically the same world.[3] Qualitatively different possible worlds need not be numerically distinct.

This view does not imply that qualitatively different possible worlds are never numerically distinct. In addition to the common thought that the world could have been different, the thought seems to be intelligible that there could have been a different world, one numerically distinct from this one. Just above we drew the distinction with respect to doubts about whether this is the best of all possible worlds.

Necessarily, twice two is four. Does this mean merely that twice two would still have been four however the world might have gone, and that twice two will continue to be four in any event, however the world might go on from here? We take this necessity to be stronger. 'True in all possible worlds' implies 'true in any world there might possibly be', which appears stronger than 'true in this world however it might possibly be or have been'. Possible-world semantics for some modal statements require possible worlds numerically distinct, by anyone's manner of counting, from the actual world.

161

If P, then Q

Most of the conditionals we care about concern inhabitants of this world. Possible-world semantics for these conditionals usually need not refer to any worlds in addition to this one, as it is, as it might have been, and as it might turn out to be. The central relational notions of the semantics, *true in world w_i*, and *more similar to world w_i than to world w_j*, can be applied without obtaining agreement about just what kinds of items w_i and w_j are. The assumption (A) that, for any contingent falsehood p, there is one possible world in which p is true that is more relevantly similar ('closest') to the actual world than any other possible world in which p is true can be made or denied without presupposing that we are talking about worlds numerically distinct from this one. The egg was not in fact dropped. 'The world as it would have been had the egg been dropped into a vat of molten iron' and 'The world as it would have been had the egg been dropped on a tile floor' are different descriptions of numerically the same world, this one. If the world had been the second way it would have been 'closer', more similar, to it as it actually was than if the world had been the first way. According to assumption A, there is one way the world could have been in which the egg was dropped that is closer to the way the world actually was than any other way the world could have been in which the egg was dropped. Here I quantify over numerically distinct *ways* in order to refer to different actual and possible states of a single thing, the world. Of course possible-world semantics can and does proceed with just the *ways the world might be* as the numerically distinct possible worlds. I will persist a while longer with the conception that the different possible worlds we talk about are usually all this single world under the different aspects of the ways it might be or have been. Questions of validity and logical truth can be treated just as they were treated before on the more usual understanding of possible worlds. Should you regard conditional excluded middle as a logical truth? It depends on what assumptions you make and on the details of your definitions. The degree of plausibility of these assumptions and details need not turn on a settled view of just what a possible world is. Is contraposition a valid principle for subjunctive conditionals? Again, the construction of an abstract counterexample depends on structural considerations, on the nature of the relations in the semantic theory rather than on the nature of the *relata*.

A logic of conditionals is one thing; and a theory of the truth, acceptability, and meaning of conditionals is another. Recall truth-functional semantics. It grounds a useful notion of validity and a useful notion of logical truth. While conditionals that are false as material conditionals are false on anyone's theory, true truth-functional, material, conditionals include many which most theorists regard as untrue. One can regard conditional premises as truth-functional when enquiring about the validity of an argument yet refuse to accept these same conditionals as true on merely truth-functional grounds. The application of possible-world semantics to conditionals provides an analogous situation: it supports and organizes judgments of validity without offering as much useful guidance in the evaluation of particular statements.

If we take a possible world to be this very world as it might possibly be or have been, some of the theoretical, reductive advantages of possible-world semantics seem to be lost. According to the standard line, the modal notions of what is possible (or necessary) are reduced to non-modal quantifications: true in some (or all) worlds. Conditional notions of 'what would happen if' are reduced to categorical assertions about what does happen in the relevant world or worlds. In my attempt to sketch a 'one world' view of possible worlds that handles conditionals about things in this world as well as any possible-worlds theory, I have freely used the very modal and conditional notions that are allegedly reduced. Terminological or formal innovations could remove the impression that various attempted reductions fail, but these would only perpetrate an illusion. The 'one world' view explains modality and conditionals as well as any possible-worlds account. If it does not go very far, neither do the others. If others appear to go farther, the appearance is an illusion.

If the egg had been dropped, it would have broken. In this world as it would have been if the egg had been dropped and things had been as relevantly similar as they could be to things as they actually were, the egg broke. Although this account introduces something, the notion of similarity between worlds, that is entirely absent from the original conditional, nothing in the original conditional is reduced. *If* and *would* are explained by

163

means of *if* and *would*. We can take pains not to use 'if' and 'would' in our descriptions of possible worlds, and we can return to a more usual notion in which different possible worlds are always numerically different and a possible world in which the egg was dropped is an abstract entity of some kind that represents this concrete world as it would have been if the egg were dropped. Such reversion to the more usual conception of possible-world semantics, I claim, adds nothing to our understanding of the meaning of conditionals or what makes some true and others false.

Modal realism at this point may appear to offer the depth of understanding that more cautious versions of possible-world theory fail to provide. Possible worlds like our world, according to the modal realist, are just as full-blooded, concrete, and spatio-temporal as our world. Other possible worlds really exist just as much as our world really exists. A modal realist who also adopts an indexical account of actuality does not take 'really' and 'actually' to be stylistic variants. Of all the worlds that really exist, we say only one actually exists, the one we inhabit. The real but non-actual existence of a possible world containing a relevantly similar dropped egg that breaks seems to offer a more substantial basis for the truth of our egg-drop conditional.

Although modal realism need not suppose that every possible world is spatio-temporal and contains causal processes, the following sketch of how to distinguish worlds applies only to worlds that are spatio-temporal and causal. Spatio-temporal regions are directly connectible if and only if an occurrence in one can causally affect an occurrence in the other.[4] Regions related by the ancestral of 'directly connectible' are connectible: A and B are connectible if they are directly connectible, or if something C is directly connectible both to A and to B, or if there is a pair of directly connectible things C and D such that A is directly connectible to C and B is directly connectible to D, or if there is a triplet . . ., and so on.[5] Regions are parts of the same world if and only if they are connectible. If there is a world distinct from our world, you can't get there from here, one can't get there from any place from which one could get here, you can't get to any place one can get to from there, and so forth. According to modal realism, nothing in the possible world in which an egg, quite similar to the undropped egg in this world, is dropped and breaks is connectible with this world.

Like many philosophers, I disbelieve in the existence of worlds distinct from this world. Perhaps that is because, like many philosophers, I lack a quality of intellect possessed by David Lewis, the chief advocate of modal realism.[6] Instead of attacking modal realism directly, I will try to appear to do it one better. I will describe modal super-realism.

As we have been using the term 'world' up to now, worlds are closed under connectibility. If *A* is part of world *W*, and *B* is connectible to *A*, then *B* is also part of world *W*. On this conception, 'another world far, far away and long, long ago' is inconsistent: nothing any distance away, and thus nothing far, far away, is in *another* world. (The similar view that nothing temporally related to us, and thus nothing long, long ago, is in another world, requires some additional support.) Modal super-realism is concerned with less inclusive regions, which for the next few paragraphs I will call 'WORLDS' (which can be pronounced 'subworlds' when one reads aloud). Many non-overlapping WORLDS can occupy a single world. The boundaries of WORLDS are relative to particular applications of possible-world semantics, just as, in the ordinary use of the term *world*, boundaries and extents depend on the interests at hand. The world of modern dance, the world of high finance, and their own little worlds in which our eccentric and slightly mad friends live are none of them all-inclusive. None includes everything connected or connectible to it. Modal super-realism assumes that many modal and conditional statements can be treated by reference to WORLDS that are less than totally inclusive. The conditional about a dropped egg does not need a world thousands of light-years across and millions of years old. A few minutes in a WORLD the size of a kitchen should be world enough. Such WORLDS must, of course, be similar in all the relevant respects to the original, actual set-up. A conditional about the collision of planets requires very large WORLDS, but presumably still not WORLDS nearly so large as galaxies. There are WORLDS as large as you need to treat modal and conditional statements about large things, according to modal super-realism; but none is all-inclusive. All the WORLDS are connectible with us; they are all parts of the actual world. The closest WORLD in which the

165

egg was dropped may be next door next week, it may be north of Hudson Bay nine thousand years from now, it may be on a planet that circles a star visible to the naked eye from Earth, or it may be in a region that is remote to the twelfth degree from everything directly connectible to us.

Probably the most frequently entertained form of super-realism holds, usually not under just this description, that Euclidean space–time extends infinitely in every direction along every dimension. The universe is large enough to be partitioned into infinitely many non-overlapping subregions, each no smaller than a given minimum size. Its space–time structure is simple enough for no regions to be remote to more than the first degree: regions not directly connectible to each other, because of the finite limit on the speed of causal influence, are always each directly connectible to some third region. The principle of plenitude reigns, for there is world enough and time. Every possibility, no matter how elaborate and no matter how spatio-temporally extensive, is realized infinitely many times. Some of your counterparts live in galaxy clusters just like ours, although numerically distinct; some live in galaxy clusters very like ours, but differing in this or that little detail, for example, in one more or less freckle, hair, twitch, or twinge; and some live in galaxy clusters more or less unlike ours. Everything in our world, from frying-pans to industrial revolutions, has counterparts in other WORLDS. Modal super-realism is a fantasy of a kind common to childish musing and to science fiction: 'What if there is someone just like me living somewhere in surroundings just like these?'

If space–time is not Euclidean and everywhere infinite, it might be multiply infinite in other ways. Black holes, big bangs, big whimpers, and such singularities might, despite assertions to the contrary by physicists who ponder such matters, mark a route of direct connection between regions that are not otherwise directly connectible. Certain looking-glasses, wardrobes, and doors at the back of the closet play a similar role in fantasy literature: there is some place not too far away that you cannot get to from here by travelling in a straight line; you must pass through the appropriate portal, which happens not to lie on a straight-line path between you and your destination. If the universe seems too small to contain all the WORLDS modal super-realism requires, remember that there may be paths of connectibility as yet undiscovered.

Is the universe large enough to contain, as it does according to modal super-realism, all the situations of any kind a possible-world semantics should require to handle modal statements or subjunctive conditionals? That depends, of course, both on the size of the universe and the number of situations required. Not all infinite cardinals are equal. An infinite universe can contain infinitely many distinct WORLDS of any given spatio-temporal size yet be unable to accommodate a number of such WORLDS equal to the power of the continuum. It is not obvious to me just how many possible worlds an adequate semantics requires. However many that might turn out to be, modal super-realism can attempt coherent descriptions of single worlds, as defined above, large enough to contain enough sufficiently large non-overlapping spatio-temporal regions. This is one of many problems that a serious, thorough treatment of modal super-realism should handle. This chapter does not pretend to be such a treatment. Here I am mainly concerned to compare typical uses of possible worlds, as conceived by modal realism, with typical uses of WORLDS, as conceived by modal super-realism, in the treatment of modality and conditionals.

A natural objection to modal realism is that, on its conception of possible worlds, what occurs in other possible worlds is irrelevant to what would have or might have happened in our world. Some who state this objection tend to misstate the position of modal realism, so a reply can deflect attention away from the objection to the misstatements. I believe that the force of this objection does not depend on misdescribing or misunderstanding the view under attack. I hope that the notion of modal super-realism will help in stating an objection to modal realism without misdescribing the view. Modal super-realism is useful for this purpose because the objection under discussion to modal realism applies as well to modal super-realism in a very vivid way: on the super-realist conception of WORLDS, what occurs in other WORLDS is irrelevant to what must have or would have or might have happened closer to home. Suppose that the nearest WORLD pertaining to the egg-drop conditional is right across the street. How can the behaviour of another dropped egg across the street be essential to the truth conditions for a conditional concerning this egg right here on our side of the street? Once it seems plausible to deny the relevance of the occurrences in more or less distant WORLDS to modal and conditional statements about objects closer to home, the next step is to argue that the worlds of modal realism are no more relevant to explaining modal and conditional statements than the WORLDS of modal super-realism.

Each world of modal realism includes everything connectible to everything it includes, while the WORLDS of modal super-realism are not similarly all-inclusive. The worlds of modal realism are disconnected from each other and from our world, while the WORLDS of modal super-realism are all connected. Why should these differences matter at all to the appropriateness of WORLDS for the explanation of modality and conditionals? The non-inclusive nature of WORLDS requires that one consider the whole conditional, and not just its if-clause, before deciding how large a WORLD should be suitable to test the conditional. As we have seen, there are reasons independent from the peculiar problems of super-realism for considering both clauses of a conditional together while subjecting it to some test.

The following argument uses the contention that the WORLDS of modal super-realism are just as useful for semantics as the possible worlds of modal realism:

> What happens elsewhere in the universe is irrelevant to what this egg would have done had it been dropped. What happens in another WORLD happens elsewhere in the universe. What happens in the WORLDS of modal super-realism and what happens in the possible worlds of modal realism are equally relevant to accounts of conditionals. Therefore, what happens in other possible worlds (as conceived by modal realism) is irrelevant to what this egg would have done had it been dropped.

This blunt argument has some force, I think, despite the fact that it requires various qualifications. I shall question its first premise.

Nothing so like as eggs. Suppose two eggs to be in circumstances that are very similar in all respects relevant to whether an egg will break when dropped. One egg breaks after being dropped. The other egg remains undropped. 'It would have broken if it had been dropped' can scarcely mean, or have as a truth condition, that the first egg broke when dropped. On the other hand, the behaviour of the first egg in the circumstances described gives one reason to accept the conditional about the second egg. The fact that a very similar egg broke when dropped supports the assumption that this egg would have broken if it had also been dropped. The problem of explaining the reasonableness or grounds of this support is the problem of induction. What occurs in one spatio-temporal region is taken to provide evidence about what will, or would, or might occur in other relevantly similar spatio-temporal regions.

The strength of connection between the traditional problem of induction and possible-world semantics for conditionals depends on what can count as a relevant similarity. Eggs dropped on the kitchen floor back home have mostly broken. The inference of similar behaviour for eggs dropped in locally similar circumstances in a WORLD at greater spatial and temporal distances from us than any distances astronomy recognizes pushes induction to one of its limits. The inference of similar behaviour for eggs dropped in locally similar circumstances in worlds disconnected from ours, in the possible worlds of modal realism, appears to push induction beyond the limits of this world and to transform the problem of this-world induction into the problem of trans-world induction. This appearance dissipates, however, when we remember that sameness or near-sameness of laws counts as a relevant respect of similarity in a possible-world semantics for counterfactual conditionals. Before possible-world semantics became fashionable, discussions of these three topics were often found together: the riddles of induction, old and new; the distinction between laws and accidentally true generalizations; and the distinction between acceptable and unacceptable counterfactual conditionals.[7] These days, reference to similarity of laws is generally unaccompanied by much discussion of the nature of law; and problems of induction are left to the side.

Possible-world treatments of conditionals place great importance on the comparative similarity between worlds. The phrase 'relevant similarity' suggests that some similarities are irrelevant. My use of the phrase suggests that the distinction between the relevant and irrelevant is an important theoretical goal. Once this

169

goal is attained, there is little further use for possible worlds or for WORLDS in evaluating contingent conditionals. Relevant respects of similarity do much of the work in possible-world semantics; and, once these respects are specified, they can do the same work by themselves, apart from other WORLDS or possible worlds.

'If the egg had been dropped, it would have broken.' Why is that true? On the possible-world account, it is true because a dropped egg in relevantly similar circumstances did break. On the suggested alternative, it is true because of the circumstances the egg was in (circumstances such that any egg that is dropped in relevantly similar circumstances breaks). The relevant facts about the circumstances, in virtue of which the egg would have broken had it been dropped, do not depend on these circumstances being duplicated (in another 'possible world'). On the other hand, the similarity between a relevant possible world and this world does depend on the relevant facts about the circumstances in this world. Facts about this world ground both the conditional and possible-world treatment of the conditional. The possible-world treatment, when spelled out, requires reference to facts about this world which, when adequately specified, make reference to possible worlds unnecessary.

I shall attempt to support a proposal of this kind in the remaining chapters. Before ending this chapter, I want to mention one way indeterminism causes difficulties for possible-worlds treatments of conditionals. Suppose that rolling dice is indeterministic. As I toss the dice, the state of the world may be causally sufficient for the dice coming up some way or another, but the state of the world at that time does not make any one of the 36 possible combinations more probable than any other. The dice in fact come up 1–1. I say 'If you had thrown the dice just as I did, they would have come up 1–1.' What I say here is false, by hypothesis. If you had thrown the dice, they *might* have come up 1–1; the chances of their coming up 1–1 would have been 1 in 36. One problem for possible-world semantics is avoiding classifying this unacceptable conditional as acceptable.[8] Since the dice came up 1–1 when I threw them, they come up 1–1 in the most similar world in which you throw them.

In this example, no world in which you throw the dice is close enough to the actual world to be suitable for testing the conditional. There are no respects of relevant similarity. By hypothesis, there are no facts about the actual circumstances that ground any conditional of the form 'if you had thrown the dice just as I did, they would have come up %–#' where '%–#' stands for any one of the 36 combinations. An absence of relevant respects, as much as a presence, can obtain independent of other possible worlds. Just as conditionals can be understood to be true without looking at other possible worlds, so can conditionals be understood not to be true.

CHAPTER XI

Laws and Conditions

Once, as I recall, he spent a whole night analyzing
for us the word *circumstance*, the word *condition*,
and the word *consistent*.

The discussion in the last several chapters points backward past theories of probability and possible worlds to treatments of conditionals of the kind developed by Roderick Chisholm and Nelson Goodman forty years ago.[1] Goodman wanted to avoid purported reference to anything not in the actual world, and his ontology of actually existing things was sparse. In his example about scratching a match, it is facts about the actual circumstances together with laws about match-behaviour that support the counterfactual conditional. Although the laws imply that certain describable situations are impossible (damp matches will not light), there is no mention of situations that are possible but not actual.

In Chapter V we saw a number of difficulties with covering law accounts of subjunctive conditionals. Laws and lawlike statements are usually statements of incompossibility. Given that the resistance and the voltage are such and such, the current cannot be other than so and so. This relationship is formally similar to one we discussed while treating deductive inference. When a number of statements are jointly inconsistent, the argument to the negation of any one of them from those remaining is deductively valid. A theory of logical inconsistency cannot by itself tell you what inferences to draw. When a number of values are, in the circumstances, jointly inconsistent with the relevant law, the argument to the negation of any one of them from those remaining is similarly valid. The argument from scratching and

172

non-dampness to lighting is as valid as the argument from scratching and non-lighting to dampness. The relevant law usually cannot by itself tell you which conditional to accept, for the law indicates nothing about the direction or structure of dependence.

Simple appeals to temporal priority are insufficient to pick out the preferred direction of causation. In this respect, the scratching-and-lighting example may be misleading. Rather than datable brief events, in many cases of causation the causal relation connects more or less long-standing states. In some cases of causation, cause and effect appear to be simultaneous. Even if proper formulations of laws or lawlike statements should somehow provide a way of distinguishing acceptable from unacceptable conditionals, when these conditionals are supported by just the same laws, there would still be a problem of distinguishing acceptable from unacceptable conditionals that are not based on any law. The following are variations on the example concerning interest rates at the end of Chapter V:

> If you bought a thousand dollars' worth of Tandy Corporation stock at its 1975 low, it would have been worth over eighty thousand dollars in 1982.
> If we had bought one more artichoke this morning, we would have had one for everyone at dinner tonight.

Some people do ardently seek to discover the laws that, together with relevant facts that obtain at a certain time, entail the later performance of the stock market. We do not have to believe that there are any such laws to accept the conditional above. The relevant facts that support the conditional concern the actual performance of Tandy Corporation stock between 1975 and 1982 together with the reasonable assumption that your buying a thousand dollars' worth would not have greatly affected its price. The second conditional is similarly supported by the fact that the number of people coming for dinner tonight exceeds by one the number of artichokes we bought this morning. Our confidence in the conditional exceeds our confidence about what happens in the closest possible world in which we buy one more artichoke this morning. Who can say about this world just which people in it we impulsively invite for dinner and of those just how many accept?

It is not obvious that there are laws – if only we knew them – that could answer such questions. Examples like these, and also like the dice-throwing case at the end of the last chapter, cause problems for several accounts of conditionals cast in terms of possible worlds.

The concept of physical or causal law cannot by itself solve our problem of causal dependency. Goodman's troublesome match example certainly seems to call for some reference to the direction of dependence or direction of causation. Scratching matches makes them light; scratching matches does not make them damp. Reflection on examples like this leads the linguist James McCawley to assert that there is a simple connection between conditionals and a direction of dependence:

> The English counterfactual construction, like all conditional constructions in English, is normally used only when the antecedent is temporally and/or causally and/or epistemologically prior to the consequent, as in the examples discussed [earlier] such as
>
> a. If you touch me, I'll scream.
> a'. You'll touch me only if I scream.
>
> The *if*-clause must be temporally/causally/epistemologically prior even if it is modified by *only*, contrary to the usual claim of introductory logic texts that 'If A, B' and 'A only if B' are 'equivalent'.[2]

We should believe McCawley on the relation between *if* and *only if* before we believe the standard introductory logic texts. And we should take the if-clause always to be prior in some way to the main clause before we simply neglect questions of priority, as do so many treatments of conditionals. I will argue nevertheless that McCawley's generalization sweeps far too broadly. There is no single central pattern but a variety of patterns of dependence and priority that back up acceptable conditionals. Understanding these patterns of dependence allows us to understand the acceptability of conditionals.

Before emending McCawley's claim, I shall restate it in terms of *conditions*:

> The conditional construction in English is normally used only

when the antecedent mentions a condition of what the consequent mentions, as in the examples such as

a. If you learn to play the cello, I'll buy you a cello.

a'. You will learn to play the cello only if I buy you a cello.

The *if*-clause must mention a temporal, causal, or epistemological condition of what the main clause mentions even if it is modified by *only*, contrary to the usual claim of introductory logic texts.

In this passage, written in imitation of McCawley, example (a) would normally be understood as stating a sufficient condition of my buying you a cello. There could be other, alternative, sufficient conditions as well: If you pass algebraic topology, or if you stop leaving dirty socks under the bed, or if you learn to play the cello, I'll buy you a cello. Example (a'), in contrast, would normally be understood as stating a necessary condition of your learning to play the cello. There could be other additional and supplementary necessary conditions as well: You will learn to play the cello only if I buy you a cello and hire you a teacher, and you practise almost every day. (a) and (a') together put you, the hopeful beginner, in a bind: you cannot learn to play unless I buy you the instrument, and it sounds as though I am unwilling to buy you a cello until you have already learned to play.

Nelson Goodman's exemplary counterfactual conditional about lighting the match is acceptable because scratching, in the circumstances, is a sufficient condition for lighting. The circumstances include a number of necessary conditions for lighting. The standard competing example about the match becoming damp is an unacceptable conditional because scratching, in these circumstances and in most circumstances, is not a condition of being or becoming damp or of being or becoming dry. What Goodman calls the 'problem of relevant conditions' is the problem of locating, without first assuming a conditional of the very kind for which you are attempting to account, which conditions are relevant in the treatment of a given conditional. Goodman writes as if anything that actually occurs or obtains is a condition. The oxygen in the vicinity is a condition of the match's becoming damp, although it presumably is not a condition relevant to a conditional about the dampening of the match if it were scratched. I suggest that neither the oxygen in the vicinity nor the scratching of the match is any kind of a condition of the match's becoming damp. We should view the problem of relevant conditions as a problem of *conditions*. What is it for something to be or not to be a condition of something else? We can assume that any condition of A is a relevant condition of A. What we need is a way of distinguishing conditions of A from non-conditions.

The passage quoted from McCawley conflicts with the usual textbook treatment of *if* and *only if*. The rewritten passage conflicts with the usual textbook treatment of *necessary condition* and *sufficient condition*. This is no mere coincidence; the topics are connected. One usually treats *if* and *only if* in the context of truth-functional propositional logic. Given the methodological assumption to treat all conditionals as material conditionals, the logic textbooks are quite correct in their usual claims. At the first step of the move from a natural language conditional to a formula in a logical system, 'If *P*, *Q*' naturally goes to '*P* ⊃ *Q*' while '*P* only if *Q*' goes first to 'Not *P* unless *Q*' and then to 'not-*Q* ⊃ not-*P*'. By contraposition, which is valid for '⊃', the two material conditionals are equivalent. Sometimes necessary and sufficient conditions are treated with the same logical resources used to treat *if* and *only if*. But, even if the full resources of standard modal logic are employed, there is a similar problem. The resources are inadequate to reveal a relevant distinction. The problem we had with law is still unsolved, for laws typically say only that certain joint occurrences or joint instantiations of values of variables are impossible. 'Scratching is sufficient for lighting' is represented as 'It is not possible that there is scratching without lighting.' (Of course this is not true in the absence of certain background factors.) 'Oxygen is necessary for lighting' is represented as 'It is not possible that there is lighting without oxygen.' 'It is not possible that there is A without B' is taken to express what is meant both by 'A is sufficient for B' and by 'B is necessary for A.' These last two schematic sentences, moreover, are not distinguished respectively from 'A is a sufficient condition of B' and 'B is a necessary condition of A.' So these last two are regarded as equivalent. According to the standard treatment, A is a sufficient condition of B if and only if B is a necessary condition of A; and A is a necessary and sufficient condition of B if and only if B is a necessary and sufficient condition of A.

These results can work philosophical mischief. Consider a statement of Aristotle's sea-battle example in terms of conditions:[3]

The occurrence of a sea battle tomorrow is a necessary and sufficient condition for the truth today of the statement 'There will be a sea battle tomorrow.'

Now rewrite this in accord with the alleged equivalence:

The truth today of the statement 'There will be a sea battle tomorrow' is a necessary and sufficient condition of the occurrence of a sea battle tomorrow.

The first is sensible while the second has things backwards. The statement about the battle, if true, is true because of the occurrence of the battle. The battle does not occur because of the truth of the statement. Notice that this is not a clearly causal example. The occurrence of the battle does not *cause* the truth of the statement. Another apparently non-causal example concerns a topic that introductory philosophy classes frequently cover:[4]

The truth of P is a necessary condition for your knowing that P.
Your knowing that P is a sufficient condition for the truth of P.

The first is standard doctrine while the second suggests that things are true *because* you know them. Causal examples are easily found:

Guzzling cyanide is a sufficient condition of death.
Death is a necessary condition of guzzling cyanide.

Although you can't guzzle cyanide without dying, that does not mean that you can't guzzle cyanide without dying first. While some take cyanide in order to die, none die in order to take cyanide. The direction of causation runs from the ingestion of poison to death. The second sentence above suggests that the causation runs in the opposite direction.

The orthodox symmetry theses about the connection of necessary conditions and sufficient conditions can be abandoned

177

without giving up the view that *necessary condition* and *sufficient condition* are interdefinable. Georg Henrik von Wright suggests the following pattern of definition:[5]

A is a necessary condition of B =df the absence of A is a sufficient condition of the absence of B.
A is a sufficient condition of B =df the absence of A is a necessary condition of the absence of B.

These two patterns of definition together suggest the generalization that A is a condition of B if and only if the absence of A is a condition of the absence of B. The patterns of definition do not support the orthodox generalization, a thesis that deserves rejection, that A is a condition of B if and only if B is a condition of A. When applied to the true sentences in the examples considered above, the definitions yield further truths:

Avoiding guzzling cyanide is a necessary condition of avoiding death.
The falsehood of *P* is a sufficient condition for your not knowing that *P*.
The non-occurrence of a sea battle tomorrow is a necessary and sufficient condition of the falsehood today of the statement 'There will be a sea battle tomorrow.'

Parallel transformations on falsehoods yield further falsehoods. For example:

Avoiding death is a sufficient condition of not guzzling cyanide.

The pattern of defining 'necessary for' and 'sufficient for' sketched above is useful and straightforward. Our laws and theories tell us that certain combinations of factors, events, occurrences, states, values, and so forth, cannot be co-instantiated. 'It cannot be that A without B' can be read either as 'A is sufficient for B' or as 'B is necessary for A' so long as these expressions by themselves are not understood to say something about conditionship. The following two arguments are fallacious in the same way:

178

A is a condition.
A is sufficient for B.
Therefore, A is a sufficient condition of B.

John is a son.
John is considerate of Mrs Smith.
Therefore, John is a considerate son of Mrs Smith.

Just as the second conclusion requires not merely that John is a son, but that he is a son of Mrs Smith, the first requires not merely that A is a condition, but that it is a condition of B. If it is impossible that A should obtain without B's obtaining as well, then we might as well say that A is sufficient for B, or that B is necessary for A. But this impossibility by itself does not indicate what is a condition of what.

Necessary condition and *sufficient condition* are not purely technical terms. As persons uncorrupted by philosophy classes and logic textbooks ordinarily understand them, they do not satisfy the biconditional symmetry thesis: A is a necessary condition of B if and only if B is a sufficient condition of A. Neither does our ordinary understanding imply generally that *condition of* is a symmetric relation: A is a condition of B if and only if B is a condition of A. The ordinary view is scarcely disproved by being shown to be inconsistent with the textbook definitions. On the contrary, the textbook definitions are inadequate because they are inconsistent with the ordinary view. Well-formed textbook definitions possess a virtue, however, that ordinary views lack: it is clear what they contain and imply. On the ordinary view, it is not so clear and obvious whether conditionship is asymmetric or non-symmetric. If A is a condition of B, does it follow that B is not a condition of A? Or does nothing of the kind follow, neither that B is a condition of A nor that it is not? Although I do not know how to argue for definite answers to these questions, I can describe some examples favouring the view that conditionship is non-symmetric.

Consider two meshed gears. Neither can turn without the other turning. The rotation of either one, I think it is natural to say, is a necessary and sufficient condition of the rotation of the other. The first might turn the second, or the second might turn the first. It is also possible that neither turns the other and that each is turned by something else, but this would be unusual. Usually the direction of causation is one way or the other through the two meshed gears. In a mechanism such as this in which conditionship is reciprocal, causation can go in either direction. Not all such examples deal with the straightforward kinematic transfer of motion. Consider a gas container with a fixed volume. Given that the volume and the number of gas molecules is fixed, values for the temperature and pressure of the contained gas come in pairs. The gas's having temperature t is a necessary and sufficient condition of its having pressure p, and its having pressure p is a necessary and sufficient condition of its having temperature t. Again, the direction of causation can be in either direction. The pressure can be increased (or decreased) by an increase (or decrease) in temperature. The temperature similarly can be increased (or decreased) by an increase (or decrease) of pressure. These instances of causation are in accord with the gas laws, but the laws by themselves say nothing about the direction of causation.

According to our treatment of these examples, if A is an occurrent sufficient condition of B, it does not follow that A causes B. Although the temperature of the gas may be an occurrent sufficient condition of its having a certain pressure (this depends on the circumstances), it may be that the temperature is due to the pressure, rather than the other way round. An appeal to the direction of causation in a particular instance in order to determine the direction of conditionship has another difficulty. Not all conditions are causal. A necessary condition of knowing that the number $\sqrt{2}$ is irrational is that the number $\sqrt{2}$ be irrational, but it is difficult to see how the irrationality of the number $\sqrt{2}$ can cause, or contribute to the cause, of anything. This example also serves to cast doubt on another proposal for accounting for the direction of conditionship, that A is a condition of B only if A occurs earlier than B. Since the irrationality of the number $\sqrt{2}$ is timeless, it cannot occur earlier than anything. The temporal criterion works poorly even for purely causal examples. Although causes are often earlier than their effects, and it is not obvious that effects ever precede their causes, simultaneous causation appears to be common. (The increase in the pressure of the enclosed gas does not *come after* the increase in temperature.)

If we do not attempt to account for the direction of conditionship by reference to the direction of causation, the way is left open for an account that goes the other way, explaining the direction of causation by reference to the direction of conditionship. The suggestion is not to analyse causation just in terms of conditions, or even just in terms of causal conditions. The suggestion presupposes, rather, that we have acquired an adequate understanding of causal ordering, of what it is for items to be causally connected in a direct line, and what it is for something to be causally between two others. If C is causally between A and B, this causal ordering does not determine the causal direction, which may be from A to C to B, or the other way, from B to C to A. The appeal to causal conditionship is supposed to help determine causal direction once causal order has been independently established. If A and B are occurrences causally connected in a direct line, if A is a causal condition of B while B is not a causal condition of A, then A is a cause of B. (If A and B are causal conditions of each other, this account requires that one look for some larger causal order of which they are a part to look for some one-way conditionship that imparts a direction on the whole connected order.) Flipping the switch turns on the lights because switch position is a causal condition of the light's being on. The light's being on is not a condition of the switch's being in or put in the 'on' position.

If the suggestion to explain the direction of causation by reference to the occurrence of one-way conditionship is promising, this puts even more pressure on the attempt to provide an account of conditionship. I have already claimed that we can best deal with Goodman's problem of relevant conditions by taking the notion of *condition* more seriously. McCawley's suggestion that the antecedent of a conditional typically mentions a condition of what the consequent mentions will have more substance once we develop a theory of conditionship. Before addressing this project, however, I will return to the question whether conditionals typically exhibit a single, forward pattern of dependence. The next chapter will deal mainly with David Lewis's notion of counterfactual dependence and his treatment of backtracking conditionals.

181

CHAPTER XII

Counterfactual Dependence
and Backtracking

> HENRY: Buddy Holly was twenty-two. Think of
> what he might have gone on to achieve. I mean,
> if Beethoven had been killed in a plane crash at
> twenty-two, the history of music would have been
> very different. As would the history of
> aviation, of course.

The water pressure in my house does not depend on the operation of an electric pump. But, if I had a well, the water pressure would depend on an electric pump. Although we might have said that this is a counterfactual dependence, a dependence considered counterfactually, we do not say this; for 'counterfactual dependence' has received a different meaning. An event E depends counterfactually on an event C just when each of a pair of counterfactual conditionals is true: if C had occurred, E would have occurred; and if C had not occurred, E would not have occurred. Neither of these conditionals need have dependence as subject matter. One supposes that a kind of dependence, counterfactual dependence, obtains in virtue of the truth or acceptability of the conditionals.

Counterfactual dependence has become a term of the trade in recent years. Writers of philosophy often use it without explanation. Some writers repeat the explanation that David Lewis originally provides in his article 'Causation'.[1] One would expect that writers on causation would not adopt the term 'counterfactual dependence' in Lewis's sense unless they largely agreed with Lewis about which counterfactuals are acceptable, but the facts are curiously otherwise. Some, disagreeing with Lewis, admit without apparent qualms that causes can depend counterfactually on their effects although they have no inclination to conclude in such cases that causes depend causally on their effects or that the notion of one-way causal dependence is an illusion. They attempt, rather, to account for our common beliefs about causal priority in terms of counterfactual dependence, despite the fact that the direction of counterfactual dependence is often the reverse of the direction of causal dependence.

I turned the switch knob on the floor lamp, but the lamp did not go on. No wonder: the lamp was not plugged in. I unplugged it myself yesterday when I was looking for a place to plug in the vacuum cleaner; and I forgot to plug the lamp back in. If the lamp had gone on, then it would, some time earlier, have been plugged back in. This last conditional is a *backtracking conditional*. We do not think of the replugging in of the lamp as depending on the lamp's subsequent lighting. The dependence runs in the opposite temporal direction – what is later depends on what is earlier – which we regard as the normal temporal direction of causal dependence. If Stevenson were President of the United States in February 1953, he would have been elected in November 1952.[2] (Stevenson and Eisenhower ran against each other in 1952, and Eisenhower won the November election.) Each backtracking conditional like this casts doubt on the generality of McCawley's claim about the priority of the antecedent in English conditionals. Not all acceptable backtrackers are causal. Some non-causal examples are familiar philosophic principles. If S knows that *P*, then *P*. 'Ought' implies 'can'. If *a* and *b* share exactly the same properties, *a* is identical to *b*. It is not, in this last case, a perennially controversial claim, that numerical identity is achieved by attaining total qualitative identity; numerical identity, rather, is claimed to be a necessary condition of total qualitative identity.

David Lewis acknowledges that we sometimes accept backtracking conditionals; but he maintains that backtrackers are accepted only on extraordinary interpretations, only on non-standard resolutions of indeterminacy. On the standard resolution, acceptable conditionals track forward and backtracking conditionals are ruled out. There is standardly an asymmetry of counterfactual dependence: when A counterfactually depends on B, then B does not counterfactually depend on A. That is, when each of the pair of counterfactual conditionals required for a

183

dependence is true, at least one of the pair of conditionals required for the reverse dependence is not true. Lewis puts the asymmetry of counterfactual dependence to some important philosophic uses. It accounts for causal asymmetry; and it accounts for the asymmetry of openness, the inescapable but often inexplicable feeling that the future is open in a way that the past is not:

> The literal truth is just that the future depends counterfactually on the present. It depends, partly, on what we do now.
>
> Likewise, something we ordinarily *cannot* do by way of 'changing the past' is to bring it about that the past is the way it actually was, rather than some other way it would have been if we acted differently in the present. The past would be the same, however we acted now. The past does not at all depend on what we do now. It is counterfactually independent of the present.
>
> In short, I suggest that the mysterious asymmetry between open future and fixed past is nothing else than the asymmetry of counterfactual dependence. The forking paths into the future – the actual one and all the rest – are the many alternative futures that would have come about under various counterfactual suppositions about the present. The one actual, fixed past is the one past that would remain actual under this same range of suppositions.[3]

I will summarize the argument in Lewis's 'Counterfactual dependence and time's arrow' for the asymmetry of counterfactual dependence by quoting several passages from Lewis, with my order of presentation the reverse of Lewis's.

Our world happens to exhibit a pervasive asymmetry of overdetermination:

> Any particular fact about a deterministic world is predetermined throughout the past and postdetermined throughout the future. At any time, past or future, it has at least one *determinant*: a minimal set of conditions jointly sufficient, given the laws of nature, for the fact in question. (Members of such a set may be causes of the fact, or traces of it, or neither.)[4]

When simultaneous disjoint states of the world each determine the same fact, that fact is overdetermined. According to Lewis, there happens to be vastly more overdetermination of facts by later states of the world than by earlier states of the world. He illustrates the asymmetry of overdetermination by discussing an example of Popper's:

> There are processes in which a spherical wave expands outward from a point source to infinity. The opposite processes, in which a spherical wave contracts inward from infinity and is absorbed, would obey the laws of nature equally well. But they never occur. A process of either sort exhibits extreme overdetermination in one direction. Countless tiny samples of the wave each determine what happens at the space–time point where the wave is emitted or absorbed. The processes that occur are the ones in which this extreme overdetermination goes toward the past, not those in which it goes toward the future. I suggest that the same is true more generally.[5]

If there is an asymmetry of overdetermination, as is here alleged, there is also an asymmetry of miracles. Again quoting Lewis:

> It takes a miracle to break the links between any determinant and that which it determines. . . . The more overdetermination, the more links need breaking and the more widespread and diverse must a miracle be if it is to break them all.[6]

Since there are relatively few localized links running in the earlier-to-later direction, a small, localized miracle is sufficient to break them all. If the first of two possible worlds is deterministic, and a second possible world matches it perfectly up to time *t*, only a small, local violation in the second world of the laws of the first is necessary for the two worlds to diverge after *t*. Since there are many determining links running in the later-to-earlier direction, a large, widespread violation of law is necessary to bring about a convergence of worlds. If the first of two possible worlds is deterministic, and a second possible world matches it perfectly after time *t*, a large, widespread violation of laws in the first world is required for the two worlds to converge at *t* if they did not match perfectly before *t*.[7]

The thesis of the asymmetry of miracles, which employs a distinction between local and global miracles, coordinates with Lewis's ranking of respects of world-similarity quoted in Chapter VII. To repeat: 'It is of the first importance to avoid big, widespread violations of law. It is of the second importance to maximize the spatio-temporal region throughout which perfect match of particular fact prevails. It is of the third importance to avoid even small, localized, simple violations of law.'[8] Approximate similarity of particular fact, no matter how important to us, is of little importance in applying possible-world semantics to conditionals. Lewis implies that it is probably of no importance at all. This ranking of respects of similarity, remember, was intended to handle conditionals about how a little difference of a certain kind would have made a big difference. The problem of dealing with these conditionals is different from the problem of explaining the asymmetry of counterfactual dependence. In treating this second problem, Lewis appeals both to his ranking of respects of similarity and to his thesis of the asymmetry of miracles.

If the actual world is deterministic, then any possible world that sometimes but not always matches the actual world perfectly will violate some of the laws of the actual world. Global violations produce a greater dissimilarity between worlds than local violations. If the actual world is indeterministic, then there need be no miracle, not even a little one, in a possible world that diverges from the actual world. Lewis appears to hold that, if the actual world is indeterministic, there is something analogous to the asymmetry of miracles that might be called the *asymmetry of indeterministic microevents*. Only one such microevent is needed to make worlds diverge, but a coordinated global system of microevents is required to bring divergent worlds back together.

Jonathan Bennett questions Lewis's treatment of backtracking and asymmetry on a number of points. In connection with the topic of convergence, Bennett remarks, 'Lewis's real topic is *re*convergence miracles, that is, events through which worlds which were alike and then unalike become alike again.'[9] The difficulty of reconvergence helps possible-world semantics fit *if a tiny difference, then a huge difference* conditionals. It does not by itself imply an asymmetry. Although, given a certain kind of divergence, reconvergence may be difficult, given a certain kind

186

of convergence, prior divergence may be equally difficult. Bennett describes counterexamples to some of Lewis's claims about divergence and convergence, and there may be other kinds of counterexamples as well. The exercise of inventing such examples, however, does not touch the heart of Lewis's thesis of the asymmetry of counterfactual dependence, to which the thesis of the asymmetry of overdetermination provides the ultimate support.

The asymmetry of overdetermination is an illusion. Consider an example of wave expansion more easily observed than the propagation of light. An acorn falls into the middle of a quiet pond, and circular waves move outward on the pond's surface. Now it is true that, given the extra information that this is a quiet pond, its surface disturbed from the outside at just one spatio-temporal point at most, there is an asymmetry of overdetermination. But the extra information is essential; once it is explicitly taken into account, the appearance of asymmetry vanishes. Consider two rather small spatio-temporal regions, each spatially a sphere ten centimetres in diameter and temporally one-tenth of a second in duration. One contains the acorn's sudden entry into the pond. The other contains the passage of a small part of the crest of the first wave ten metres away from where the acorn fell. Each occurrence within one of these regions is compatible with a great number of different things happening in the other. The occurrences in neither region determine the occurrences in the other because the occurrences in neither region determine that the surface of the pond is undisturbed except for the entry of the acorn. Neither precludes, for example, the sudden landing in the pond by a pair of mallard ducks a little after the acorn enters and a little before the wave crest passes. Every time-slice of the world at time t that determines the state of the world at space-time point p, whether p is earlier or later than t, includes every point at t causally connectible to p, every point in the slice not outside p's light cone. Wave expansion does not illustrate an asymmetry of overdetermination.

How then should we regard backtracking conditionals? We should regard some of them as true or as acceptable as any forward-tracking conditional. Many backtrackers accord quite well with Lewis's ranking of similarities (although, if they didn't, that would be so much the worse for the rankings). If the lamp had lighted, the lamp would have been plugged in. That is, if the lamp had lighted five minutes ago, when I turned the switch, the lamp would have been plugged in. Five minutes ago the lamp was not plugged in; so if we treat this conditional with a possible-worlds semantics, and we take the world as it was up to five minutes ago to be the actual world to which other possible worlds will be compared, we must address a difficult question: what sort of world in which a lamp lights at time *t* is closest to the world in which a lamp is not plugged in at *t*? Should we say that, if the lamp had lighted, then it would have lighted without being plugged in? We should, rather, try to release ourselves from a fixation on the if-clause of the conditionals we treat. Although it was five minutes ago that I turned the lamp switch, a look at the entire conditional reveals that a longer period of earlier time is probably relevant. When – most likely – would the lamp have been plugged back in if it had been plugged in? Yesterday, when I was operating the vacuum cleaner. For comparison purposes, then, the actual world is this world up to yesterday. That allows us to count this backtracking conditional as true without positing any big, widespread violations of law. (PROFESSOR'S UN-PLUGGED LAMP LIGHTS!) If the actual world is indeterministic, having the lamp plugged in yesterday may require no violation of law at all. And, if the actual world is deterministic, the localized violation may be too small to notice. An unexciting headline: PROFESSOR REMEMBERS TO REPLUG LAMP! The possible world most like the actual world in which the lamp lighted five minutes ago matched the actual world perfectly up to yesterday. Then they diverged. In the actual world, I forgot to plug the lamp back in; in this other possible world, I did not forget.

As I tell this slight domestic story, if the lamp got plugged in, it got plugged in yesterday. Such a high degree of specificity is only for the purpose of illustration. The conditional itself neither implies nor requires anything so specific. If the lamp had been plugged back in, just when would this have occurred? Although we may have no idea how to defend a specific answer to this question, we can still be confident that it would have to have been plugged back in sometime if it had lighted five minutes ago. Such confidence does not require the ability to pin down the closest possible world in which the lamp was replugged.

The standard acceptability of backtracking counterfactual conditionals conflicts with the asymmetry of counterfactual dependence. One of them must go, namely the second. No single pattern of dependence correlates with the acceptability of standard conditionals. Counterfactual dependence explains neither the asymmetry of causation nor the temporal asymmetry of openness. In the passage quoted above from Lewis about the asymmetry of openness, we should strike out the word 'counterfactual' when it occurs in the phrase 'counterfactual dependence'. I mean to question the very notion of counterfactual dependence. When we read the passage from Lewis to be simply about the dependence of the later on the earlier, and the non-dependence of the earlier on the later, then it is a useful explanation of what we mean by 'The future is open while the past is fixed.'

The claim can be questioned. There often are, or seem to be, alternative ways for something to come about:

> Kira took the bus to the airport. If she had missed the bus, she would have taken a cab; so her arriving at the airport did not depend on her taking the bus.
> The electric clock is running on line current. If the line current had gone off, the clock would be running on the current from stand-by batteries; so the running of the clock does not depend on the line current.

Causal and temporal examples which are not briefly, idiomatically, and appropriately described by using the word 'depend' do not all involve stand-by or back-up or overdetermining factors. 'The pine tree died because the beetles got it; the beetles caused the pine to die' is closer to idiom than something like 'The death of the pine tree depended on the beetles.' While we should not despise attempts to provide conceptual analyses, although they are out of fashion at present, I shall not attempt to provide an analysis of 'depend'. Instead of recommending direct solutions to the problems raised by the examples above, I shall continue talking about *dependence* and continue to write as if there are correlations between 'causes' and 'depends' more neat and simple than examinations of ordinary language may reveal. My usage, then, is somewhat technical and theoretical. The theoretical convictions are widely shared, I think; and the ordinary language

189

of dependence comes close enough to expressing these convictions for us to prefer it to an artificial, explicitly technical vocabulary.

Hume inspires Lewis on causation, and the two of them, together and separately, inspire other philosophers to attempt to provide conditional accounts of causation. When a conditional is true in virtue of some causal dependence, however, the direction of causation need not be from the occurrence the if-clause mentions to the occurrence the main clause mentions. I describe several patterns of dependence in the next chapter. When something causally depends on something, certain conditionals are true in virtue of this dependence. The occurrence of causation typically supports the truth of subjunctive conditionals, particularly conditionals of the form Lewis uses to define 'counterfactual dependence'. (Such conditionals can be undermined by extraordinary complications.) There is thus a close connection between causation and conditionals, and accounts of this connection commonly turn things around. Some conditionals are true in virtue of causation. Instances of causation do not occur in virtue of the truth of certain conditionals. Instead of attempting to explain dependence in terms of acceptable conditionals, we should attempt to explain the acceptability of conditionals in terms of dependence. That means that to avoid circularity we should not account for the direction of dependence solely in terms of the acceptability and unacceptability of associated conditionals. (I attempt to avoid circularity by providing such an account in Chapter XIV.)

Not all dependence is causal dependence; and not all acceptable conditionals are true in virtue of one or another pattern of dependence, causal or otherwise. Most of the examples to follow are nevertheless tied to various patterns of causal dependence. I will often describe them in terms of necessary conditions and sufficient conditions. In so doing, I assume the central contention of the last chapter: conditionship is not symmetric. The lamp's being plugged in is a necessary condition of its lighting. (Its lighting is not a sufficient condition of its being plugged in – as if we might cause a lamp to get plugged in, or to have been plugged in, by turning it on.) The backtracking conditional discussed above is true for these reasons. The if-clause mentions something for which a necessary condition is mentioned by the main clause. Acceptable back-trackers of this kind are common.

We know about the direction of dependence relevant to our lamp-lighting conditional because we know enough about how electric lamps work. Our knowledge of relevant directions of dependence is often due simply to our knowledge of how the world works. The relevant direction is not indicated by the simple conditional form *If P, then Q*. Sometimes the antecedent is prior to the consequent only by coming earlier in the sentence. What the consequent mentions can be temporally prior, causally prior, and otherwise prior to what the antecedent mentions when an *if P, then Q* or *if it had been P, then it would have been Q* conditional is true. Conditionals of other forms, however, can indicate something about the direction of dependence just by their forms. A prime example is *P only if Q*. Conditionals of this form are often accepted because what *Q* mentions is a necessary condition of what *P* mentions. It would be odd to accept or assert them just because what *P* mentions is a sufficient condition of what *Q* mentions. The presence of backtracking in a subjunctive conditional can also be indicated by certain grammatical complications in the main clause. 'If the lamp had gone on, it would *have had to have been* plugged back in.'

Necessary condition of and *sufficient condition of* indicate two patterns of dependence in virtue of which conditionals are frequently true. They are not the only such patterns, however. The next chapter provides some examples of some additional patterns.

CHAPTER XIII

Patterns of Dependence

This chapter begins with variations on an example illustrating different patterns of dependence that can ground the conditional:

If Smith was fired, so was Wilson.

Although the example is in the indicative for the sake of simplicity, the corresponding subjunctive conditional connects with the same variety of patterns. The minimal structure of the conditional sentence form, *if P, Q*, indicates nothing very strongly about which directions of dependence are relevant. The subject matter also offers no hint along these lines. One who lacks enough background information about the Smith–Wilson situation to form a belief about the direction of dependence between their firings can nevertheless believe, perhaps just on testimony, that, if Smith was fired, Wilson was fired.

Here are descriptions of five different ways in which the firings of Wilson and Smith might be related so as to make this conditional true: (1) If Smith was fired, Wilson was fired as a result. Smith's firing is a sufficient condition of Wilson's firing. (2) If Smith was fired, it was as a result of Wilson's firing. Wilson's firing is a necessary condition of Smith's firing. Smith was fired only if Wilson was fired. (3) The firing of either Smith or Wilson would result in the firing of the other. Each is a sufficient condition of the other. (4) If Smith was fired, then it resulted from something from which Wilson's firing was a result. A necessary condition of Smith's being fired is a sufficient condition of Wilson's being fired. (5) The firings of Smith and Wilson are completely independent in that neither resulted from the other, and there is nothing from which each resulted. But Wilson definitely was or will be the first to be fired. If anyone was fired, Wilson was fired.

The following brief stories distinguish these cases and show their possibility:

(1) Wilson was Smith's trusted assistant. Smith wouldn't have fired Wilson; but, if Smith was fired, so was Wilson, because, whenever a head is fired, so are all the assistants. A new head gets to bring in his own assistants. If Smith was fired, Wilson was fired as a result.

(2) Smith was *Wilson's* trusted assistant. Wilson wouldn't have fired Smith. The only way Smith would have been fired is for his boss Wilson to be fired; for, whenever a head is fired, so are all the assistants. If Smith was fired, it was as a result of Wilson's firing.

(3) Management has no reason to fire one rather than the other, but it did have reason to fire one or the other. In the opinion of management, the work done by Smith and Wilson together could be done by either one of them alone. Smith and Wilson are close friends. If one were fired and the other not, the one remaining would cause a lot of trouble by complaining about management's treatment of the other. It would be less trouble to hire and train a new person to replace the pair of them. The firing of either Smith or Wilson would result in the firing of the other.

(4) Management was considering eliminating the unit for which Smith, Wilson, and several others work. They were not considering reorganizing the unit by firing some but not others, and they were not considering transferring some in the unit elsewhere. If the unit was eliminated, everyone in it, including Smith and Wilson, was fired. If Smith was fired, then it resulted from something, the decision to eliminate the unit, from which Wilson's firing was another result.

A full enough story for (5) was told the first time around. Wilson was fired if anyone was. So Wilson was fired if Smith was, although the firings are completely independent.

The fact that there are at least five different ways in which 'If Smith was fired, so was Wilson' can be true does not show that the sentence is ambiguous. I maintain that it is unambiguous. Providing distinguishable grounds for the truth or acceptability of a sentence need not also provide distinguishable meanings. Someone can accept this conditional sentence without having any idea which pattern of dependence, if any, backs it up. Such a person does not have a very specific idea of what makes the conditional true, but does not thereby have an ambiguous belief. Unspecificity is not ambiguity. The claim that any one of several patterns of dependence might support a conditional bears on the truth and the acceptability of the conditional. It does not obviously bear on the analysis of its meaning.

In a passage quoted in Chapter V, Ted Honderich urges that we recognize a simple distinction:

> There are *two* questions, one of them that of specifying the meaning of conditionals, the other the general analysis of their *grounds* or *premises*. It is in fact this latter problem to which philosophers have addressed themselves, despite their mis-description of it, and they have had arguable things to say about it. Their efforts must be seen in a proper light, not the one they supply.[1]

Honderich argues as follows against the typical conflation of grounds and meaning when the purported analysis of meaning is stated schematically by means of propositional variables:

> What is being proposed is that something of the form *if p then q* is equivalent in meaning to something of the form *r & (if p & r then q)*. But the latter is ground for the former. What we have in fact is that something, *if p then q*, is represented both as consequence and its own ground. It is represented as a logically distinct entailer of itself, which thing it does not itself entail.[2]

Even if those who provide traditional analyses of meaning might encounter this objection without falling silent, I recommend adopting the objection's intended moral: explaining what a conditional means is different from explaining why it is true.

How, then, should we explain what a conditional means? Honderich suggests that, once questions about the meaning of conditionals are distinguished from questions about grounds, questions of meaning will have little philosophical interest:

> Another thought is that the question of the analysis of

conditionals themselves does not deserve the name of problem. 'If the door is shut the room is warmer' wears *its* meaning on its words. It is not about windows and the like, or a connection between other than the door's being shut and the room's being warmer. Nor does it mean that it isn't the case that the door is shut and the room not warmer. Clearly that could not be the whole of the meaning, or we would have the result that a conditional, of the form *if p then q*, would always be true when ~(*p* & ~*q*) was true, which evidently it is not.

What the conditional means can be variously expressed: on condition, or given, or in the case that the door is shut, the room is warmer. Or: the possible situation in which the door is shut is also one in which the room is warmer. What the conditional means can be best expressed by nothing other than itself: if the door is shut the room is warmer.[3]

The first paragraph in this passage ends with a highly controversial claim. As we saw in Chapter III, despite the (alleged) fact that there is no difference in truth value between *if p then q* and ~(*p* & ~*q*), explanations are available for the differences in assertability between them. Although I expressed admiration for Grice's larger programme, I did not accept the inessential part of it that treats conditionals. Other philosophers have been more ready than Honderich or I to accept a view similar to Grice's. David Lewis holds that the indicative conditional simply is the truth-functional conditional, but the assertability of the conditional is equal to the conditional probability of its main clause on its if-clause.[4] Frank Jackson argues in a rather different way for the same conclusion.[5]

A distinction between truth conditions and assertability conditions for conditionals, which these last views draw, does not require that a truth-functional account of the meaning of conditionals provides the truth conditions. For appeals to probability or possible worlds or connections or something else, including patterns of dependence, can also provide truth conditions. The distinction between truth conditions and assertability conditions also does not require that both conditions are relevant to conditionals of every kind. Some theorists hold that subjunctive conditionals lack truth conditions and thus are never literally true or false, although they are more or less assertable.

Some theorists hold that a truth-functional account of indicative conditionals is only partial: some indicative conditionals are true; some are false; and some, especially those with false if-clauses, are neither true nor false.

In this chapter I advance the view that conditionals are acceptable in virtue of a number of different patterns of dependence and independence. The question is thus naturally asked: do I suggest truth conditions, or assertability conditions, or what? Do I assert or deny that subjunctive conditionals have truth-values? Do I assert or deny that indicative conditionals with unfulfilled antecedents have truth-values? When discussing topics in the vicinity of these questions in earlier chapters, I have sometimes employed apparently evasive disjunctions such as 'the truth or acceptability of the conditional'. Which exactly then do I mean, truth or acceptability? What I mean, in fact, is the disjunction rather than either disjunct. I cannot find and do not care to stipulate a sharp division between assertability conditions and truth conditions. 'Assertability-or-truth conditions' – clumsy, disjunctive phrase – fits my view that one conditional can be true in virtue of the satisfaction of a certain condition *C*, a second conditional can be false in virtue of the non-satisfaction of *C*, a third conditional, not happily called either *true* or *false*, can be acceptable because it does not definitely fail to satisfy *C*, and a fourth conditional, also neither true nor false, can be unacceptable because the satisfaction of *C* is implausible, unlikely, or bizarre.

It is true that, if the egg had dropped, it would have broken, because, in the circumstances, dropping the egg would definitely have resulted in its breaking. It is neither true nor false, in my opinion, that, if Julius Caesar had lived in the United States during the 1950s, he would have become fond of French fries, Coca-Cola, and cheeseburgers. The question whether Caesar's encountering the United States of the 1950s would result in his adopting certain indigenous food preferences has no obvious definite answer. (The question can be regarded as radically ambiguous between a number of much more complicated and specific questions, which each have definite *yes* or *no* answers. But such appeals to radical ambiguity are difficult to contain: once ambiguity is found in these cases which involve specific details never previously considered, it can be found everywhere.) In general, questions about what results, or would result, from what can sometimes be answered with enough definiteness to make a conditional true, or false, and can sometimes be answered with less definiteness, not enough to make a conditional true or false, but enough to make it acceptable, or unacceptable. The same holds for other patterns of dependence.

Some conditionals have truth-value; some do not; and the unsharp, fuzzy distinction between the two kinds does not coincide with any well-entrenched category such as the distinction between indicative and subjunctive conditionals. On this view, the connection between the meaning of a conditional and its truth conditions is not especially privileged. There is equally a connection between meaning and conditions for assertion, acceptance, belief, and so forth. Assertable truth and assertable non-truth lie along a continuum unseparated by a precise dividing line. Explanations of meaning by reference to truth conditions and explanations of meaning by reference to assertability conditionals similarly lie in a continuum. Nothing is forbidden in explanations of the meaning of conditionals, or anything else, so long as we remember that genuine explanations have specific audiences and purposes. Explanations vary at least as much as purposes. Requests for the meaning of conditionals, made in the context of abstract philosophical interest in meaning, can be answered as Honderich recommends: the conditionals mean just what they say. The different patterns of dependence I describe are grounds or premises of conditionals, but, in certain contexts that require explanations of the meaning of a conditional, describing a pattern of dependence also specifies meaning. The satisfaction, or non-satisfaction, of a pattern of dependence can explain why a conditional has, or does not have, a truth value.

When a conditional is true in virtue of one or another pattern of dependence, one should ideally have the pattern in mind when investigating the truth of the conditional. (In so far as this view advocates searching for real relations or connections between the if-clause and the main clause of a truth conditional, it is quite old-fashioned.) As suggested earlier, the selection of relevant factors from the circumstances is easier when we know how the factors are supposed to fit into a pattern of dependence. It matters whether we are looking for factors in the circumstances that make A, in those circumstances, a sufficient condition of B, or we are looking for factors that make B, in those circumstances, a necessary condition of A. The if-clause of a conditional, a time *t* to which it pertains, and the state of the actual world at *t* are insufficient to determine which facts about the actual world are relevant to evaluating a conditional. Given two conditionals with the same if-clause pertaining to the same time, but with different main clauses, different factors may be relevant because different patterns of dependence are relevant. If we have no pattern of dependence in mind, a primary object of our investigations should then be to get one in mind. We can accept a conditional for a specific reason, for example, on authority, without having a specific theory about why it is true. A true conditional is true for some specific reason, so an investigation that fails to come up with any specific grounds for accepting a conditional thereby produces grounds of some weight for rejecting it.

What depends on what can depend on something else; what is a condition of what can itself be conditioned. Patterns of dependence can be as complex structurally as any conditional statement might require. Both the if-clause and the main clause in the following example are conditionals:

> If Daria will sing with the band only if they get someone else to play keyboards, then Eric will continue to play guitar with the band only if they get someone else to sing.

Although my treatment of conditionals emphasizes patterns of dependence, I acknowledge that acceptable conditionals sometimes appear to have nothing to do with dependence, independence, or non-dependence, simple or complex. Some theorems of elementary logic in conditional form, such as 'If *P & Q*, then *Q & P*', appear to be acceptable for reasons unrelated to dependence. The *A* and *E* categorical statements of traditional-term logic are routinely re-expressed in modern predicate logic as quantified conditionals. Statements of the form *All Fs and Gs* are translated into corresponding statements of the form *For anything, if it is an F, then it is a G*; while *No Fs are Gs* goes to *For anything, if it is an F, then it is not a G*. Some statements of these kinds are true in virtue of species/genus or determinate/determinable relations; and these relations, it seems, are not usefully explained in terms of dependence or conditionship. Many statements of these kinds are true simply in virtue of class inclusion or class exclusion. This does not say much – *All Fs are*

Gs is true when and only when all Fs are Gs – and it says little that requires explanation in terms of dependence. I shall not attempt to provide a complete enumeration, an exhaustive list, of schematic reasons for which a conditional can be acceptable or true. Many, if not all, of the puzzles about conditionals that attract philosophical attention are tied up with issues about patterns of dependence, and to a discussion of such conditionals we will now return.

Point to any small region in my yard. One can truthfully say of this region that, if I had sprayed it with herbicide, poison ivy would have been growing nearby. Should one therefore conclude that my yard is disposed to grow poison ivy in places where I spray herbicide? Such an inference would be a blatant instance of what Alan Gibbard calls the *dispositional fallacy*.[6] The truth about dispositions in this example is, of course, that I am disposed to spray herbicide only in places where poison ivy grows. The presence of this noxious plant is a necessary condition of my spraying. My spraying is not a sufficient condition of the presence of the plant. Indeed, I hope it will prove to be a sufficient condition of the absence of the plant. The substance I spray has a disposition to kill poison ivy. Any plausible general principle connecting dispositions with conditionals must be explicit about the direction of dependence in virtue of which the conditional is acceptable.

In an article that has had a rather delayed effect, Peter Downing tells a story about characters named Jim and Jack.[7] Bennett gives Downing's puzzle prominence in his 1974 review article on Lewis's *Counterfactuals*.[8] In a 1984 article, Bennett treats backtracking conditionals differently. He also retells Downing's story, substituting more memorable characters for schematic Jim and cardboard Jack:

> Mr D'Arcy and Elizabeth quarreled yesterday, and she is still very angry. We conclude that if he asked for a favour today, she would not grant it. But wait: Mr D'Arcy is a proud man. He never would ask for a favour after such a quarrel; if he were to ask her for a favour today, there would have been no quarrel yesterday. In that case, Elizabeth would be her usual generous self. So if Mr D'Arcy asked Elizabeth for a favour today, she would grant it after all.[9]

The story appears to be consistent. The story appears to support each of a pair of opposite conditionals, one of the form *if P, then Q* and the other of the form *if P, then not Q*. The opposite conditionals, however, appear to be inconsistent. At least one of these appearances misleads.

Other stories in the literature have the same structure. There is a story about jumping out of the window.[10] If you jump, you will hurt yourself, because it is a long way down. On the other hand, if you jump, you will not hurt yourself, because you will not jump unless you know a safety net is securely in place. Gibbard tells a story about some riverboat poker-players in which the opposite conditionals are indicative.[11] If Pete called Stone's raise, Pete won, because Pete knows, with the help of a cheating confederate, just which cards Stone holds, and Pete would not lose on purpose. On the other hand, if Pete called Stone's raise, Pete did not win, because he has a flush and Stone has a full house.

In all these stories, the opposite conditionals hold in virtue of two quite different patterns of dependence. If Mr D'Arcy should ask Elizabeth for a favour today, this request will be a sufficient condition in the circumstances of Elizabeth's present anger for her refusing it. On the other hand, a necessary condition of Mr D'Arcy's asking Elizabeth for a favour today is that they not have quarrelled yesterday, and this, in the circumstances, is a sufficient condition of her granting any reasonable request by Mr D'Arcy today. A failure to distinguish these different patterns of dependence can lead one to regard the original two conditionals as inconsistent. There is nothing inconsistent, however, about the following scheme:

A is a sufficient condition, in the circumstances, for B.
C is a necessary condition, in the circumstances, for A; and A and C together, in the circumstances, are sufficient for the absence of B.

It does follow from these two together that neither A nor C obtains; in the circumstances, they could not obtain. But it does not follow that B, or anything else, both obtains and does not obtain. The opposite conditionals about the prudent potential window-jumper and about the poker-player who cheats exemplify similar patterns. Pete's (dishonestly obtained) knowledge that he would win is a necessary condition of his calling: if Pete called, he won. Given the actual comparative values of Pete's and Stone's hands, Pete's calling Stone's raise is a sufficient condition of Pete's losing: if Pete called, he did not win. As before, two conditionals together imply something neither implies separately, that the common if-clause is false. They do not imply an inconsistency. A misleading appearance of inconsistency can produce the illusion of paradox in these stories of equally supported opposite conditionals.

The simple conditional form 'If *P*, then *Q*' is neutral and uninformative about which pattern of dependence, if any, is relevant to its truth. Other conditional forms provide more information. We have already discussed 'only if'. Since 'if' has a meaning apart from 'only' and 'only' has a meaning apart from 'if', we might expect to explain the meaning of the compound 'only if' by referring to its components.

One uses 'only' to select some member or members from a group and to exclude the remaining members. The constitution of this group is highly context-sensitive in ways that I understand only poorly. This last sentence is not an ideal example. For a better illustration of the general principle, let us consider 'We ate only bread and cheese.' The group from which we exclude all members except bread and cheese is not simply all the things we might eat. Although our words do imply that we did not eat eggs, or fruit, or meat, they do not imply that we did not eat proteins, fats, or carbohydrates, and neither do they imply that we did not eat scraps of paper or bits of pencil eraser.

Many inferences we gladly make fit the form 'Only As are Fs. Therefore, some As are Fs.' The form itself, however, is invalid. One way to see this is to recognize that the following three forms of statement are consistent: 'Only As are Fs.' 'Only Bs are Fs.' 'No As are Bs.' The three together entail that no As are Fs. Since 'Only As are Fs' is thus consistent with 'No As are Fs', it does not imply 'Some As are Fs.' 'Only persons under eighteen years of age who were born in North Dakota are eligible for the Sanfordian Prize', for example, does not imply that there actually is anyone eligible for the Sanfordian Prize. It is consistent with 'Only persons who can fluently translate Greek poetry into Japanese are eligible for the Sanfordian Prize' and 'No one under eighteen years of age who can fluently translate Greek poetry into Japanese was born in North Dakota.'

If only we had a firmer theoretical grasp of 'only', we could proceed with more confidence to its contribution to 'only if'. The following paraphrase looks promising:

P only if *Q* = *P* in no event other than one in which *Q*.[12]

This attempt respects the meaning of 'only', for there certainly is a tight connection between *only* and *no . . . other than*, for example:

Only Kate carried her dishes to the kitchen = Kate carried her dishes to the kitchen and no one other than Kate did.

Still, the 'no event other than' paraphrase appears not to distinguish '*P* only if *Q*' from '*Q* if *P*' and thus not to capture the directionality of 'only if'. It does not distinguish 'Mary cooks oatmeal only if Bill washes the pot' from 'Bill washes the pot if Mary cooks oatmeal.'

I am unsure whether I can explain how *only if* acquires its rather specific directionality from its components. Here is a tentative suggestion:

P only if *Q* = *P* on the one condition that *Q*.

Although the following idiom is part of my idiolect, I do not know how widespread it is:

You may borrow this book on one condition – that you return it before noon tomorrow.

That is, you may borrow this book only if you return it before noon tomorrow. I suspect that we can easily paraphrase all idiomatic uses of 'on one condition' in terms of 'only if'. I am less confident that we can easily paraphrase all or nearly all idiomatic uses of 'only if' in terms of 'on one condition' in ways that do not permit similar paraphrases for 'if'.

If and only if inherits the directionality of *only if*. Biconditionals, 'if and only if' conditionals, appear frequently in the writings of logicians, philosophers, and other theorists. The three-letter 'iff' (for 'if and only if') increasingly appears in non-technical writing. The material or truth-functional biconditional commutes; corresponding statements of the forms $P \equiv Q$ and $Q \equiv P$ always have the same truth-value. Introductory logic texts teach the same lesson about 'if and only if'. They claim that 'P if and only if Q' and 'Q if and only if P' are interchangeable and equivalent. Natural-language examples show some important differences in this respect between 'if and only if' and '$\equiv$':

You will be nominated if and only if the executive committee suggests you.
The executive committee will suggest you if and only if you are nominated.

The cactus flowers if and only if it rains.
It rains if and only if the cactus flowers.

Each sentence is naturally interpreted as being based on a condition that is both necessary and sufficient. *Necessary and sufficient condition of* is a non-symmetric relation. In each of these pairs, one expects it to hold in one direction but not the other. The executive committee's suggesting you is a necessary and sufficient condition of your nomination; your nomination depends on the committee's suggestion. This is by no means equivalent to your nomination being a necessary and sufficient condition of the committee's nominating you, so that the committee's suggestion depends on your nomination. Similarly, rain in the desert is a necessary and sufficient condition of the cactus flowering. Whether or not this is strictly true in the circumstances that the context specifies, it sounds all right. 'It rains if and only if the cactus flowers', on the other hand, sounds as if it expresses a superstition. The cactus flowering is not a condition of any kind of rain in the desert.

Some biconditionals are better expressed without 'if and only if.' 'Mary and Morton each agree to sing only if the other agrees as well' should sound different from 'Mary and Morton each agree to sing if the other agrees as well.' These are statements of mutual conditionship, the first of conditions that are mutually necessary, and the second of conditions that are mutually

203

sufficient. We can express the second as a conjunction of conditionals: 'Mary agrees to sing if Morton agrees to sing as well, and Morton agrees to sing if Mary agrees to sing as well.' Standard doctrine equates '(P if Q) and (Q if P)' with '(P if Q) and (P only if Q)'. The non-equivalence of 'Q if P' and 'P only if Q' explains why these two conjunctions of conditionals do not have exactly the same meaning.[13]

Many biconditionals hold in virtue of an unmentioned condition. 'The wine is cold if and only if the beer is cold' does not typically hold because the coldness of one beverage is a necessary and sufficient condition of the coldness of the other. There is something, rather, such as a certain length of time in the refrigerator, that is a necessary and sufficient condition of both the wine and the beer's being cold.

Directed conditionship is irrelevant to some biconditionals. 'The card has a vowel on one side if and only if it has an even number on the other side' may be accepted on purely truth-functional grounds. It is significant that subjects in the conditional reasoning experiments perform better with subject matter unlike letters and numbers in which there is a causal or conventional connection between what the clauses of a conditional mention.

Although biconditionals follow many patterns, the cactus flower pattern seems most common. *P if and only if Q* is true, or is accepted, because what makes Q true is a necessary and sufficient condition of what makes P true. Biconditional non-commutation is thus easily explained by the non-symmetry of *is a necessary and sufficient condition of*. What needs still to be explained is biconditional commutation. Why is it that sometimes both a biconditional and its commutation are quite acceptable even though the direction of conditionship goes one way? I suggest that the relevant considerations are epistemic.

The following examples are selected in part to deflect the suggestion that appeal to temporal priority can always explain the apparent non-symmetry of conditionship:

The kiln is hot enough for firing if and only if the ceramic cone is soft.
The solution is acidic if and only if the moistened litmus paper is red.

204

From the point of view of objective dependence, these might well both seem backwards. The colour of litmus paper does not make the solution acidic. Neither does the softening of the pyrometric cone cause the kiln to reach the correct firing temperature. Yet neither biconditional is normally taken to express bizarre back-to-front views about causation. What runs counter to the direction of causation in these cases is the direction of inference. Litmus is technically called an indicator; and the purpose of a pyrometric cone, as its name suggests, is to measure high temperatures. One gains knowledge that a solution is acidic by observing the colour of an indicator. One gains knowledge that a kiln has reached a certain temperature by observing a pyrometic cone soften. When the natural direction of inference and the direction of objective dependence are opposite, biconditionals commute without strain.

In similar inferential contexts, the direction of anticipated inference can overwhelm the normal directionality of *only if*. Do not be concerned that we are about to run out of petrol, I say:

The tank is nearly empty only if the warning light is on.

The warning light is off, as you can see; so you can rest assured that the tank is not yet nearly empty. We do not assume here that the activity of the warning light is a condition of any kind of the amount of petrol in the tank. The petrol level does not depend on the warning light.

Unless displays as much directionality as *only if*, and this directionality is as much neglected by standard logic textbooks, which often inform students that statements of the form *P unless Q* are equivalent to corresponding conditionals of the form *If not-P, Q*. Given contraposition, which is uncontroversial for the material conditional, and principles of double negation, it follows that *unless* commutes. *P unless Q* is equivalent to *Q unless P* because *If not-P, Q* is equivalent to *If not-Q, P*. But there must be something wrong with the view that:

P unless *Q* = *Q* unless *P*.

Few 'unless' sentences retain their senses when their clauses are transposed. Consider the following:

Jane will love him for ever unless he goes bald.
He will go bald unless Jane loves him for ever.

He won't come unless we will buy him a ticket.
We will buy him a ticket unless he won't come.

Comparing the members of such pairs reveals the directionality of 'unless'. The first says that his not going bald is a necessary condition of Jane's loving him for ever. The second says that Jane's loving him for ever is a sufficient condition of his not going bald, that is, in an awkward but equivalent formulation, Jane's not loving him for ever is a necessary condition of his going bald. In the second pair, there is a difference between saying that his coming depends on our buying him a ticket and saying that our buying him a ticket depends on his coming. If a conditional paraphrase of 'unless' statements is desired, an 'only if' conditional works best:

P unless Q = *Not-P* only if Q.

Another form that bothers philosophers and linguists is *even if*. One reason they provide mutually incompatible theories is that they have incompatible beliefs about the character of the linguistic data they want to explain. Do conditionals of the form 'P even if Q' imply 'P, in any event'?[14] I shall explore several putative counterexamples to this pattern in order to learn something about 'even'. Consider:

Even if you bring him a bottle of cheap red wine, he will be pleased.

Does it imply that he will be pleased in any event? Not in absolutely *any* event:

Even if his house burns down, and he loses everything, he will be pleased.

'Even' picks out something as occupying an extreme position – less probable, more surprising, contrary to expectation, and so forth – in a contextually determined range of alternatives. A general understanding of 'even' requires a theory – which I do not have – about how words in a context determine ranges. We do not need a general theory to be confident that the range of relevant alternatives in the last example does not include *the burning down of his house*. Perhaps we should modify 'in any event' to read 'no matter which of the relevant alternatives occurs'. What are the relevant alternatives, then, for this example? The range does not include just anything it is possible for you to bring him:

Even if you bring him a sack of rabid bats, he will be pleased.

Although we do not have a genuine context in this example and thus no way of deciding in the context which gifts of food, flowers, plants, pottery, spirits, glassware, and so forth, belong to the range *Your bringing him a bottle of cheap red wine* indicates, we should have no trouble in deciding that something so bizarre as the last example is out of the range.

The following example introduces another problem in understanding 'even if':

Even if you drop your camera into sea water for just a minute, it will be destroyed.

This sounds all right, although it may not be strictly true that a minute in the ocean is enough to destroy your camera. Assertable conditionals need not be strictly true. If the next conditional is not true, it is for a reason very different from the last conditional:

Even if you drop your camera into molten iron for just a minute, it will be destroyed.

Although the destruction of a camera by immersion in molten iron may be a very rare and surprising event, if a camera is immersed in molten iron, there is nothing surprising, unexpected, or improbable about the fact that it is immediately destroyed. 'Even' is definitely out of place in this conditional. Some writers, relying on a sharp distinction between truth conditions and assertability conditions, would hold that, although such a conditional is true, it is very strange to assert because it violates assertability conditions. While I have attempted to produce an example that is comfortably classified neither as true nor as false, I see slight hope for consensus on the semantic classification of 'even if' conditionals.

Some of the ways in which 'even' and 'only' operate are similar, and 'only if' is highly directional. Although many 'even if' conditionals are highly directional, 'even' seems not to limit the patterns of dependence in virtue of which a conditional can be true. Consider this modification of the first example in this chapter:

Even if Smith was fired, so was Wilson.

This conditional can be true in virtue of just the same patterns of dependence as the original. For different patterns, 'even' will sometimes identify events at the extreme of different ranges of events:

Even if Smith was fired, Wilson was fired as a result.
Even if Smith was fired, it was as a result of Wilson's firing.

In the first, Smith's firing is an extreme case in the range of events that can result in the firing of Wilson. In the second, Smith's firing is an extreme case in the range of events that can result from the firing of Wilson.

This return to the earlier examples of the chapter returns also to my claim that conditionship is non-symmetric. I have supported the claim by examples, but I have yet to support it by theory. The next chapter attempts to provide an account of objective dependence that can back up my claims about conditions.

CHAPTER XIV

Objective Dependence

If ever the search for a tranquil belief should end,
The future might stop emerging out of the past,
Out of what is full of us. . .

Near the end of Section VII, Part II, of *An Enquiry Concerning Human Understanding*, David Hume provides two famous definitions of *cause*. We will not be concerned here with the second definition, '*an object followed by another, and whose appearance always conveys the thought to that other*'. The 'first definition' of *cause* (also quoted in the Introduction) appears really to consist of two definitions:

Similar objects are always conjoined with similar. Of this we have experience. Suitably to this experience, therefore, we may define a cause to be *an object, followed by another, and where all the objects similar to the first are followed by objects similar to the second*. Or in other words where, *if the first object had not been, the second never had existed*.

David Lewis quotes from this passage at the beginning of his article 'Causation'.[1] The many present-day regularity analyses of causation descend from Hume's definition in terms of similarity. A cause–effect pair is an instance of a lawlike regularity. Lewis's proposal to replace regularity accounts of causation with an analysis in terms of counterfactual conditionals derives from Hume's 'in other words where, *if the first object had not been, the second never had existed*'.

Both the attempt to explain causation in terms of regularities and the attempt to explain causation in terms of conditionals

209

seem to me to head in the wrong direction. Heating this strip of metal does not cause it to expand because heated metal objects regularly expand; heated metal objects regularly expand, rather, because heat causes metal to expand. Flipping this switch does not cause the light to go on because the conditional 'If this switch had not been flipped, the light would not have gone on' is true; the conditional is true, rather, because flipping this switch caused the light to go on. Other conditionals are true in virtue of other patterns of causal dependence, and still others are true in virtue of patterns of dependence and independence that are not causal.

Although for a long time there have been a few philosophers who regard causal notions with suspicion, many philosophers, most scientists, and most ordinary folk continue to talk and think with explicitly causal concepts. I can recognize instances of causal conditions, causal necessity, causal possibility, and causal explanation when I encounter them, or so I think; and my classifications under these categories would mostly coincide with those made by others independently of me. Despite this confidence of mine about classifying the causal, I cannot recommend any theory of causation for its adequate explanation of these classifications or of technical notions such as *causally connected in a direct line* that we used in Chapter XI. We identify instances of events that are causally connected in a direct line, and instances of events that are not, even without an explanation. Attempts to explain the direction of causation can take the notion of causal connection in a direct line as primitive, at least for the time being – later we may attempt to explain it. Saying just that two events are causally connected in a direct line does not by itself say in which direction causation runs from one to the other, so accounting for the direction of causation is an additional task. In this chapter, I shall attempt to account not just for causal dependence, but for dependence generally.

Two-place, or binary, relations are *symmetric*, *asymmetric*, or *non-symmetric*. Definitions of the following form leave implicit the quantified variables that textbook definitions standardly employ:

Relation R is symmetric: no two things are related in just one direction by R. No two things, for example, are related in just one direction by *has the same birthday*. If *a* has the same birthday as *b*, then *b* has the same birthday as *a*, so *has the same birthday as* is symmetric.

Relation R is asymmetric: no two things are related in both directions by R, and no single thing is related by R to itself. No two things, for example, are related in both directions by *is older than*, and nothing is older than itself. If *a* is older than *b*, *b* is not older than *a*, so *is older than* is asymmetric.

Relation R is non-symmetric: R is neither symmetric nor asymmetric; that is, there are two things related in just one direction by R, and there are also either two things related in both directions by R or a single thing related by R to itself. *Loves* is a non-symmetric relation because love is sometimes reciprocated and sometimes not.

A common problem for theories of causation is the unwanted implication that causation is symmetric. (For example, a theory that holds a cause to be a causally necessary and sufficient condition, and that also defines 'necessary condition' and 'sufficient condition' so that 'is a necessary and sufficient condition of' is symmetric, thereby implies that causation is symmetric.) The central task of an 'account of the direction of causation' is to explain why causation typically (or always) runs in one direction and not the other.

There is nothing mysterious about using only symmetric relations in formulating a condition sufficient for the existence of an asymmetric relation. Consider the symmetric relation 'is related by blood': A is related by blood to B if and only if B is related by blood to A. The negation of any symmetric relation is itself a symmetric relation, so 'is not related by blood' is symmetric: A is not related by blood to B if and only if B is not related by blood to A. What we will call *being lined up* is another symmetric relation. *A is lined up with B* means: either A is an ancestor of B or B is an ancestor of A. Suppose that:

A and B are not related by blood.
A is lined up with C.
B is lined up with C.

It follows from these suppositions that A and B are each ancestors of C. 'Ancestor of' is an asymmetric relation: if C is an ancestor of A, then A is not an ancestor of C.

This derivation of asymmetry loses still more air of mystery when we supply the meaning of 'is related by blood', namely, 'have an ancestor in common'. Although A and B do not have an ancestor in common, each is either an ancestor of C or has C as an ancestor. A and B cannot both have C as an ancestor, for then they would be related by blood. Neither can just one have C as an ancestor, for it would then have the other as an ancestor, and thus be related by blood. The only alternative consistent with the suppositions is that neither A nor B has C as an ancestor. Both A and B must be ancestors of C.

A similar pattern explains asymmetric dependence generally. The relation *is independent from* is symmetric, and so, therefore, is its negation *is not independent from*. Consider the following schematic supposition:

A and B are independent.
A is not independent from C.
B is not independent from C.

Do these suppositions imply that C depends on both A and B? Certainly many cases of dependence fit this pattern. The position of the light switch and the integrity of the light bulb are independent of one another, and neither is independent of the light's being on. The light's being on depends on the position of the switch and the integrity of the light bulb. In the classic match-lighting example, the dryness of the match is independent of the presence of oxygen; and neither is independent of the match's lighting, which depends both on the dryness and on the oxygen. In such patterns of dependence, the dependence need not be causal. The *meaning* of 'The moon circles the earth' is independent of the moon's circling the earth; and neither is independent of the *truth* of 'The moon circles the earth', which depends both on facts about meaning and on facts about the moon. Multiplying examples of the purported pattern of implication does nothing, unfortunately, to show that there are no counterexamples. Given the pattern of independence and non-independence presented above, why must we assume that C depends on both A and B rather than that both A and B depend on C? Cannot A and B be mutually independent effects of their common cause C? The door's being shut both caused the room to become warmer and caused the room to become quieter, where the quiet and the warmth of the room are independent of each other.[2]

A certain distinction still remains between independent causes and independent effects. We shall define *independent with respect to* as follows: A and B are independent with respect to C if and only if, in the absence of C, A can occur without B, and B can occur without A. The relation is symmetric in its first two places: A and B are independent with respect to C if and only if B and A are independent with respect to C. In the examples above where something C depends on A and B, A and B are independent with respect to C. A match can be surrounded by oxygen without being dry, and a match can be dry without being surrounded by oxygen, both in the absence of the match's lighting. On the other hand, in the example where something A and something B each depend on C, A and B are not independent with respect to C. Although the room can be warm without being quiet, and can be quiet without being warm, in the particular circumstances in question, without the door's being shut it can be neither warm nor quiet.

Familiar conditionals used to explicate so-called counterfactual dependence, uncomplicated by references to independence and non-independence, do not capture this last asymmetry. In the circumstances, to be sure, if the door had not been shut, the room would not have become warm. In the same circumstances, if the room had not become warm, the door would not have been shut. The counterfactual conditionals by themselves do not indicate a direction of genuine dependence. Reference to independence and non-independence plays a useful role in explaining objective dependence.

There is a close connection between dependence and conditionship. If C depends on A, A is a condition of C. If A is a condition of C, it is possible that C depends on A. In some set-ups, there is mutual conditionship without mutual dependence: the direction of dependence between A and C is due to something other than the relations of conditionship between A and C. When two gears are meshed, as in the example that appears in Chapter XI, the rotation of either one is a condition of the rotation of the other; and this does not determine whether the first gear turns the second, the second turns the first, or both are being turned synchronously by something else.

213

Laws about the properties of gases, also alluded to briefly in Chapter XI, are prominent in philosophical arguments about causal priority.[3] The equation of state for ideal gases illustrates several relevant points about physical laws, dependence, and asymmetry:

$$PV = nRT.$$

P, V, n, and T are variables for pressure, volume, the number of moles of gas, and temperature; R is a universal constant. By assuming that certain of the variable quantities in this equation are fixed, one can derive simpler gas laws such as the general gas law (n fixed), Charles's law (n and P fixed), and Boyle's law (n and T fixed). These laws, like other physical laws, imply that certain quantities are not independent. The volume and temperature of a gas, for example, are not independent. According to my suggestions about understanding dependence, we can determine a direction of dependence by finding appropriate patterns of independence and non-independence. Laws of nature, cast as equations, certainly pertain to one-way dependence; for they bear on two-way non-independence. We should not expect to discover asymmetries, either fundamental, global asymmetries, or local instances of one-way causal or temporal dependence, by studying familiar equations. Equations, merely by having the form of equations, are unfit to tell us by themselves what depends on what. Physicists may discover some fundamental asymmetries in nature, but philosophers need not wait for any such discoveries of sensational asymmetries before accepting the objectivity of causal and temporal priority in ordinary situations.

To prepare a standard demonstration of Charles's law, securely fasten a balloon to the neck of a bottle and devise a way to heat the gas (air) inside the bottle. To explain what this set-up demonstrates, mention the idealizing assumptions that the atmospheric pressure remains constant, that the pressures inside and outside the balloon are equal, and that no gas molecule passes between the balloon–bottle system and the surrounding environment. The values for n and P are thus supposed to be fixed, so that values for T and V vary directly with each other. That is just what Charles's law says and what the simple demonstration bears out. As the gas enclosed in the balloon–bottle system heats up, the balloon expands. Measurements of temperature and volume are required to obtain a more precise confirmation (or disconfirmation) of Charles's law, but the introduction of units and techniques of measurement are unnecessary to support the simple causal claim that the gas expands because it heats up.

Heating the gas inside the balloon–bottle system causes it to expand. The gas does not heat up, in this case, because it expands. The increase in volume does not cause the increase in temperature. Although this asymmetry does not follow from Charles's law, or, apparently, from any other law, philosophers should resist the temptation to conclude that the apparent causal asymmetry is merely apparent. This set-up fits the general pattern for one-way dependence. There are several mutually independent factors, including heating up, each necessary for the increase in volume. Although we assume that there is a tight seal between the inside and the outside of the balloon–bottle system and thus assume that the number of molecules of gas remains constant, when we look for patterns of independent and non-independent factors, neither the assumption that a value of n is fixed, nor what makes this assumption approximately true, precludes considering the number of gas molecules. For the volume to increase in direct proportion to the increase in temperature, gas inside the balloon cannot leak out through a loose seal or through pin holes in the surface of the balloon. The tightness of the seal and the integrity of the balloon are both necessary in the circumstances for the particular increase in volume and independent, or virtually independent, of the heating of the gas. The constancy of pressure is another such factor, independent of the temperature increase but not independent of the volume increase. In these circumstances, the increase in temperature and the increase in volume apparently do not fit into a pattern of the same kind but in reverse order. The increase in volume is not one of several mutually independent factors each necessary for the increase in temperature.

A condition of something is often necessary for it; and typically, when condition A is necessary for C, there is something independent from A that is also necessary for C.[4] When A is a condition of C, and C is not a condition of A, then there is nothing independent from C that is necessary for A.

The dryness of a match may not be necessary for its lighting in every possible circumstance, but it is necessary in the ordinary circumstances we consider. The presence of oxygen is also necessary in these circumstances for the lighting. As mentioned above, the dryness and the presence of oxygen are independent of each other. In various circumstances, different factors are necessary for the match to be dry; and these will, in turn, be necessary for the match to light.[5] Nothing necessary for the match to be dry is independent from the lighting of the match. This objective asymmetry accounts for the one-way direction of conditionship, when it obtains. Dryness is a condition of the lighting; the lighting is not a condition of the dryness.

Nor, for reasons of just the same sort, is non-lighting a condition of dampness. I invoked my notion of non-symmetric conditionship to deal with Nelson Goodman's problem of relevant conditions, which should be taken, I suggested in Chapter XI, as a problem of relevant *conditions*. The following conditionals compete:

If match *M* had been scratched, it would have lighted.
If match *M* had been scratched, it would not have been dry.

The same lawlike incompossibility seems to support each: it is impossible for a scratched, well-made, dry match in adequate oxygen not to light. How, without begging the question, can the fact that the match did not light be excluded as a relevant condition? My answer is that it is not a condition at all of the dampness or of the dryness of the match, and in this chapter I support this answer with an account of objective dependence.

It is important for a theoretical account of conditionals both to exclude non-conditions as irrelevant and to include as relevant genuine conditions. In Chapter XIII, I claimed that a variety of patterns of dependence and independence can support conditional statements. One will take different factors to be conditions relevant to an assessment of a conditional statement according to which pattern one assumes to be operative. The understanding of dependence cannot be directly based on a distinction between acceptable and unacceptable conditionals without the explanation of conditionals being so tightly circular as to be uninformative.

One cannot talk at any length about many topics, including

dependence and conditions, without using conditionals. It serves no good purpose to develop or present a theory of conditional sentences and deliberately to avoid at the same time any use of conditional sentences. Here I have tried only to defend a general theory that distinguishes acceptable from unacceptable conditionals and that does not, in particular applications, assume the very distinctions it attempts to explain.

In the rest of this chapter, I will discuss several more examples of dependence including the one-way direction of explanation and the one-way direction of time.

When the sun is at a certain angle above the horizon, a vertical flagpole of a certain height standing near a sufficiently large horizontal area casts a shadow of a certain length. Given that light travels in straight lines but not through flagpoles, the laws relevant to calculating shadow length belong to plane geometry or trigonometry. These laws imply nothing by themselves about what depends on what; they license inferences in all directions, from angle and height to length, from angle and length to height, and from height and length to angle. There are more directions of possible inference, in most cases, than there are directions of objective dependence.[6] In our example, the length of the shadow depends on the height of the flagpole and the angle of the sun. The angle of the sun and the height of flagpole do not depend on each other, and neither depends on the length of the shadow. In the circumstances, everything necessary for the flagpole to have a certain height is necessary for the shadow to have a certain length. In contrast, many factors necessary for the shadow to have a certain length are not necessary for the flagpole to have a certain height. There is the angle of the sun, already mentioned, and there are all the factors necessary for the sunlight to pass in a coherent way by the side of the flagpole on its way to the ground, the absence of clouds, the absence of heavy fog, of dense smoke, of other opaque objects, and so forth, none of which are necessary for the height of the flagpole or the angle of the sun. A number of mutually independent factors, including the height of the pole and the angle of the sun, are each necessary in the circumstances for the length of the shadow. The length of the shadow does not similarly figure as one of a number of mutually independent factors each necessary in the circumstances for the height of the pole or the angle of the sun.

The velocity of light is finite, and no signal can be transmitted faster than it. The velocity of light is so great, however, that, when we consider the distance from the top of the flagpole to a point on the ground a few yards from the base, light might just as well, so far as we can determine, be transmitted instantaneously. If the transmission of light were instantaneous, shadows would look no different. The judgment of one-way dependence in the flagpole case, that the length of the shadow depends on the length of the pole, is not based on some judgment of temporal priority. I shall return to the topic of temporal priority after some more discussion of explanation.

Explanations typically rely on a one-way dependence. Bromberger's example of a flagpole or building that casts a shadow shows that inferential relations licensed by laws do not always suffice to account for the natural direction of dependence or the direction of explanation. Of course explanations too come in many varieties. Like 'by'-statements and some conditionals, some explanations are most naturally understood in terms of goals, plans, strategies, purposes, or final causes. It is nevertheless very common for an explanation of the occurrence of an event to mention other events or conditions upon which the occurrence of the first event depends. Any adequate general account of dependence, causal and non-causal, will be helpful in understanding explanations of this type.

In an article entitled 'Time and counterfactuals' that I mentioned in Chapter V, Michael Slote appeals to the notion of explanation to deal with Nelson Goodman's problem of relevant conditions.[7] Of the factors relevant to spelling out the grounds for an acceptable counterfactual conditional, Slote requires that they, perhaps in conjunction with the antecedent, help explain the consequent. When we consider once more Goodman's competing pair, we see that while the dryness of the match, together with its scratching, helps to explain its lighting, the non-lighting of the match, even together with its scratching, does not help to explain its non-dryness. I draw similar distinctions in terms of conditions. Slote's appeal to non-symmetric explanation and my appeal to non-symmetric conditionship and dependence are not only compatible; when we apply them to the most familiar puzzle cases, they have just the same results. I nevertheless deny that our suggestions are virtually identical except in terminology.[8] A theory of one-way dependence and conditionship, as I said before, helps to explain non-symmetric explanation. The notion of non-symmetric explanation, on the other hand, does not help to explain one-way dependence. It is not because the height of an opaque object helps to explain the length of the shadow it casts that the length of the shadow depends on the height of the object. Rather, it is because the length of the shadow depends on the height of the object, and not the other way around, that the height of the object helps to explain the length of the shadow, and not the other way around.

I claim that my account of conditionals in terms of conditions and dependence is more general and basic than Slote's in terms of explanation. This claim is an instance of a move that is common when theories compete. When consequences of competing theories diverge, an advocate of a theory tries to show that its consequences should be preferred to those of the other. When consequences of competing theories are strikingly similar, an advocate of one theory tries to subsume the other. 'My theory accounts for everything in your theory that is correct, and it accounts for more as well!' Hence, I, in the role of advocate, claim that my theory in terms of conditions subsumes Slote's in terms of explanation.

Theories of conditionals in terms of probability invite attempts at subsumption. There are some extreme cases in which it is inappropriate to assert a conditional according to the probability of the consequent conditional on the antecedent, yet it is appropriate to assert this same conditional according, say, to the dependence of the consequence on the antecedent. For the most part, however, dealing with non-extreme cases, my account and theories of conditionals assertable according to conditional probability count the same conditionals as assertable. A full attempt at subsumption would require something I do not even begin in this book, investigations of different theories of probability. On whatever theory, when the probability of the match's lighting conditional on its scratching is high, I say that is because the scratching is a sufficient condition in those circumstances of the match's lighting, and not the other way around. The probability of lighting is high because scratching causes lighting; scratching does not cause lighting (or so I claim) because the probability of lighting conditional on scratching is high.

Standard explanations of causal priority appeal to temporal priority rather than conditional probability. One can invoke the physical principle that there is a maximum velocity for the transmission of a signal to show that many apparent cases of simultaneous causation are merely apparent. As you lift the spoon to your mouth, for all you can tell, the bowl of the spoon and the end of its handle move together, at exactly the same time. But the world contains more discrepancies, more gaps and twists and folds, than we can discover with unaided observation. It takes a brief while for the transmission of motion from the handle to the bowl of the spoon, much too brief for you to notice, and similarly with the transmission of motion through apparently rigid larger objects such as rakes, shovels, wrenches, and connecting rods. Some cases of apparent simultaneous causation seem not to conflict with the principle that no signal can be transmitted instantaneously. When the high temperature of a body causes it to radiate, for example, there seems to be no relevant spatial interval that needs to be traversed. In many apparent cases of simultaneous causation, some of which are merely apparent and some of which may be genuine, we do not base our judgments about the direction of causation on our judgments of temporal priority.

My view of non-symmetric conditionship does not invoke the direction of time to account for the direction of conditionship. An explanation of the causal priority in terms of one-way conditionship thus accords with the common-sense view that simultaneous causation is possible. It also allows for the possibility of *backward* or temporally reversed causation.[9] While we may doubt whether causal dependence ever runs from later to earlier, we can easily accept that what is earlier depends on what is later in some familiar (although non-causal) mode of dependence. If I rashly predict that the local baseball team will win its next game, then the truth of the prediction I made this morning depends on the Durham Bulls winning their game this evening. The team's winning the game is a necessary and sufficient condition of my prediction's being true. The truth of my prediction is not a condition of any kind of the Bulls winning their game. Predictions and statements about other future contingencies are similar: they depend on future occurrences for their truth, but the occurrences of the events predicted do not depend on the truth of their predictions.

If we do not use temporal priority to explain non-symmetrical conditionship, can we then use non-symmetrical conditionship to explain temporal priority? Much as questions of causal priority are distinct from questions of causal ordering, questions of temporal ordering and temporal priority are distinct.[10] Events ordered by *temporal betweenness* are not thereby ordered by *earlier* and *later*, and I would no more attempt to account for temporal betweenness with my present resources than I would attempt to account for causal betweenness: I shall not try to explain in general what it is for two items to be temporally related. I am concerned rather with the temporal direction involved in the persistence of ordinary objects through time.

Persistence through time provides a very common example of the dependence of the later on the earlier.[11] Consider a book sitting on a shelf. (If you like, consider it as unread, unmoved, unnoticed, and untouched for months at a time.) The book as it is today, its existence, location, and character, depends on the book as it was yesterday. Not so in the reverse order: the book as it was yesterday did not depend for its existence, location, and character on the book as it is today. Does my account of one-way conditionship help explain this kind of one-way dependence through time?

The existence, location, and so forth, of the book as it was yesterday is not completely sufficient for the existence, location, and so forth, of the book as it is today. Any number of things could have destroyed, moved, or changed the book. Interventions between yesterday and today have temporally asymmetric effects: they affect what becomes of the book after the intervention but not what became of it before. The absence of such current interventions and interferences, therefore, is necessary for the book's relatively unchanging persistence from today onwards, and is not necessary for the book's relatively unchanging persistence up to yesterday. Although *absences* may appear to be second-class candidates for conditions, they are as genuinely necessary as presences for future occurrences and non-occurrences of all sorts. (The real difference between presences and absences will not detain us here.) Yesterday the book was right there on the shelf. Between yesterday and today, the water pipes in the ceiling over the bookshelf did not burst. In the circumstances, these two states of affairs were each necessary for the book's being right there on the shelf today. And, most important for this attempt at explanation, they are independent. There are no connections of dependency between the location of the book yesterday and plumbing disasters during the following twenty-four hours. Two earlier states of affairs, independent of each other, each are necessary for a later state of affairs. This pattern fits our account of conditionship.

Finding that a pattern fits in one direction cannot explain a one-way dependence unless the same pattern does not fit just as well in the opposite direction. Does the pattern just described figure just as frequently in the other temporal direction? Are mutually independent states each necessary for some earlier state? If some sort of interference was possible in the evolution of the later state from the earlier state or the production by it, then it was possible for the earlier state to obtain without the later. In a primary sense of *not necessary for*, A is not necessary for B if B can exist, obtain, or occur without the existence, obtaining, or occurrence of A. In our example, the later state is in this sense not necessary for the earlier state. The later depends on the earlier in a way that the earlier does not depend on the later.

The last point, put in terms of *earlier* and *later*, is put more commonly in terms of *past* and *future*: the future depends on the past in a way that the past does not depend on the future. The past is earlier, and the future later, than the present; and the present has a dubious ontological status that the past and future inherit. A standard metaphysical question: is there an objective present independent of any mind or consciousness? If the search for a tranquil belief ends with the end of consciousness, then one can interpret the epigraph of this chapter to imply that all of the future, present, and past – all of the future emerging out of the past – depends on consciousness for its existence. This view is compatible with the view just sketched about the objective dependence of the later on the earlier. Later states of the world can continue to emerge out of earlier states no matter how bereft of mind and will the world becomes.

Is temporal dependence a special case of causal dependence? I doubt whether our conception of causation is definite enough to answer this question with confidence. Although the theoretical difference between causal and non-causal is none too clear, the distinction between instances of causal and non-causal dependence is clear enough for many purposes. *Sam signalled by extending his arm* is an example of a kind frequently discussed in the theory of action. The asymmetrical relation between Sam's extending his arm and his signalling is not a causal relation. It nevertheless fits the general pattern of one-way dependence developed in this chapter. The motion of Sam's arm and the appropriate signalling convention are, in the relevant sense, independent.[12] In the circumstances, both the arm motion and the convention are necessary for signalling. Like conditional sentences, 'by'-sentences can be true or acceptable for many different reasons. When an 'A by B' sentence holds in virtue of a one-way dependence of A on B, the asymmetry of dependence can often be explained by reference to one-way conditionship, whether causal or non-causal.

What depends on what, and what explains what, can vary with the circumstances. Wilfrid Sellars tells a tale in which Harry stands nearby with a full pail ready to douse any scratched match.[13] In that case, the acceptability of Goodman's two competing conditionals is reversed. It is not true, in these circumstances, that, if match M had been scratched, it would have lighted. It would, rather, have been damp. Its scratching would, through the instrumentality of Harry the fireman, have caused it to be doused. Nor is this the only pattern of dependence in virtue of which it can be true that:

If match *M* had been scratched, it would not have been dry.

The laboratory was testing the behaviour of damp matches, and the experimental design required that only damp matches be scratched. In these circumstances, a match's dampness is a necessary condition of its being scratched.

The discussion is moving back to the topic of the previous chapter, how conditionals are supported by different patterns of dependence and independence. The next chapter will deal with the topic of how different patterns of dependence bear on the validity of arguments with conditional premises. The specific account of causal and non-causal dependence offered in this chapter is not assumed elsewhere in this book. Readers of the book will believe, I hope, that there are objective dependencies that can be understood otherwise than through a theory of conditionals. My attempt to provide such an understanding is my argument that it is possible. Those disinclined to accept my account can develop or adopt alternatives (although I have no alternatives in mind to recommend). My claims about the relations between dependence and conditionals require only my most general claims about the nature of dependence.

CHAPTER XV

A Problem with Validity

Our previous results have ruined Things.

Contraposition and hypothetical syllogism are valid forms of argument for material conditionals and for strict conditionals. In Chapters VI and VII, we saw several reasons for thinking that these forms are invalid for natural-language conditionals. There are natural-language arguments of these forms with premises that appear to be true and with conclusions that appear to be false. Also, alternative semantics for conditionals explain theoretically how the premises can be acceptable while the conclusion is unacceptable. Probabilistic semantics and most versions of possible-world semantics ruin some classically valid argument forms.

Some examples seen in Chapters VI and VII are repeated here:

If Smith dies before the election, Jones will win the election.
If Jones wins the election, Smith will retire after the election.
Therefore, if Smith dies before the election, Smith will retire after the election.

If I were president of General Motors, I would be very wealthy.
If I were very wealthy, I would drive a Jaguar.
Therefore, if I were president of General Motors, I would drive a Jaguar.

If I had drawn a flush, I would not have drawn a straight flush.
Therefore, if I had drawn a straight flush, I would not have drawn a flush.

If we had more than two children, we would not have had more than ten children.
Therefore, if we had more than ten children, we would not have had more than two children.

It is worth noting here that some of these examples work as well in the indicative as in the subjunctive:

If I draw a flush, I will not draw a straight flush.
Therefore, if I draw a straight flush, I will not draw a flush.

If we have more than two children, we will not have more than ten children.
Therefore, if we have more than ten children, we will not have more than two children.

The example about Smith and the election is already in the indicative. Theories that claim that hypothetical syllogism and contraposition are valid for indicative conditionals, even if they are invalid for subjunctive conditionals, are evidently mistaken. Here, and elsewhere, it is difficult to find a general distinction of theoretical interest that coincides with the distinction between indicative and subjunctive conditionals.[1] Particular pairs of corresponding conditionals, one indicative and one subjunctive, sometimes illustrate an interesting sharp contrast, such as between truth and falsity. Can we also find a pair of corresponding arguments, with the constituents of one indicative and the other subjunctive, that illustrates the contrast between validity and invalidity? The president-of-General-Motors argument above may serve:

If I am president of General Motors, I am very wealthy.
If I am very wealthy, I drive a Jaguar.
Therefore, if I am president of General Motors, I drive a Jaguar.

This argument looks valid: there seems to be no way for the premises both to be true when the conclusion is false. On the other hand, the argument is too strange to fit into a normal context. (Perhaps my amnesia is so extensive that I remember nothing about my position, worth, and possessions?) Ernest W. Adams uses examples to illustrate the contrast between justified and unjustified conditionals that I adapt here as a pair of contrapositions:

If someone shot Kennedy in Dallas, then Oswald did.
Therefore, if Oswald didn't shoot Kennedy in Dallas, then no one else did.[2]

If someone would have shot Kennedy in Dallas, then Oswald would have.
Therefore, if Oswald hadn't shot Kennedy in Dallas, then no one else would have.

The second argument, cast in subjunctive conditionals, does not seem not to be a counterexample to the validity of contraposition. The first argument, in contrast, appears to be an invalid contraposition, although it consists of indicative conditionals.

The title of this chapter, 'A problem with validity', refers to the problem of accounting for valid substitution instances of invalid argument forms. In Chapter II I emphasize the point that invalid argument forms can have valid instances. I admit here that the examples one provides to illustrate this point often seem to be contrived. Chapter II ends with the following valid instance of the invalid form *denying the antecedent*:

If she has any living relatives, her father's youngest brother is still alive.
She has no living relatives.
Therefore, her father's youngest brother is not still alive.

This argument seems contrived because its conditional premise is superfluous. The conclusion follows from the second premise by itself. As the argument stands, this entailment of the conclusion by the second premise depends on the meanings of the component terms and is not a purely formal matter. Although the argument is a valid instance of denying the antecedent, it is not valid because it has this form. Its being an instance of *denying the antecedent* is incidental to its validity.

Both hypothetical syllogism and contraposition have both valid and invalid instances. Many valid instances, unlike the example directly above, seem to be valid in virtue of the argument form in question. The valid hypothetical syllogisms are somehow valid because they are hypothetical syllogisms. The valid contrapositions are somehow valid because they are contrapositions. The evasively unspecific 'somehow valid' signals a peculiarity here in the relation between validity and form. The contrapositions and hypothetical syllogisms are not valid by being instances of the valid forms *hypothetical syllogism* and *contraposition*. These are not valid forms, because not all their instances are valid. I repeat yet again: an invalid form can have valid instances. How then is the validity of these instances to be explained? The fact that these arguments are instances of *hypothetical syllogism* or *contraposition* is not incidental to their validity, or so it appears. Can this appearance be defended?

Specific examples illustrate this problem and make it more vivid. The following are instances of hypothetical syllogism that are valid in the sense that it is impossible for the conclusion to be false when the premises are true:

If the power should go off, the sump pump would stop.
If the sump pump should stop, the basement would flood.
Therefore, if the power should go off, the basement would flood.

If I draw a flush, I will win at least one big pot tonight.
If I win at least one big pot tonight, I will buy you a new pair of shoes.
Therefore, if I draw a flush, I will buy you a new pair of shoes.

The following instances of contraposition are valid in the same sense as the preceding arguments:

If I draw a flush, I will win at least one big pot tonight.
Therefore, if I do not win at least one big pot tonight, I will not draw a flush.

If that is a left-over piece of your birthday cake, it will be very stale.
Therefore, if that is not very stale, it is not a left-over piece of your birthday cake.

My appeal to different patterns of dependence at this point should not surprise readers of earlier chapters. Distinctions between different patterns of dependence help explain distinctions between valid and invalid instances of some classical argument forms. In the examples above of valid arguments, the premise-conditionals are of the normal 'healthy' kind: if the conditional is true what the main clause is about depends on or results from – or would depend on or result from – what the if-clause is about. If I draw a flush, I will win at least one big pot tonight *as a result*. (Since there may be other ways for me to win a big pot tonight besides drawing a flush now, and perhaps even other ways for me to win this big pot, my winning at least one big pot may not depend on my now drawing the flush.) 'If A occurs, then B will happen as a result' is a specified form of conditional that contraposes. If B does not happen, then A, from which it would have resulted, will not have occurred.

Although the staleness of the cake does not result from its being a left-over piece of your birthday cake, its being a left-over piece of your birthday cake can figure in an explanation of its staleness. Other explanatory factors might be today's date, the date of your birthday, the manner in which the left-over cake was stored, and what kind of cake you had for your birthday (not, for the aptness of this example, the kind completely soaked in brandy or rum). Can the cake's being stale explain why it is a piece of your left-over birthday cake? I do not see how such an explanation would go. In certain circumstances, the cake's being stale might help explain how you *know* that it is a piece of your left-over birthday cake. For example, you might know that of the five kinds of cake now in the refrigerator, four were fresh this afternoon, and one is left over from your birthday last month. Not every order of possible inference is an order of possible explanation. The cake became stale because it sat around for a week after it was baked; it did not sit around for a week after it was baked because it became stale. The direction of explanation is from if-clause to main clause. 'If A, then that explains why it is that B' is a specified form of conditional that contraposes. If it is not so that B, then it will also not be so that A, which would have explained B.

Now I shall look at a new example of a conditional that does not validly contrapose. The product in question is Sassoon anti-dandruff shampoo:[3]

If you use it, no one will know.

No one will know what? It makes a difference what one takes to be the unspecified object of absent knowledge. 'If you use it, no one will know whether or not you use it' leads to no paradox by way of contraposition. The following argument, in contrast, jumps the track:

> If you use it, no one will know that you use it.
> Therefore, if someone will know that you use it, you do not use it.

What is wrong with the conclusion of this purported argument? No argument, including this one, provides a counterexample to the validity of the contraposition of the material conditional. We will never find a conditional with a true if-clause and a false main clause that is the contrapositive of a conditional with either a false if-clause or a true main clause. The conditionals above have a different peculiar relation. Let us say that a conditional is *friendly* if it is possible for both of its clauses to be true. Contraposition fails, I assume, when a friendly conditional has an unfriendly contrapositive. The conclusion of the argument above is definitely unfriendly, for the truth of the main clause, *you do not use the shampoo*, is a sufficient condition of the falsity of the if-clause, *someone will know that you use the shampoo*. Equivalently, in the form more familiar in the theory of knowledge, the truth of *you do use the shampoo* is a necessary condition of the truth of *someone will know that you use the shampoo*. The premise-conditional is friendly enough; there is no difficulty in its being true both that you use the shampoo and that no one will know that you use it. So far as general principles of epistemology can show, your using the shampoo is not a condition of any kind, necessary or sufficient, of general ignorance that you use it.

Our examples of suspect contraposition all involve arguments from friendly to unfriendly conditionals. It is possible to draw a flush and not draw a straight flush, while it is impossible to draw a straight flush and not draw a flush. Drawing a flush is a necessary condition of drawing a straight flush. The first conditional rests on the claim that this necessary condition will not itself be or be part of any sufficient condition for drawing a straight flush. (And it may be true that no cards remaining in the deck can make my hand into a straight flush.) The contrapositive of the conditional says that if I draw a straight flush, then a condition necessary for drawing a straight flush will be absent. Someone who would prop up fallen soldiers in the last battle to defend contraposition should maintain that this conditional is only an unusual vehicle for the assertion that I will not draw a straight flush. There seems, however, to be a significant modal jump in this contraposition. If it is impossible for me to draw a straight flush in this game, that is because of the distribution of cards in this game so far. The cards will be distributed differently in the next game. But the impossibility of drawing a straight flush without drawing a flush is not relative to card distribution in this or any game. It is a logical impossibility.

The 'if we have more than two children' example is logically very similar to the 'if I draw a flush' example. The conditional 'If we have more than ten children, we will not have more than two children' is definitely unfriendly, since the falsity of the main clause is a logically necessary condition of the truth of the if-clause.

It is tempting here to start multiplying senses. Contraposition is valid for conditionals that certain patterns of dependence back up but not valid for those that certain other patterns support. So why not distinguish conditionals according to the associated patterns of dependence? The validity of contraposition will then appear to depend on *which kind* of conditional is involved. Conditionals will turn out to suffer from hitherto unnoticed logically important ambiguities.

This motive for finding multiple meanings might lure us away from the position on the meaning of conditionals I advocate in Chapter XIII. We should stand fast. Whether a conditional is supported by one pattern of dependence or another, it means the same thing. We can retain an uncluttered theory of meaning by paying the price of working with less neat theories of validity. This price will not be too high if the theories of validity pay for themselves by solving more problems than they were designed to handle.

Circumstantial validity is the ordinary validity of an argument to a conclusion from the grounds of the premises of the

231

argument. By 'grounds' here I mean 'reason why something is true' as opposed to 'reason why something is believed to be true'. If you tell me that you were born at sea, and I believe you because you tell me, this does nothing to explain why it is true that you were born at sea. Grounds, in this sense, are not always easily available. Circumstantial validity is called *circumstantial* because the grounds for token premises of the same type can vary in different circumstances. This is as vague as the notion of grounds is vague, which is, I think, not so vague as to be useless. While 'If I draw a flush, I will win at least one big pot tonight' says nothing about dependence, it is supposedly grounded on the fact that my drawing a flush will, together with other factors obtaining in the circumstances, result in my winning a big pot. Whatever follows validly from this complex fact follows with circumstantial validity from the original conditional.

It is of theoretical interest, when an argument is classified as valid, whether the validity is classical or circumstantial. Consider these arguments from disjunctions:

You may have coffee or tea.
Therefore, if you have coffee, you may not have tea.

She will attend medical school or law school.
Therefore, if she should attend medical school, she would not attend law school.

The classical validity of the first argument provides evidence for the existence of *exclusive disjunction* in natural language. The classical validity of the second provides evidence for the existence of *intensional disjunction*. An exclusive disjunction implies that its disjuncts are not all true. (Disjunctions in which the disjuncts are strongly incompatible obviously cannot demonstrate the existence of exclusive disjunction; for the conclusion of exclusivity will be true on its own, without any assistance from a disjunctive premise.) An intensional disjunction implies a corresponding subjunctive conditional. Suppose that the ground or reason for the truth of 'She will attend medical school or law school' implies, if she should attend one, she would not attend the other. Then the conclusion follows with circumstantial validity. If we do not distinguish circumstantial from classical validity, it is natural

232

enough to say simply that the conclusion follows validly. But, once we draw the distinction, we can see that the case for the existence of intensional disjunction in English rests on the difficult requirement that the validity of the target disjunctive arguments be classical rather than circumstantial. The case for exclusive disjunction is difficult for much the same reason. While there are many circumstances in which a 'not both' conclusion follows with circumstantial validity from a disjunctive premise, it is hard to defend the view that it follows with classical validity.

We can treat circumstantially valid arguments as a variety of enthymeme, an argument in which one or more premises are implicit. We can regard the relevant statement of grounds as the unmentioned extra premise.[4] Such an enthymeme would be of a special kind, however, since usually the extra premises of an enthymeme can come from anywhere, without restriction, and the extra premises of this variety must include grounds of the explicit premises. In this case, moreover, the extra implicit premise will typically render superfluous the explicit premise for which it is a ground. Once we make all the premises of the enthymeme explicit, and remove superfluous premises, at least some of the original premises are gone. Although there are similarities between circumstantial validity and the enthymemic validity, it is best not to subsume one under the other.

The view that conditionals can be supported by different patterns of dependence together with the view that conditionals with different grounds need not thereby have different meanings or senses gives the notion of circumstantial validity some work to do. The concept of circumstantial validity and the view that patterns of dependence provide the truth and acceptance conditions of conditionals are nevertheless independent: one can accept both, reject both, or accept either one without the other.

Troublesome cases of contraposition can be adapted to provide troublesome cases of hypothetical syllogism:

If I draw a straight flush, then I will draw a flush.
If I draw a flush, I will not draw a straight flush.
Therefore, if I draw a straight flush, I will not draw a straight flush.

The first premise is a necessary truth, and the second premise is familiar from earlier examples. The conclusion is unfriendly. Regarded as a material conditional, the conclusion is logically equivalent to 'I will not draw a straight flush', which the second premise does indeed entail. Disagreements about the aptness of material conditional interpretations of natural-language conditionals have boiled and simmered for years; and I will not claim at last to leave the topic cool, clear, and tranquil. Anyone who insists can continue to read these conditionals as truth-functional. I see no plausible patterns of dependence or independence that can make the last conditional true, so I count it as untrue.

The standard examples of invalid hypothetical syllogism we can understand as involving different degrees of similarity between relevant possible worlds and the actual world. (I shall treat the forthcoming familiar example without using special symbols and also without casting the comparisons so they refer to just one world, as it is, as it might have been, and as it might be.) The worlds in which I am very wealthy that are closest to the actual world are worlds in which I drive a Jaguar. The worlds in which I am president of General Motors that are closest to the actual world are worlds in which I am very wealthy. It does not follow that the worlds in which I am president of General Motors that are closest to the actual world are worlds in which I drive a Jaguar, an automobile manufactured by a competing firm. For the worlds in which I am president of General Motors that are closest to the actual world are farther from the actual world than the closest worlds in which I am very wealthy. We can recast this diagnosis of invalidity in terms of conditions. My being very wealthy is a sufficient condition, in the circumstances, of my driving a Jaguar. My being president of General Motors is a sufficient condition, in the circumstances, of my being very wealthy. Does it follow that my being president of General Motors is a sufficient condition, in the circumstances, of my driving a Jaguar? It follows only if 'the circumstances' that the two premise statements refer to are the same, or are nearly the same, which in this case they are not. An 'in the circumstances' qualification is relevant to any statement of sufficient conditions or necessary conditions that are not concerned with strict logical necessity or sufficiency. When patterns of dependence are expressed in the language of conditions, the accompanying 'in the circumstances' qualifications allow for distinctions between relevantly different circumstances that are parallel to distinctions between relevantly different possible worlds. The parallel is not an identity. Circumstances can consist of factors that each actually obtain in the actual world. Circumstances can thus be different only because the factors of which they consist are not exactly the same: two different circumstances can each be as completely actual as two different trees.

Enquiry into the circumstantial validity of a hypothetical syllogism reveals distinctions between relevantly different circumstances, for a full statement of grounds mentions the circumstances. The grounds for 'If I were president of General Motors, I would be very wealthy' include factors that are not included in the grounds for 'If I were very wealthy, I would drive a Jaguar.'

The notion of circumstantial validity helps explain the validity of certain instances of argument forms that, although classically valid, are invalid according to well-received, non-classical semantics. Perhaps the notion of circumstantial validity can also help explain the apparent validity of instances of argument forms that come out invalid on everyone's semantics, classical or non-classical. Consider the following example:

If someone pushes the button next to the front door, the chimes play 'How dry I am'.
(Brief pause.) Why, the chimes are playing 'How dry I am' right now!
Therefore, someone must have pushed the button next to the front door.

This is a textbookish example of affirming the consequent, an invalid form. It is logically possible for this argument to have true premises and a false conclusion, for it is consistent with the conditional premise that there be many reasons why the chimes should play 'How dry I am' in addition to someone's pushing the button next to the front door. The premises do not logically rule out, for example, that, because the previous owner followed a misguided scheme for marking the passage of time with music, the chimes play that same tune every five minutes, night and day. Other argument instances of the same logical form seem nevertheless to be much more illogical, such as:

235

If someone thinks that his beliefs and desires are controlled by radio waves from the planet Venus, that person has at least heard of Venus.
The editor of *Nous* has heard of Venus.
The editor of *Nous* therefore thinks that his beliefs and desires are controlled by radio waves from the planet Venus.

The conclusion of this ridiculous argument is so implausible that we know it cannot follow from reasonable premises. The conclusion of the earlier argument that affirms the consequent, in contrast, is not implausible (except, perhaps, in the choice of tune). This contrast between the two arguments provides a case for thinking that the apparent differences between them have nothing to do with logic but have only to do with subject matter. I would suggest that there is, nevertheless, a logical difference. The first argument, but not the second, is a borderline case of being circumstantially valid.

When the corresponding biconditional replaces the conditional premise in the argument form *affirming the consequent*, the resulting argument form is valid by every classical criterion:

P if and only if *Q*. *Q*. Therefore, *P*.

The grounds for a conditional are often, but not always, grounds for the corresponding biconditional. Although our examples of inferences are fictional, and the circumstances are thus also fictional, it is difficult to imagine how the grounds for:

If someone thinks that his beliefs and desires are controlled by radio waves from the planet Venus, that person has at least heard of Venus,

would also be grounds for the converse conditional that the biconditional requires:

If someone has at least heard of Venus, that person thinks that his beliefs and desires are controlled by radio waves from the planet Venus.

On the other hand, grounds for accepting:

If someone pushes the button next to the front door, the chimes play 'How dry I am',

can easily support the relevant converse conditional:

If the chimes play 'How dry I am', someone has pushed the button next to the front door.

Treating all conditionals as if they were biconditionals leads to trouble. Psychological experiments on conditional reasoning appear to show that normal subjects often treat conditionals as biconditionals even when nothing in the context supports the converse conditional. In the so-called selection task devised by Peter Wason, the subject understands that each card has a letter on one side and a numeral on the other.[5] The task is to select which cards to turn over to determine the truth of the conditional:

If a card has a vowel on one side, then it has an even number on the other side.

Subjects frequently elect to turn over a card that shows a 4, although this cannot disconfirm the conditional. A card that shows a 4 can, however, disconfirm the associated biconditional. Indeed, any card in this set-up can disconfirm the biconditional; but very few subjects choose to turn over all the cards. The common failure to turn over the card that shows a 3 reveals that contraposition is quite difficult for normal subjects. Our previous results have shown that the credentials of contraposition are suspect. But I see no support for the view that normal subjects have a deep yet inarticulate wisdom about the invalidity of contraposition that textbook-trained psychologists lack. The classically valid contrapositions that experimental subjects overlook are circumstantially valid as well. An overriding incompetence about contraposition makes it difficult to determine the exact extent to which normal subjects treat conditionals as biconditionals.

However often subjects reason from conditionals as if they were biconditionals, such inferences are at least sometimes circumstantially valid. It is too much to expect them all to be circumstantially valid. Treating conditionals as if they were biconditionals assumes a stance in the permanent, unresolvable conflict between these two ideals: to believe every truth and yet to believe nothing false. If we have somehow an inherent tendency to treat conditionals as biconditionals, is the increase in important true beliefs acquired worth the accompanying increase in acquired dangerously false belief? If reasoning from conditionals as if they were biconditionals were limited to circumstantially valid inferences, there should be no doubt that we would be better off: the increased number of truths accepted would outweigh the increased number of accepted falsehoods. In many circumstances, true premises imply only true conclusions with circumstantial validity; and more true conclusions follow from true premises with circumstantial than with classical validity. This bonus of extra truth does not have comparable extra falsehood as its price, since for every circumstantially valid argument there is a classically valid argument in which the premises, once formulated, are seen to be nearly as secure as the premises of the original argument.

The theory of classical validity is a beautiful thing, and useful too. I would never suggest that we discard it. I recommend, rather, that we extend or supplement it with the notion of circumstantial validity. This notion helps to distinguish acceptable from logically unacceptable inferences without any appeal to an independently unmotivated multiplication of senses or meanings. It may also help, in the psychology of reasoning, to understand the prevalence of certain inferences that are classically invalid.

I have contended that distinguishing different patterns of dependence helps to explain the distinction between valid and invalid instances of argument forms such as contraposition. This contention is unaccompanied by suggestions for new connectives and other new symbols, new methods of diagramming, new axioms and rules, new theorems and metatheorems. My own preliminary attempts along these lines are not so startling in their promise to provide fresh insights that they should appear here at any cost. In a book like this that tries to avoid formalism, merely routine formalism at the end is out of place. Still, if my suggestions have promise, there is honest and original work to be done in formal logic. Our various current symbolisms do not indicate direction of dependence, so, if direction of dependence is logically important, we should devise some economical symbolism that indicates it. That is not a difficult first step. While I have not given up on taking the next step after that, I hope that some genuine logician, persuaded that my approach to conditionals is worth formalizing, takes it before me.

Philosophers and other writers sometimes entertain the fleeting feeling that they have finally disposed of a subject once and for all. In calling upon some unnamed logician to devise a system and prove some theorems, I swerve away from the temptation of spurious closure (and swerve toward the temptation of spurious seminal originality). Apart from the prospects of my own contributions to the theory of conditionals, the historical survey imposed by the format of this book provides an independent reason for doubting that disputes about the nature of conditionals are at last about to end. Few theoretical disputes, in philosophy or elsewhere, have had such staying power. Given a little luck necessary for the continued existence of philosophers and crows, it is a good bet that, for some thousands of years to come, the crows on the roofs will caw about the nature of conditionals.

Notes

Introduction   Conditionals in Everyday Life and in Philosophy

The literary examples in this chapter are from *Macbeth*, I. vii. 1–2; Aristotle, *Nicomachean Ethics*, X. 7; Yeats, 'Lapis lazuli', 12–15; Dylan, 'If you see her, say hello', *c.* 1974, Rams Horn Music; *Twelfth Night*, I. i. 1; Matthew 5. 40; Psalms 137. 5; and Shelley, 'Ode to the west wind', 70.

1 See the reference to McCawley, 1981, in Chapter XI, note 2.
2 Two very influential twentieth-century treatments of conditionals and their relation to freedom are Moore, 1912, Chapter VI, 'Free will', and Austin, 1956. Most of Austin's criticisms of Moore, in my opinion, can be answered. Roderick Chisholm's criticisms of conditional analyses of freedom, in Chisholm, 1964, pp. 21–2, and elsewhere, can be answered only by modifying the account under attack.
3 Kneale and Kneale, 1962, p. 244.
4 Ashworth, 1974, p. xi.
5 Kneale and Kneale, 1962, besides being an authoritative history of logic, also provides an excellent introduction to the subject. The Kneales' refusal to translate anything from Latin, however, will frustrate some readers.
   Bochenski, 1961, is a rather different comprehensive history of logic that collects, organizes, and annotates passages from the original sources. The long article by several hands, edited and organized by A. N. Prior, 'Logic, history of' in Edwards, 1967, is also a valuable reference.

Chapter I   Ancient History

The epigraph is by Callimachus as reported by Sextus Empiricus, *Adversus Mathematicos*, i. 309.

1 Whitehead, 1929, p. 63.
2 The question why there was mutual hostility rather than co-operation

240

between the Aristotelian and Stoic logicians calls for subtle scholarship. See Mueller, 1969, and Frede, 1974.

3 See Mates, 1953, Chapter 5, and Kneale and Kneale, 1962, pp. 158–72, for discussion of the Stoic logical systems.

4 Does every valid argument have a valid argument form? One's answer to this question depends on one's definition of argument validity.

5 The letters of the Roman alphabet most often used as propositional variables are P and Q. Some writers use upper-case, some lower-case, some italics, and some not. I will use upper-case italics except when discussing passages that use other typographic conventions.

6 See Geach, 1976, Chapter 14, for recommendations about current use of the Stoic term *themata*. Some beginning textbooks present logical systems that are really systems of themata, for example Lemmon, 1978, and Pospesel, 1984, which derives from Lemmon.

7 This is the formulation in Mates, 1953, p. 45.

Chapter II Medieval and Post-medieval History

1 See Boh, 1982, and Kneale and Kneale, 1962, pp. 274–97.

2 See Boehner, 1951, Moody, 1953, Moody, 1967, and especially M. M. Adams, 1973, to which my discussion of Ockham is indebted.

3 Perhaps he is John of Cornwall. See McDermott, 1972, p. 273.

4 McDermott, 1972, p. 290.

5 Rather than use propositional variables or metalinguistic variables, medieval writers typically describe such argument forms by using structural descriptions such as: the inference from a conditional and its antecedent to its consequent.

6 See Ashworth, 1974, p. 121.

7 The first premise of this argument is superfluous. Examples of valid arguments with a familiar invalid form frequently have one of the following peculiarities: a premise is superfluous, the premises are inconsistent, or the conclusion is a necessary truth. The following example has none of these features:

Queen Elizabeth is older than Prince Charles.
Queen Elizabeth is not older than Quine.
Therefore, anyone older than Quine is older than Prince Charles.

By following common practice in paraphrasing for this purpose, we can recast this argument as a categorical syllogism:

All persons identical to Queen Elizabeth are persons older than Prince Charles.
No persons identical to Queen Elizabeth are persons older than Quine.
Therefore, all persons older than Quine are persons older than Prince Charles.

Although this is a valid argument, and it is a categorical syllogism, it is not valid as a categorical syllogism. Its syllogistic form is invalid:

All As are Bs.
No As are Cs.
Therefore, all Cs are Bs.

An argument of this form can be invalid. This particular argument is valid because of properties of the relation *older than*.

Someone with a little experience with logic exercises of this kind who thinks at first that adding the extra premises that *older than* is asymmetric and transitive will produce an argument that is valid in virtue of its form should consider the relation *ancestor of*, which is also asymmetric and transitive. When *ancestor of* is substituted for *older than*, the resulting argument has true premises and a false conclusion. Not all Quine's ancestors are ancestors of Queen Elizabeth. A difference between the relations crucial to the validity of the corresponding arguments is that *not older than* is transitive, while *not an ancestor of* is non-transitive.

Chapter III   Rediscovery of the Material Conditional

1 Van Heijenoort, 1970, p. 1. The phrase is from van Heijenoort's introduction. This book contains a translation of Frege's *Begriffsschrift*.
2 Frege, 1980, pp. 68–9.
3 Frege, 1979, p. 186. The passage quoted comes from a manuscript entitled 'Introduction to logic'.
4 *Collected Papers*, 3.441. References to the *Collected Papers* customarily give volume and section numbers. This reference is to Peirce, 1933, p. 279.
5 Whitehead and Russell, 1962, p. 99.
6 Whitehead and Russell, 1962, p. 7.
7 ibid.
8 Lewis, 1912, p. 522.
9 Johnson, 1921, p. 39. Von Wright says that as far as he knows Johnson coined the term 'paradoxes of implication' (Von Wright, 1957, p. 170.)
10 MacColl, 1908, pp. 151–2.
11 Russell, 1908, p. 301.
12 Moore, 1922, pp. 295–6.
13 The argument relies on the principle that competent speakers are prepared to assert *if p, then q* whenever the following condition is satisfied: there is a set S of true propositions such that *q* is inferable from *p* together with S (Faris, 1962, p. 117).

14 Grice, 1961, p. 445.
15 Grice, 1967. See Strawson, 1986, for an exposition and discussion of Grice on truth-functional conditionals and for a presentation of an alternative 'consequentialist' account.
16 Cohen, 1971, p. 63.
17 Stevenson, 1970, p. 28.
18 Strawson, 1952, p. 86, p. 77.
19 Quine, 1966, p. 148.

Chapter IV   Rediscovery of the Strict Conditional

1 Quine, 1966, p. 175.
2 Quine, 1951, p. 23.
3 Quine, 1982, pp. 50–1.
4 Russell, 1906, p. 161.
5 Russell, 1906, p. 162.
6 W. E. Johnson, rather than distinguish use from mention, distinguishes primary from secondary propositions. 'A secondary proposition is one which predicates some characteristic of a primary proposition' (Johnson, 1921, p. 50). His discussion of Russell anticipates Quine's:

> When the compound proposition 'If p then q' is rendered, as Mr Russell proposes, in the form 'Either not-p or q,' the compound is being treated as a *primary* proposition of the same type as its components p and q. When on the other hand we substitute for 'If p then q' the phrase 'p implies q,' or preferably 'p would imply q,' the proposition is no longer primary, inasmuch as it predicates about the proposition q the adjective 'implied by p' which renders the compound a secondary proposition. (Johnson, 1922, pp. xvi–xvii)

7 Russell, 1908, p. 301. Cf. note 8 of Chapter IV.
8 A series of articles in *Mind* and the *Journal of Philosophy* started with Lewis, 1912, and culminated in Lewis, 1918, which contains a system of strict implication.
9 Preface to the 1960 Dover reprint of Lewis, 1918, p. vii.
10 Clear, concise introductions to modal logic are provided by Kneale and Kneale, 1962, pp. 548–68, and by Prior, 1967b. Hughes and Cresswell, 1968, is recommended as a comprehensive treatment. For more recent developments, consult Bull and Segerberg, 1984.
11 See the 'Historical part' of Bull and Segerberg, 1984, pp. 2–16.
12 See Hughes and Cresswell, 1968, Chapter 4.
13 Additional properties of the relation increase the number of systems that can be distinguished. See the figure in Chellas, 1980, p. 164.

14 Lewis and Langford, 1959, p. 250. The phrase 'rule of inference' does not occur in this passage.
15 Moore, 1922, p. 291. See various entries in Moore, 1962, that show Moore's persistent interest in conditionals and in entailment.

Chapter V Subjunctive Conditionals and Covering Laws

1 Chisholm, 1946, p. 489. Chisholm's article begins with a historical survey of the importance of the topic of contrary-to-fact conditionals. Two later surveys that include bibliographies are Schneider, 1953, and Walters, 1967.
2 Ramsey, 1931, p. 248.
3 Chisholm, 1946, p. 482.
4 Anderson, 1951, p. 37.
5 Goodman, 1955, p. 4.
6 ibid.
7 Articles that explicitly locate and question the assumption in question include Anscombe, 1975, Smiley, 1984, and Dudman, 1984.
8 Chisholm, 1946, p. 491.
9 Adams, 1970a, p. 90.
10 Chisholm, 1946, p. 486.
11 Goodman, 1955, p. 3.
12 Schneider, 1953, p. 623.
13 Mates, 1970, pp. 303–4.
14 Chisholm, 1946, p. 490.
15 Honderich, 1982, p. 300.
16 See, for example, Walters, 1961, and Mackie, 1966. Mackie advanced a somewhat different view of conditionals in Mackie, 1973, and Mackie, 1974, but still a view on which subjunctive conditionals are not literally true. For a critical discussion of Mackie's reasons for denying truth-value to conditionals, consult Honderich, 1982.
17 Goodman, 1955, p. 11. As an early reviewer points out, 'Prof. Goodman has apparently not quite made up his mind whether his S is to be regarded as a sentence or as a class of sentences: he speaks of it as a class of sentences, but applies to it the operation of conjunction of the sentential calculus, and speaks of sentences having S.A as antecedents' (McKinsey, 1947, p. 139). Such equivocation between symbols for classes and symbols for their members is common in formal philosophy. So far as I can see, it leads to no genuine confusion in Goodman's treatment of conditionals. When sliding over this distinction, or the use-mention distinction, does not contribute to fallacious reasoning, it can be difficult to draw the further distinction between rigour and pedantry.
18 Chisholm, 1946, pp. 493–5.
19 Quine, 1960, p. 222.
20 Quine, 1982, p. 23.

21 Goodman, 1955, p. 15.
22 Slote, 1978, pp. 4–5.
23 ibid., pp. 14–15.
24 Parry, 1957, p. 89; Cooley, 1957, p. 298.
25 Goodman, 1957a, pp. 443–4.
26 Goodman, 1957b, p. 532.
27 Slote, 1978, pp. 17–18. Slote's entire requirement is more intricate and uses his notion of a *despiteness relation* that he explains in turn by reference to valid explanations involving no extraneous elements.
28 Kvart, 1986. Kvart provides a quick summary of his general approach in Kvart, 1980.

Chapter VI Belief and Probability

1 Ramsey, 1931, p. 247, note. Quoted by Chisholm, 1946, p. 489. Chisholm quotes two Ramsey passages in reverse order: p. 248, p. 247.
2 Rescher, 1964, p. 18.
3 Stalnaker, 1968, p. 43.
4 ibid., p. 44.
5 Harper, 1981, p. 5. An earlier formulation of the Ramsey test appears in Harper, 1976, p. 97.
6 Stalnaker, 1970, pp. 114–15.
7 Harper, 1981, p. 11.
8 The general philosophical public had to wait for the publication of Lewis, 1976.
9 Jeffrey, 1981, p. 82.
10 Jeffrey, 1981, p. 84. Those who seek a full proof of the triviality result can look at Lewis, 1976, or Jeffrey, 1981, or any of the following: Appiah, 1985, chapter 9, Appiah, 1986, Skyrms, 1980, pp. 169–76. In his discussion of the proof, Skyrms points out the algebraic fact of life that 'it is not in general true that mixtures of quotients are quotients of mixtures' (p. 171).
11 Lewis himself, in Lewis, 1976, develops the notion of *imaging*, an alternative to conditionalization. For futher discussion of imaging, see Gärdenfors, 1982.
12 Ramsey, 1931, p. 247, note.
13 Von Wright, 1957, p. 131. See the long essay 'Conditionals' in Mackie, 1973, pp. 64–119, for further defence of the view that conditionals often lack truth-value.
14 Quine, 1982, p. 21.
15 Stalnaker, 1970, pp. 113–14.
16 Adams, 1965, p. 175.
17 ibid., p. 173.
18 ibid., pp. 176–7.
19 Adams, 1975, p. 101, note 16.

20 ibid., p. 3, where the sentence quoted here is set in italics. The principle, appropriately called 'Adams' Hypothesis', as in Appiah, 1985, p. 4, pp. 173–6, is what Harper calls 'Stalnaker's Hypothesis' (see note 7). Adams certainly published (Adams, 1964) before Stalnaker. Others such as Richard Jeffrey and Brian Ellis were also thinking similar thoughts in the mid 1960s. If there is a definite, correct answer to the question 'Who formulated the principle *first*?' I do not know what it is.

21 Adams, 1975, pp. 9–11. I use one-dimensional representations mainly to show that it can be done. Two-dimensional representations seem to be more perspicuous, although I cannot explain why this is so. If we want to represent many probabilistically independent propositions and we want each representation of a proposition to be topologically connected, there is no limit to the number of dimensions that could be required.

22 ibid., p. 10.

23 Adams doubts that a theory of conversational implicature can explain the absurdity of the premise (ibid., p. 29). The absurdity of the premise, at any rate, sets a nice exercise for theories of implicature.

24 Lewis, 1976, pp. 305–8 (as reprinted in Harper, Stalnaker, and Pearce, 1981, pp. 137–8); Jackson, 1979, *passim*.

25 Skyrms, 1980, p. 88.

26 Adams, 1970b, pp. 2–3.

27 Adams develops an intricate probabilistic counterexample to his own treatment of subjunctive conditionals, Adams, 1975, pp. 129–33. For further discussion of this example, consult Skyrms, 1980, pp. 97–9.

Chapter VII   Possible Worlds

The epigraph is from *Candide*, The World Publishing Company, Cleveland and New York, 1947, Chapter 6, p. 31.

1 The explicit doctrine that necessity is truth in all possible worlds is difficult to find in Leibniz's writings. Following commentators' references without ever finding the doctrine allegedly referred to, I abandoned my search after learning from William Lycan that he found all such page references to be specious. See Lycan, 1979, p. 274, note.

2 Lewis, 1943, p. 243. A slightly revised version of this passage occurs in Lewis, 1946, pp. 56–7.

3 Carnap, 1947, p. 9.

4 Sellars, 1948. When Sellars returns to the topic of subjunctive conditionals in Sellars, 1958, he does not talk about possible worlds.

5 Stalnaker, 1968, acknowledges the collaboration of Richmond Thomason on the formal development of the theory.

6 Lewis, 1973b, refers to Lewis, 1968, which in retrospect looks like preliminary work for Lewis's treatment of subjunctive conditionals. According to Stalnaker, Lewis's account was developed independently.

J. Howard Sobel reports that Lewis delivered a talk on subjunctive conditionals to Richard Montague's seminar in November, 1967 (Sobel, 1970, p. 448, note 26).

7 Stalnaker, 1968, p. 44.

8 ibid., pp. 44–5.

9 Stalnaker, 1981, p. 89. Stalnaker, 1984, p. 133.

10 Lewis, 1973b, p. 13.

11 There are not really an infinite number of possible heights greater than 75 inches and less than 76 inches, although there is also no precise upper limit. Nothing counts, for example, as a's being 10^{-133} inches taller than b.

12 A two-dimensional diagram could represent the region occupied by C-worlds as connected. See the diagram in McCawley, 1981. p. 314. The diagram in Lewis, 1973b, p. 34, to illustrate the failure of hypothetical syllogism represents one of the premises as a semifactual. My one-dimensional diagrams represent only comparative similarity to the leftmost point. Two worlds located at the same point are equally similar to the world located at the leftmost point no matter how much or little they resemble each other. A two-dimensional representation allows the locations of two such worlds to be nearer or farther from each other while they remain equidistant from the location of the actual world. Lewis's diagrams display a set of concentric circles centred on the actual world, and he talks about *spheres* of accessibility around a world i. Although we ordinarily think of spheres as three-dimensional, there is no limit to the dimensionality of the logical space of possible worlds; for there is no limit to the number of possible worlds that can be equally similar to each other.

13 Stalnaker, 1981, pp. 99–101. Stalnaker, 1984, pp. 142–6.

14 Nute, 1984, pp. 404–9, refers to his earlier work, such as Nute, 1980, and the work of others on 'small change' theories which Nute contrasts with 'minimal change' theories. There is a sympathetic discussion of Nute's approach in McCawley, 1981, pp. 321–6.

15 Bennett, 1974, p. 395.

16 Fine, 1975, p. 452. Lewis quotes this passage in Lewis, 1979, p. 467.

17 Lewis, 1979, p. 467.

18 ibid., p. 472.

19 Jackson, 1977, p. 7.

20 ibid., p. 9.

21 Davis, 1979, p. 554.

22 Bennett, 1984, p. 73.

23 Pollock, 1976, p. 21.

24 The relation of minimal difference generates a partial ordering of worlds. Unlike the Lewis–Stalnaker relations of marginal similarity, it does not generate a simple ordering (Pollock, 1976, p. 23). Pollock provides elaborate theories of minimal change in terms of *historical antecedent*. See Pollock, 1984, chapter 4.

25 But I will not attempt to mention every difference between different theories of conditionals or even briefly to mention every significant theory. In this chapter it would have been appropriate to discuss treatments by Nelson Blue, Angelika Kratzer, Pavel Tichý, and many others. Nute, 1984, provides a pretty full discussion of recent possible-worlds treatments of conditionals, although it is not comprehensive. Tichý, 1984, also discusses several theories.

Chapter VIII Inference, Entailment, and the Purposes of Theories

1 The same point holds for non-conditionals. J. L. Austin rejected the view that constatives are always true or false. 'How can one answer this question, whether it is true or false that France is hexagonal? It is just rough, that is the right and final answer to the question of the relation of "France is hexagonal" to France. It is a rough description; it is not a true or a false one' (Austin, 1962, p. 142).
2 Von Wright, 1957, p. 181.
3 Anderson and Belnap, 1975, pp. 155–6.
4 ibid., pp. 176–7.
5 ibid., p. 177.
6 See Johnson, 1921, pp. xxxiii–xxiv, 2–3, 38–47, and Johnson, 1922, xv–xvii, 7–10.
7 Johnson, 1922, p. 8.
8 Stebbing, 1961, p. 215. Stebbing appears to be influenced by Broad, 1933, p. 193, but, unlike Broad, she does not advocate the 'relevance-logic' view of inconsistency of Nelson, 1930. Broad acknowledges Nelson's influence in Broad, 1933, p. liv.
9 Hare, 1970, p. 16.
10 Mackie, 1973, p. 67. See Prior, 1960, for another kind of difficulty with the logical powers view, and Belnap, 1962, for a response.
11 Ryle, 1950, p. 308.
12 ibid., p. 307.
13 ibid., p. 312.
14 Harman, 1984, pp. 107–8. Harman makes the same point in several other publications.
15 Appiah, 1985, p. 176.
16 Jackson, 1979, p. 578.
17 Appiah, 1985, p. 237.
18 Gärdenfors, 1986, p. 81.

Chapter IX Problems with the Ramsey Test, Possible Worlds, and Probability

The epigraphs are from T. S. Eliot, 'Burnt Norton', I, 4–5, *The Complete Poems and Plays, 1909–1950*, New York, Harcourt, Brace and Co., 1952, p. 117, and Theodore Roethke, 'The lady and the bear', 23–4, *Words for the Wind*, London, Secker & Warburg, 1957, p. 136.

1 In Ithaca, New York, in the summer of 1949, Wittgenstein and Malcolm began to discuss some of the famous anti-sceptical papers by G. E. Moore, 'Proof of an external world' and 'A defence of common sense'. One result of these conversations was Malcolm, 1952. Another is the collection of remarks Wittgenstein began that summer and continued until soon before his death in 1951 that was eventually published with the title *On Certainty* (Wittgenstein, 1969).

2 Malcolm, 1952, p. 189.

3 Malcolm, 1963, p. 71.

4 Wittgenstein, 1969, section 245.

5 ibid., sections 380–2.

6 ibid., sections 613–14.

7 Ramsey, 1931, p. 247, note.

8 'How might I be mistaken in my assumption that I was never on the moon?'

   'If I were to say "I have never been on the moon – but I may be mistaken", that would be idiotic' (Wittgenstein, 1969, sections 661–2).

9 Frege, 1984, pp. 400–1.

10 Appiah, 1985, pp. 219–22.

11 V. H. Dudman uses the conditional 'If Her Majesty is in this room she's invisible' to make a point that I repeat in this chapter. 'What sort of bearing can the probability have that Her Majesty is in the room when it is understood on all sides that she is not?' (Dudman, 1987, p. 76).

Chapter X   Various Visions of Possible Worlds

The epigraph comes from *Paradise Lost*, VIII, 175–8.

1 Lewis, 1973b, p. 86.

2 Kripke, 1980, pp. 19–20.

3 The world in all the ways it might be provides possible worlds suitable for S4 (the Lewis system of modal logic discussed on p. 82). Let 'it is necessary that p' mean 'p is true as the world is now and will remain true however the world might go'. The relation between the world as it is at time t_1 and the world as it might be at a later time t_2 is reflexive and transitive, but not symmetric, and thus appropriate for the semantics of S4. According to Prior, 1967a, p. 27, Kripke proposed this 'branching time' matrix of S4 in 1958.

4 Lewis advises me that super-realism can deal better with the contingency of physical laws if direct connection is defined so as not to require causal connection. According to realism, if the maximum velocity of light might have been greater, there is some world in which it is greater. According to super-realism, there is some

WORLD in which it is greater, some region of this huge universe in which the maximum velocity of light is greater than it is in the region we inhabit. If the physical laws could have been very different, then some WORLDS are so different from 'adjoining' WORLDS that there can be no causal connection between them. A definition of direct connection in purely spatio-temporal terms escapes this difficulty.

There are two reasons I have not followed this good advice. First, I do not propose modal super-realism as serious competition for modal realism; I can use super-realism to express misgivings about realism without regarding it as a genuine alternative. Second, one can see the point of distinguishing direct from indirect connection more easily when direct connection is causal. Distinguishing direct from indirect spatio-temporal relations requires a more sophisticated and technical treatment.

5 By quantifying over classes, one can define the ancestral of a two-place relation without resorting to 'and so on'. A and B are indirectly connectible if and only if B belongs to every class which contains A and everything directly connectible to members. The form of this concise formulation comes from Quine, 1982, p. 293. The first definition of the ancestral appears in Frege, 1879.

6 As Lewis remarks in his Introduction to Lewis, 1983, p. ix, modal realism runs through much of his philosophy. Lewis, 1986a, is a book-length defence of modal realism.

7 The problem that Goodman later called 'the new riddle of induction' appeared in 'The problem of counterfactual conditionals' in a section subtitled 'The problem of law' (Goodman, 1955). Another influential treatment of the connections between conditionals, laws, and induction appears in Mackie, 1966, and in Mackie, 1974.

8 This difficulty is presented clearly in Tichý, 1976.

Chapter XI Laws and Conditions

The epigraph is from Thomas Bernhard, *Correction*, translated by Sophie Wilkins, Knopf, New York, 1979, p. 9.

1 Also see Reichenbach, 1976, which Chapter V rather neglects. Reichenbach's work on conditionals seems to be remembered less well than his work on many other topics in philosophy.

2 McCawley, 1981, p. 317.

3 An example of this kind appears in Wertheimer, 1968, pp. 363–4.

4 Richard Sharvy treats this example in an unpublished paper entitled 'Conditionals'.

5 Von Wright, 1974, p. 7, and in other publications. The one philosopher chiefly responsible for introducing the logic of conditions into contemporary analytic philosophy is Von Wright.

Chapter XII   Counterfactual Dependence and Backtracking

The epigraph comes from Tom Stoppard, *The Real Thing*, Faber & Faber, Boston, 1984, Scene 5.

1 Lewis, 1973a.
2 This example appears in Bennett, 1984, p. 79.
3 Lewis, 1979, pp. 461–2. Lewis provides a clear statement and criticism of several other attempts to explain the asymmetry of openness, pp. 459–61.
4 ibid., p. 473.
5 ibid., p. 475.
6 ibid., pp. 474–5.
7 This two-world idiom is more vivid, I admit, than the one-world idiom I recommend in Chapter X. For the sake of vivacity, we may speak with the learned, so long as we think with the vulgar, out of respect for plain truth.
8 ibid., p. 472.
9 Bennett, 1984, p. 64. This article retracts several points of Bennett, 1974.

Chapter XIII   Patterns of Dependence

1 Honderich, 1982, p. 300.
2 ibid.
3 ibid., p. 301.
4 Lewis, 1976, pp. 137–8.
5 Jackson, 1979.
6 Gibbard, 1980b, p. 255.
7 Downing, 1959, p. 125.
8 Bennett, 1974, pp. 391–3.
9 Bennett, 1984, p. 70.
10 This occurs in Jackson, 1977, and in Slote, 1978.
11 Gibbard, 1980a, pp. 226–9.
12 Lycan, 1984, p. 440. This is Lycan's modification of a proposal in Geis, 1973.
13 The non-equivalence of the second conjuncts does not entail that the conjunctions are non-equivalent. Some arguments of the form '*B* and *C* are not equivalent; therefore, *A* & *B* and *A* & *C* are also not equivalent' are invalid.
14 Writers inclined to accept the view that '*P* even if *Q*' implies '*Q*, in any event' include Pollock, 1976, pp. 29–31, Barker, 1980, and Lycan, 1984. Writers inclined not to accept it include Hazen and Slote, 1979, Bennett, 1982, Dancy, 1984, and Jackson, 1987, p. 45.

Chapter XIV   Objective Dependence

The epigraph comes from Wallace Stevens, 'Like decorations in a nigger cemetery', stanza v, *Ideas of Order*, New York, Knopf, 1936, p. 46; *The Collected Poems of Wallace Stevens*, New York, Knopf, 1957, p. 151.

1 Lewis, 1973a, p. 556.

2 This extends an example that originates in Honderich, 1982.

3 See Cover, 1987, especially pp. 25–6, for an appeal to Charles's law in an attempt to undermine the notion of one-way conditionship.

4 As we have seen before, generalizations about *necessary for* can fall prey to counterexamples that involve overdetermination and stand-by, back-up, or fail/safe devices. Let Lester the laser shooter stand for a host of such cases. Lester will light this match with a shot from his laser gun unless we light the match first by scratching it; so scratching is not necessary for the lighting, and neither is laser shooting, since effective scratching is still a possibility. To count scratching as relevantly necessary for lighting, we may simply neglect the presence of Lester and his ilk, so long as this negligence is principled and systematic. For an example of such principled negligence, see Honderich's notion of an *ordinary situation*, Honderich, 1982, pp. 295–6.

5 One condition of conditionship is that A is a condition of C when everything necessary for A is necessary for C.

6 A similar example appears in Bromberger, 1966, as a difficulty for deductive-nomological theories of explanation. There are sometimes also more directions of possible inference than there are directions of explanation.

7 Slote, 1978.

8 There are indeed additional differences between our treatments of conditionals. Slote rules out backtracking conditionals by fiat, while on my view, there are some acceptable conditionals in which the direction of explanation (or dependence) runs the other way.

9 Mackie, 1974, the seminal treatment of the direction of causation, is preoccupied with the possibility of time-reversed causation.

10 The analogy is incomplete, for there is no causal analogue to simultaneity. When one event is neither earlier nor later than another, the two are simultaneous. When one event neither causes nor is caused by another, the two need have no particular causal relation.

11 Recall the passage on the asymmetry of openness quoted from Lewis, 1979, in Chapter XII. Although I question whether temporal dependence should be regarded as counterfactual dependence, Lewis's suggestions about the asymmetry of openness otherwise strike me as clearly superior to available alternatives.

12 Sam might well not have extended his arm, in order to signal, unless there was an appropriate signalling convention. But he could have

extended his arm, whether or not he would have, without the convention. It is what Sam could have done, not what he would have done, that bears on the relevant kind of independence.

13 Sellars, 1958. In the version reprinted in Sosa, 1975, the story of Harry is on p. 129.

Chapter XV   A Problem with Validity

The epigraph is from the 'Table of contents' of *Appearance and Reality* by F. H. Bradley, London, Allen and Unwin, 1893.

1 I wrote this before the appearance of Dudman, 1988. Dudman claims that 'those many logicians and philosophers who take the indicative/subjunctive dichotomy as fundamental go wrong at their first step' (p. 122). If I, moving with the crowd in this way, and also in other ways that Dudman questions, go wrong at my first step, I only hope my less orthodox steps later on help turn me around in the direction of the true path.

2 The conclusion of this argument and the next one are examples taken from Adams, 1970a, p. 90.

3 This example appears in an unpublished paper by Howard Margolis entitled 'Habits of mind'. Margolis and I use the example somewhat differently.

4 Alvin I. Goldman made this suggestion.

5 Wason, 1966, resulted in enormous research and publishing activity by a number of investigators. The continuation of this activity is a good sign that definite results are hard to pin down. Evans, 1982, and Evans, 1983, contain further discussion and many references including several to philosophers who have tried to interpret the work of psychologists on reasoning.

Bibliography

A few of the entries below are not cited in the text. Most of these are either works so recent (in 1988) that they could have been included in the text only by last-minute revision or articles of my own that serve as preliminary studies for this book.

Adams, E. W. (1964) 'On the reasonableness of inferences involving conditionals', *Proceedings of the 13th International Congress of Philosophy*, vol. 5, Mexico City, pp. 1–9.

Adams, E. W. (1965) 'A logic of conditionals', *Inquiry*, vol. 8, pp. 166–97.

Adams, E. W. (1968) 'Probability and the logic of conditionals', in *Aspects of Inductive Logic*, edited by P. Suppes and J. Hintikka, Amsterdam, North-Holland, pp. 265–316.

Adams, E. W. (1970a) 'Subjunctive and indicative conditionals', *Foundations of Language*, vol. 6, pp. 89–94.

Adams, E. W. (1970b) 'Prior probabilities and counterfactual conditionals', in Harper and Hooker, 1976, pp. 1–21.

Adams, E. W. (1975) *The Logic of Conditionals*, Dordrecht, Reidel.

Adams, E. W. (1987) 'On the meaning of the conditional', *Philosophical Topics*, vol. 15, pp. 5–22.

Adams, E. W. (1988) '*Modus tollens* revisited', *Analysis*, vol. 48, pp. 122–8.

Adams, M. M. (1973) 'Did Ockham know of material and strict implication? A reconsideration', *Franciscan Studies*, vol. 33, pp. 5–37.

Anderson, A. R. (1951) 'A note on subjunctive and counterfactual conditionals', *Analysis*, vol. 12, pp. 35–8.

Anderson, A. R. and Belnap, N. D. (1975) *Entailment: the Logic of Relevance and Necessity*, vol. 1, Princeton, Princeton University Press.

Anscombe, G. E. M. (1975) 'Subjunctive conditionals', *Ruch Filozoficzny*, vol. 33; reprinted with a new prefatory note in *The Collected Papers of G. E. M. Anscombe*, vol. 2: *Metaphysics and the Philosophy of Mind*, Minneapolis, University of Minnesota Press, 1981, pp. 196–207.

Appiah, A. (1985) *Assertion and Conditionals*, Cambridge, Cambridge University Press.

Bibliography

Appiah, A. (1986) 'The importance of triviality', *Philosophical Review*, vol. 95, pp. 209–31.

Appiah, A. (1987) ' "If" again', *Analysis*, vol. 47, pp. 193–9.

Ashworth, E. J. (1974) *Language and Logic in the Post-medieval Period*, Dordrecht, Reidel.

Austin, J. L. (1956) 'Ifs and cans', *Proceedings of the British Academy*, vol. 42; reprinted in Austin's *Philosophical Papers*, edited by J. O. Urmson and G. J. Warnock, Oxford, Oxford University Press, 1961, pp. 153–80.

Austin, J. L. (1962) *How to do things with Words*, edited by J. O. Urmson, Cambridge, Harvard University Press.

Barker, J. A. (1980) ' "If" and "even if" ', *Analysis*, vol. 40, pp. 93–8.

Belnap, N. D. (1962) 'Tonk, plonk and plink', *Analysis*, vol. 22, pp. 130–4; reprinted in Strawson, 1967, pp. 132–7.

Bennett, J. (1974) 'Counterfactuals and possible worlds', *Canadian Journal of Philosophy*, vol. 4, pp. 381–402.

Bennett, J. (1982) ' "Even if" ', *Linguistics and Philosophy*, vol. 5, pp. 403–18.

Bennett, J. (1984) 'Counterfactuals and temporal direction', *Philosophical Review*, vol. 93, pp. 57–91.

Bochenski, I. M. (1961) *A History of Formal Logic*, Notre Dame, University of Notre Dame Press.

Boehner, P. (1951) 'Does Ockham know of material implication?', *Franciscan Studies*, vol. 11, pp. 203–50.

Boh, I. (1982) 'Consequences', in the *Cambridge History of Later Medieval Philosophy*, edited by N. Kretzman, A. Kenny, and J. Pinborg, Cambridge, Cambridge University Press, pp. 300–14.

Broad, C. D. (1933) *Examination of McTaggart's Philosophy*, vol. 1, Cambridge, Cambridge University Press.

Bromberger, S. (1966) 'Why-questions', in *Mind and Cosmos*, edited by R. G. Colodny, Pittsburgh, University of Pittsburgh Press, pp. 86–111.

Bull, R. A. and Segerberg, K. (1984) 'Basic modal logic', in Gabbay and Guenthner, 1984, pp. 1–88.

Carnap, R. (1947) *Meaning and Necessity*, Chicago, University of Chicago Press.

Chellas, B. F. (1980) *Modal Logic*, Cambridge, Cambridge University Press.

Chisholm, R. M. (1946) 'The contrary-to-fact conditional', *Mind*, vol. 55, pp. 289–307; reprinted with revisions in *Readings in Philosophical Analysis*, edited by H. Feigl and W. Sellars, New York, Appleton-Century-Crofts, 1949, pp. 482–97. Page references are to the revised version.

Chisholm, R. M. (1964) 'J. L. Austin's philosophical papers', *Mind*, vol. 73, pp. 1–26.

Cohen, L. J. (1971) 'Some remarks on Grice's views about the logic particles of natural language', in *Pragmatics of Natural Languages*, edited by Y. Bar-Hillel, Dordrecht, Reidel, pp. 50–68.

Bibliography

Cooley, J. C. (1957) 'Professor Goodman's *Fact, Fiction, & Forecast*', *Journal of Philosophy*, vol. 54, pp. 293–311.

Cover, J. A. (1987) 'Causal priority and causal conditionship', *Synthese*, vol. 71, pp. 19–36.

Dancy, J. (1984) 'Even-ifs', *Synthese*, vol. 58, pp. 119–28.

Davis, W. A. (1979) 'Indicative and subjunctive conditionals', *Philosophical Review*, vol. 88, pp. 544–64.

Davis, W. A. (1983) 'Weak and strong conditionals', *Pacific Philosophical Quarterly*, vol. 64, pp. 57–71.

Downing, P. (1959) 'Subjunctive conditionals, time order, and causation', *Proceedings of the Aristotelian Society*, vol. 59; pp. 125–40.

Dudman, V. H. (1984) 'Parsing "if"-sentences', *Analysis*, vol. 44, pp. 145–53.

Dudman, V. H. (1986) 'Antecedents and consequents', *Theoria*, vol. 52, pp. 168–99.

Dudman, V. H. (1987) 'Appiah on "if"', *Analysis*, vol. 47, pp. 74–9.

Dudman, V. H. (1988) 'Indicative and subjunctive', *Analysis*, vol. 48, pp. 113–22.

Edwards, P. (ed.) (1967) *Encyclopedia of Philosophy*, New York, Macmillan and the Free Press.

Evans, J. St B. T. (1982) *The Psychology of Deductive Reasoning*, London, Routledge & Kegan Paul.

Evans, J. St B. T. (ed.) (1983) *Thinking and Reasoning*, London, Routledge & Kegan Paul.

Faris, J. A. (1962) *Truth-functional Logic*, London, Routledge & Kegan Paul.

Fine, K. (1975) 'Critical notice of *Counterfactuals* by D. Lewis', *Mind*, vol. 84, pp. 451–8.

Frede, M. (1974) 'Stoic vs. Aristotelian syllogistic', *Archiv für Geschichte der Philosophie*, vol. 56, pp. 1–32.

Frege, G. (1879) *Begriffsschrift, eine der arithmetischen nachgebildete Formelsprache des reinen Denkens*, [*Begriffsschrift, a Formula Language, Modelled upon that of Arithmetic, for Pure Thought*], Halle, Nebert. Complete English translation in van Heijenoort, 1970.

Frege, G. (1979) *Posthumous Writings*, Chicago, University of Chicago Press.

Frege, G. (1980) *Philosophical and Mathematical Correspondence*, Chicago, University of Chicago Press.

Frege, G. (1984) *Collected Papers on Mathematics, Logic, and Philosophy*, Oxford, Blackwell.

Gabbay, D. and Guenthner, F. (1984) *Handbook of Philosophical Logic*, vol. II: *Extensions of Classical Logic*, Dordrecht, Reidel.

Gärdenfors, P. (1982) 'Imaging and conditionalization' *Journal of Philosophy*, vol. 79, pp. 747–60.

Gärdenfors, P. (1986) 'Belief revisions and the Ramsey test for conditionals', *Philosophical Review*, vol. 95, pp. 81–93.

Geach, P. T. (1976) *Reason and Argument*, Berkeley and Los Angeles, University of California Press.

Bibliography

Geis, M. (1973) 'If and *unless*', in *Issues in Linguistics: Papers in Honor of Henry and Renee Kahane*, edited by B. J. Kachru, Urbana, University of Illinois Press, pp. 231–53.

Gibbard, A. (1980a) 'Two recent theories of conditionals', in Harper, Stalnaker, and Pearce, 1981, pp. 211–47.

Gibbard, A. (1980b) 'Indicative conditionals and conditional probability: reply to Pollock', in Harper, Stalnaker, and Pearce, 1981, pp. 253–6.

Goodman, N. (1947) 'The problem of counterfactual conditionals', *Journal of Philosophy*, vol. 44, pp. 113–28. Reprinted as chapter I of Goodman, 1955.

Goodman, N. (1955) *Fact, Fiction, and Forecast*, Cambridge, Harvard University Press. Page references are to the 4th edition, 1983, Cambridge, Harvard University Press. In the 2nd, 3rd and 4th editions, the pagination of chapter 1 is the same; in the 1st edition, the pagination is different.

Goodman, N. (1957a) 'Parry on counterfactuals', *Journal of Philosophy*, vol. 54, pp. 442–5.

Goodman, N. (1957b) 'Reply to an adverse ally', *Journal of Philosophy*, vol. 54, pp. 531–3.

Grice, H. P. (1961) 'The causal theory of perception', *Aristotelian Society Supplementary Volume*, vol. 35, pp. 121–52.

Grice, H. P. (1967) 'Logic and conversation', in Grice, 1989, pp. 1–143.

Grice, H. P. (1989) *Studies in the Way of Words*, Cambridge, Harvard University Press.

Hare, R. M. (1970) 'Meaning and speech acts', *Philosophical Review*, vol. 79, pp. 3–24.

Harman, G. (1984) 'Logic and reasoning', *Synthese*, vol. 60, pp. 107–27.

Harper, W. L. (1976) 'Rational belief change. Popper functions and counterfactuals', in Harper and Hooker, 1976, pp. 73–112.

Harper, W. L. (1981) 'A sketch of some recent developments in the theory of conditionals', in Harper, Stalnaker, and Pearce, 1981, pp. 3–38.

Harper, W. L. and Hooker, C. A. (eds) (1976) *Foundations and Philosophy of Epistemic Applications of Probability Theory*, Dordrecht, Reidel.

Harper, W. L., Stalnaker, R., and Pearce, C. T. (eds) (1981) *Ifs: Conditionals, Belief, Decision, Chance, and Time*, Dordrecht, Reidel.

Hazen, A. and Slote, M. (1979) ' "Even if" ', *Analysis*, vol. 39, pp. 35–8.

Honderich, T. (1982) 'Causes and *if p, even if x, still q*', *Philosophy*, vol. 57, pp. 291–317.

Honderich, T. (1987) 'Causation: rejoinder to Sanford', *Philosophy*, vol. 62, pp. 77–83.

Hughes, G. E. and Cresswell, M. J. (1968) *An Introduction to Modal Logic*, London, Methuen.

Jackson, F. (1977) 'A causal theory of counterfactuals', *Australasian Journal of Philosophy*, vol. 55, pp. 3–21.

Jackson, F. (1979) 'On assertion and indicative conditionals', *Philosophical Review*, vol. 88, pp. 565–89.

Jackson, F. (1981) 'Conditionals and possibilia', *Proceedings of the Aristotelian Society*, vol. 81, pp. 125–37.

Jackson, F. (1987) *Conditionals*, Oxford, Blackwell.

Jeffrey, R. (1981) *Formal Logic: Its Scope and Limits*, 2nd edition, New York, McGraw-Hill.

Johnson, W. E. (1921) *Logic*, part I, Cambridge, Cambridge University Press.

Johnson, W. E. (1922) *Logic*, part II, Cambridge, Cambridge University Press.

Kneale, W. (1950) 'Natural laws and contrary-to-fact conditionals', *Analysis*, vol. 10, pp. 121–5; reprinted in *Philosophical Problems of Causation*, edited by T. L. Beauchamp, Encino, Dickenson, 1974, pp. 46–9.

Kneale, W. and Kneale, M. (1962) *The Development of Logic*, Oxford, Oxford University Press.

Kripke, S. A. (1980) *Naming and Necessity*, Cambridge, Harvard University Press.

Kvart, I. (1980) 'Formal semantics for temporal logic and counterfactuals', *Logique et Analyse*, vol. 23, pp. 35–62.

Kvart, I. (1986) *A Theory of Counterfactuals*, Indianapolis, Hackett.

Lemmon, E. J. (1978) *Beginning Logic*, Indianapolis, Hackett.

Lewis, C. I. (1912) 'Implication and the algebra of logic', *Mind*, vol. 21, pp. 522–31.

Lewis, C. I. (1918) *A Survey of Symbolic Logic*, Berkeley, University of California Press. Dover Publications, New York, reprinted this work in 1960 with a new preface by Lewis but without chapters V and VI.

Lewis, C. I. (1943) 'The modes of meaning', *Philosophy and Phenomenological Research*, vol. 4, pp. 236–49.

Lewis, C. I. (1946) *An Analysis of Knowledge and Valuation*, Lasalle, Open Court.

Lewis, C. I. and Langford, C. H. (1959) *Symbolic Logic*, second edition, New York, Dover. The first edition of this book was published in 1932.

Lewis, D. (1968) 'Counterpart theory and quantified modal logic', *Journal of Philosophy*, vol. 65, pp. 113–26. Reprinted in Lewis, 1983, pp. 26–39.

Lewis, D. (1973a) 'Causation', *Journal of Philosophy*, vol. 70, pp. 556–67; reprinted in Sosa, 1975, pp. 180–91, and in Lewis, 1986b, pp. 159–72.

Lewis D. (1973b) *Counterfactuals*, Cambridge, Harvard University Press.

Lewis, D. (1976) 'Probabilities of conditionals and conditional probabilities', *Philosophical Review*, vol. 85, pp. 297–315; reprinted in Harper, Stalnaker, and Pearce, 1981, pp. 129–147, and in Lewis, 1986b, pp. 133–52.

Lewis, D. (1979) 'Counterfactual dependence and time's arrow', *Nous*, vol. 13, pp. 455–76; reprinted in Lewis, 1986, pp. 32–52.

Lewis, D. (1983) *Philosophical Papers*, vol. I, Oxford, Oxford University Press.

Lewis, D. (1986a) *On the Plurality of Worlds*, Oxford, Blackwell.

Lewis, D. (1986b) *Philosophical Papers*, vol. II, Oxford, Oxford University Press.

Loux, M. J. (ed.) (1979) *The Possible and the Actual*, Ithaca, Cornell University Press.

Lycan, W. G. (1979) 'The trouble with possible worlds', in Loux, 1979, pp. 274–316.

Lycan, W. G. (1984) 'A syntactically motivated theory of conditionals', *Midwest Studies in Philosophy*, vol. 9, pp. 437–55.

McCawley, J. D. (1981) *Everything that Linguists have Always Wanted to Know about Logic* (*but were ashamed to ask)*, Chicago, University of Chicago Press.

MacColl, H. (1908) ' "If" and "Imply" ', *Mind*, vol. 17, pp. 151–2.

McDermott, A. C. (1972) 'Notes on the assertoric and modal propositional logic of the Pseudo-Scotus', *Journal of the History of Philosophy*, vol. 10, pp. 273–306.

Mackie, J. L. (1966) 'Counterfactuals and causal laws', in *Analytical Philosophy*, edited by R. J. Butler, Oxford, Blackwell, pp. 65–80.

Mackie, J. L. (1973) *Truth, Probability and Paradox*, Oxford, Oxford University Press.

Mackie, J. L. (1974) *The Cement of the Universe*, Oxford, Oxford University Press.

McKinsey, J. C. C. (1947) Review of Goodman, 1947, *Journal of Symbolic Logic*, vol. 12, p. 139.

Malcolm, N. (1952) 'Knowledge and belief', *Mind*, vol. 61, pp. 178–89. A revised version appears in Malcolm, 1963, pp. 58–72.

Malcolm, N. (1963) *Knowledge and Certainty*, Englewood Cliffs, Prentice-Hall.

Mates, B. (1953) *Stoic Logic*, Berkeley and Los Angeles, University of California Press.

Mates, B. (1970) Review of Walters, 1967, *Journal of Symbolic Logic*, vol. 35, pp. 303–4.

Moody, E. A. (1953) *Truth and Consequence in Medieval Logic*, Amsterdam, North-Holland.

Moody, E. A. (1967) 'Medieval logic', in Edwards, 1967, vol. 4, pp. 528–34.

Moore, G. E. (1912) *Ethics*, New York, Holt.

Moore, G. E. (1922) *Philosophical Studies*, London, Routledge & Kegan Paul.

Moore, G. E. (1962) *Commonplace Book 1919–1953*, edited by C. Lewy, London, Allen & Unwin.

Mueller, I. (1969) 'Stoic and Peripatetic logic', *Archiv für Geschichte der Philosophie*, vol. 51, pp. 173–87.

Nelson, E. J. (1930) 'Intensional relations', *Mind*, vol. 39, pp. 440–53.

Nute, D. (1980) *Topics in Conditional Logic*, Dordrecht, Reidel.

Nute, D. (1984) 'Conditional logic', in Gabbay and Guenthner, 1984, pp. 387–439.

Parry, W. T. (1957) 'Reexamination of the problem of counterfactual conditionals', *Journal of Philosophy*, vol. 54, pp. 85–94.

Peirce, C. S. (1933) *Collected Papers*, vol. 3, edited by C. Hartshorne and P. Weiss, Cambridge, Harvard University Press.

Pollock, J. L. (1976) *Subjunctive Reasoning*, Dordrecht, Reidel.

Pollock, J. L. (1984) *The Foundations of Philosophical Semantics*, Princeton, Princeton University Press.

Pospesel, H. (1984) *Propositional Logic*, Englewood Cliffs, Prentice-Hall.

Prior, A. N. (1960) 'The runabout inference-ticket', *Analysis*, vol. 21, pp. 38–9; reprinted in Strawson, 1967, pp. 129–31.

Prior, A. N. (1967a) *Past, Present and Future*, Oxford, Oxford University Press.

Prior, A. N. (1967b) 'Logic, modal', in Edwards, 1967, vol. 5, pp. 5–12.

Quine, W. V. (1951) *Mathematical Logic*, revised edition, Cambridge, Harvard University Press. The first edition of this work was published in 1940.

Quine, W. V. (1960) *Word and Object*, Cambridge, MIT Press.

Quine, W. V. (1966) *The Ways of Paradox and Other Essays*, New York, Random House.

Quine, W. V. (1982) *Methods of Logic*, 4th edition, Cambridge, Harvard University Press. The first edition of this book was published in 1950.

Ramsey, F. P. (1931) *The Foundations of Mathematics*, London, Routledge & Kegan Paul.

Reichenbach, H. (1976) *Laws, Modalities, and Counterfactuals*, foreword by W. C. Salmon, Los Angeles, University of California Press. The main text was first published in 1954 with the title *Nomological Statements and Admissible Operations*.

Rescher, N. (1964) *Hypothetical Reasoning*, Amsterdam, North-Holland.

Russell, B. (1906) 'The theory of implication', *American Journal of Mathematics*, vol. 28, pp. 159–202.

Russell, B. (1908) ' "If" and "Imply," a reply to Mr MacColl', *Mind*, vol. 17, pp. 300–1.

Ryle, G. (1950) ' "If," "so," and "because" ', *Philosophical Analysis*, edited by Max Black, Englewood Cliffs, Prentice-Hall.

Sanford, D. H. (1976) 'The direction of causation and the direction of conditionship', *Journal of Philosophy*, vol. 73, pp. 193–207.

Sanford, D. H. (1977) 'The fallacy of begging the question: a reply to Barker', *Dialogue*, vol. 16, pp. 485–98, especially section V, 'Alleged difficulties with disjunctive syllogism', pp. 494–8.

Sanford, D. H. (1984a) 'The direction of causation and the direction of time', *Midwest Studies in Philosophy*, vol. 9, pp. 53–75.

Sanford, D. H. (1984b) 'The asymmetry of the by-relation', *Mind*, vol. 93, pp. 410–11.

Bibliography

Sanford, D. H. (1985) 'Causal dependence and multiplicity', *Philosophy*, vol. 60, pp. 215–30.

Sanford, D. H. (1988) 'Can there be one-way causal conditionship?', *Synthese*, vol. 76, pp. 397–408.

Schneider, E. F. (1953) 'Recent discussion of subjunctive conditionals', *Review of Metaphysics*, vol. 6, pp. 623–49.

Sellars, W. (1948) 'Concepts as involving laws and inconceivable without them', *Philosophy of Science*, vol. 15, pp. 287–315.

Sellars, W. (1958) 'Counterfactuals, dispositions, causal modalities', *Minnesota Studies in the Philosophy of Science*, vol. 2, Minneapolis, University of Minnesota Press, pp. 225–308. Pp. 227–48 reprinted with the title 'Counterfactuals', in Sosa, 1975, pp. 126–46.

Skyrms, B. (1980) *Causal Necessity*, New Haven, Yale University Press.

Slote, M. A. (1978) 'Time in counterfactuals', *Philosophical Review*, vol. 87, pp. 3–27.

Smiley, T. J. (1984) 'Hunter on conditionals', *Proceedings of the Aristotelian Society*, vol. 84, pp. 241–9.

Sobel, J. H. (1970) 'Utilitarianisms: simple and general', *Inquiry*, vol. 13, pp. 394–449.

Sosa, E. (ed.) (1975) *Causation and Conditionals*, Oxford, Oxford University Press.

Stalnaker, R. C. (1968) 'A theory of conditionals', *Studies in Logical Theory, American Philosophical Quarterly Monograph*, no. 2, Oxford, Blackwell, pp. 98–112. Reprinted in Sosa, 1975, pp. 165–72, and in Harper, Stalnaker, and Pearce, 1981, pp. 41–55.

Stalnaker, R. C. (1970) 'Probability and Conditionals', *Philosophy of Science*, vol. 37, pp. 64–80. Reprinted in Harper, Stalnaker, and Pearce, 1981, pp. 107–28.

Stalnaker, R. C. (1981) 'A defense of conditional excluded middle', in Harper, Stalnaker, and Pearce, 1981, pp. 87–104.

Stalnaker, R. C. (1984) *Inquiry*, Cambridge, MIT Press.

Stebbing, L. S. (1961) *A Modern Introduction to Logic*, New York, Harper. First published in 1931.

Stevenson, C. L. (1970) 'If-iculties', *Philosophy of Science*, vol. 37, pp. 27–49.

Strawson, P. F. (1952) *Introduction to Logical Theory*, London, Methuen.

Strawson, P. F. (ed.) (1967) *Philosophical Logic*, Oxford, Oxford University Press.

Strawson, P. F. (1986) '"If" and "⊃"', in *Philosophical Grounds of Rationality: Intentions, Categories, Ends* [PGRICE], edited by R. E. Grandy and R. Warner, Oxford, Clarendon Press, pp. 229–42.

Tichý, P. (1976) 'A counterexample to the Stalnaker–Lewis analysis of counterfactuals', *Philosophical Studies*, vol. 29, pp. 271–3.

Tichý, P. (1984) 'Subjunctive conditionals: two parameters vs. three', *Philosophical Studies*, vol. 45, pp. 147–79.

van Heijenoort, J. (1970) *Frege and Gödel: Two Fundamental Texts in Mathematical Logic*, Cambridge, Harvard University Press.

Von Wright, G. H. (1957) *Logical Studies*, London, Routledge & Kegan Paul.

Von Wright, G. H. (1974) *Causality and Determinism*, New York, Columbia University Press.

Walters, R. S. (1961) 'The problem of counterfactuals', *Australasian Journal of Philosophy*, vol. 39, pp. 30–46.

Walters, R. S. (1967) 'Contrary-to-fact conditionals', in Edwards, 1967, vol. 2, pp. 212–16.

Wason, P. C. (1966) 'Reasoning', in *New Horizons in Psychology, I*, edited by B. Foss, Harmondsworth, Penguin.

Wertheimer, R. (1968) 'Conditions', *Journal of Philosophy*, vol. 65, pp. 355–64.

Whitehead, A. N. (1929) *Process and Reality*, New York, Macmillan.

Whitehead, A. N. and Russell, B. (1962) *Principia Mathematica to *56*, Cambridge, Cambridge University Press. The first edition of vol. 1 of *Principia* appeared in 1910; the second edition appeared in 1927.

Wittgenstein, L. (1961) *Tractatus Logico-philosophicus* [*Logisch-philosophische Abhandlung*], London, Routledge & Kegan Paul. First published in 1921, the first English translation of this work appeared in 1922.

Wittgenstein, L. (1969) *On Certainty* [*Über Gewissheit*], edited by G. E. M. Anscombe and G. H. Von Wright, translated by Denis Paul and G. E. M. Anscombe, New York, Harper.

Index

Bibliographic Remarks and Retrospect

In this section, I refer to the text of the first edition, that is, pages 1–265 of the book you are holding, as *If P, Then Q*. An asterisk before the year in a reference earlier than 1989 indicates that the item appears in the Supplementary Bibliography.

BOOKS ON CONDITIONALS

Frank Jackson's *Conditionals* and the first edition of my book passed each other by. Although Jackson, 1987, appears in the Bibliography of *If P, Then Q*, it receives no serious attention there. (I was shortening my manuscript in 1988, not expanding it.) Jackson develops a theory of assertibility to defend the view that the truth conditions of indicative conditionals are truth-functional. (He distinguishes 'assertibility' from 'assertability'.) According to Jackson's view, apparent counterexamples to truth-functionality are merely apparent; they are actually violations of assertibility conditions. I agree with the view in Lycan, 2001, p. 91, that Jackson's notion of assertability does not rescue the truth-functional view from a serious difficulty about the negations of conditionals. I make a similar claim about Grice's defense of truth-functionality and Charles Stevenson's example of a negated conditional (p. 62).

When Michael Woods died in 1993, he left drafts of a projected book entitled *Philosophical Logic*. A continuous section on conditionals was finished enough to warrant its editing for publication as *Conditionals* (Wood, 1997). Woods' edited text on conditionals is 92 pages long. In addition to other material, the book contains a 42-page Commentary by Dorothy Edgington. Adapting here some advise I give in Sanford, 1999b, I recommend reading Edgington's commentary before the corresponding section of Woods' text, except for the final section 8 where I recommend reading Woods before Edgington.

Chapter 2 of William G. Lycan's *Real Conditionals* (Lycan, 2001) is based on his article 'A Syntactically Motivated Theory of Conditionals' (Lycan, 1984). This title would also be a suitable subtitle for the book. Linguists and philosophers have much the same subject matter when they write about

266

conditionals. Lycan expounds, criticizes, and expands on both linguistic and philosophical research. The linguist Michael Geis is a central influence; he and Lycan are joint authors of the Appendix, 'Nonconditional Conditionals'.

SURVEYS OF RESEARCH ON CONDITIONALS

Dorothy Edgington has written three review articles in addition to her Commentary on Woods' monograph which also serves as a review article. The journal *Mind* commissioned several 'State of the Art' review articles in the 1990s. 'On Conditionals', Edgington, 1995a, is the longest and most detailed of these articles, and has the longest list of references. It expands on the central questions of Edgington, *1986, and Edgington, 1991, namely, the relations between conditionals and probability, Lewis's triviality result, and the consequences of this for the question whether conditionals have truth conditions. Somewhat shorter review articles, Edgington, 2001a and 2001b, resemble each other in organization and content. They are less complex technically than Edgington, 1995. Edgington, 1997, provides a lucid freestanding overview of the subject especially useful for its treatment of connections between conditionals and probability.

The survey article by Donald Nute and Charles Cross, 'Conditional Logic', Nute, 2002, a revision and expansion of Nute,1984, is longer than Edgington, 1995a. Although there are central topics in common to Nute and Edgington, the extent of overlap is relatively small. Nute concentrates much more with attempts to provide an adequate formal semantics and logic for various kinds of conditionals. A central figure in this enterprise is Peter Gärdenfors. Nute rapidly reviews as 'Other Topics', pp. 85–87, issues that Edgington treats more thoroughly.

COLLECTIONS ON CONDITIONALS

Frank Jackson is both the author of the book entitled *Conditionals* and the editor of a collection with exactly the same title (which is also the title of Woods' book). Jackson, 1991, is the basic 1990s collection of articles about conditionals. It includes, by alphabetical order of author's name: Dudman, 1991, Edgington, *1986, Goodman, 1947, Grice, 1967, Jackson, 1979, Lewis, 1976, 1979, and Stalnaker, 1968, *1975.

Probability and Conditionals, Eells, 1994, is a collection of essays published here for the first time and written in honor of Ernest W. Adams. These essays are generally more specialized and technical than those in Jackson, 1991. The collection ends with a complete bibliography of Adams' publications.

Some of the essays in *Conditionals: from Philosophy to Computer Science*, Crocco, 1995, also appear in this collection for the first time. There is no comprehensive bibliography, but a list of references follows each essay. The bibliography in Nute, 2002, lists only three of the essays in Crocco, 1995, but it lists other works by almost all of these authors, none of whom appear in Eells, 1994, or in the bibliography of Edgington, 1995a. Some current research programs on conditionals evidently diverge considerably from each other although they share a common heritage in the work of Goodman, Stalnaker, Lewis, and Adams. The essays in Crocco, 1995, vary in technicality from one another and sometimes from one part to another, for example, Hansson, 1995, which reviews much of the material I do in *If P, Then Q*, Chapters VI–VII.

BIBLIOGRAPHIES ON CONDITIONALS

I recommend the bibliography in this volume, *If P, Then Q*, for the history of theories of conditionals before 1987.

The bibliography at the end of Jackson, 1991, is not long but is usefully organized by topic. The somewhat longer bibliographies in Edgington, 2001a and 2002 b are very similar to each other. The bibliography in Edgington, 1995a, is more than twice the length of 2001a, 2002b. The bibliography in Lycan, 2001, which contains many references to linguists not present in any of the other bibliographies, is longer than Edgington, 1995a, although it is not so long as the bibliography in Nute, 2002, which contains many references to the formal logic of conditionals not present in the others.

Kutach, 1999, a link on the home page of Douglas Kutach, is the longest and most comprehensive nonhistorical bibliography of which I am aware. It is roughly the union of the bibliographies in Edgington, 1995a, and *If P, Then Q* (entries after 1946), some doctoral dissertations, and publications after 1995, including articles by Stephen J. Barker, V. H. Dudman, Van McGee, and several exchanges in *Mind* between Edgington and her critics.

SUBTOPICS

This is a selection of topics discussed in the books and articles by Jackson, Woods, Lycan, and Edgington.

Do Conditionals have Truth Conditions?

The Preface to the first edition of *If P, Then Q*, offers a general apology to authors I do not mention. I had a number of philosophers, logicians, and linguists in mind at the time, and Dorothy Edgington was not among them. Even if she had written nothing else on the subject, my neglect of her *1986, would have been a significant oversight. Now because of her own work and responses to it, it turns out to be a huge oversight. I am unsure, however, whether reading Edgington, 1986, would have changed my mind about her central conclusion; for she accepts a basic assumption that I reject, namely, that there being different conditions or grounds for two conditionals entails that they differ in meaning. In examples where we would agree to distinguish different grounds, she would assert (in *1986), and I would deny, that this distinction indicates an ambiguity. She seeks a unified account, and I seek to reveal diversity. For further discussion of ambiguity, see Bennett, 2001a.

'*Truth conditions, assertability conditions,* and *acceptance conditions* might all be distinguished from each other, from *grounds*, and from *analysis of meaning*', I say in *If P, Then Q*, p. 81. I agree with Ted Honderich that spelling out grounds is not the same as analyzing meaning (pp. 194–195). My positive contribution to theories of conditionals, in my opinion, is the delineation of grounds that differ in form because of different patterns of objective dependence. For the most part, when one philosopher accepts such-and-such as grounds for truth, and the other denies it is grounds for truth but agrees it is grounds for acceptance or assertability, I do not attempt to adjudicate the dispute.

Edgington, 1991, begins by asking 'which, if any, of the following conditionals are suited to stating facts (truths)?' (p. 185):

(a) If it had rained yesterday, the track would have been muddy.
(b) If it rains tomorrow, the track will be muddy.
(c) If it rained yesterday, the track was muddy.

She then outlines seven distinct ways actual philosophers respond to this question. (A list with relevantly different or additional members would increase the number of alternatives. See 'The Classification of "If"-Sentences' below.) I place myself nowhere on her list. In circumstances where it is clear enough to what 'yesterday' and 'the track' refer, for each of (a), (b), and (c), there can be facts in virtue of which it is true. But for each of (a), (b), and (c), there is not one kind of fact in all circumstances in virtue of which it is true. Some tokens of (a), (b), and (c) are true. Some, in other circumstances, are false. The distinction between conditionals with truth value and those without, moreover, can be inexact (pp. 121–122). Pronouncing that my opinions on these issues differ from Edgington's is one thing; providing overall more convincing reasons is something else. Edgington, 1991, returns to the topic of Edgington, *1986, with respectful consideration of her co-symposiast Richard Jeffrey. She returns again with impressive detail in 1995a, and again with impressive clarity in 1997. In all these treatments, she devotes more detailed attention to relations between conditionals, belief, and probability than I do in Chapter VI, 'Belief and Probability,' especially with respect to the well-known theorem named after Thomas Bayes.

The Classification of 'If'-Sentences

V. H. Dudman's subversion of commonly accepted distinctions between indicative and subjunctive so-called conditionals continues in the 1990s and continues to exert influence. See the bibliographies of Edgington, 1995a, and Kutach, 1999, for references to later Dudman. See Bennett, 1988 and 1995, for an about-face on this issue. See 'The "Indicative"/"Subjunctive" Distinction', Chapter 7 of Lycan. 2001, for a discussion of Dudman's and others' views on this topic.

The Triviality Result

David Lewis's triviality thesis, which Edgington calls 'The bombshell' (1995a, p. 271), appears concisely in *If P, Then Q*, p. 90 and I provide some further guidance with footnotes 8 to 11 (p. 245). In an earlier, longer version, in order to formulate a proof easily comprehensible to the average reader of *If P, Then Q*, I presented a step-by-step proof of this result from three basic assumptions. For the same audience I would now recommend Edgington, 1997, pp. 144–116, for an elegant proof that uses diagrams. The triviality result is an important part of her overall arguments that conditionals do not have truth conditions.

Opposite Conditionals

The title of Chapter 8 of Lycan, 2001, 'The Riverboat Puzzle', alludes to the story by Allen Gibbard that I relate on p. 200. Frank Jackson says of such examples that 'there is no question of taking two subjective conditionals with the same consistent antecedent and inconsistent consequents to be both true, and going on to infer that the common antecedent is false. The two subjunctives cannot both be true' (Jackson, 1987, p. 53). Although many agree with him, I claim otherwise in *If P, Then Q*, pp. 199–200. (There is no question that two strict conditionals with the same consistent antecedent cannot all be true so long as all three statements employ the same sense of logical possibility, but that is a different question.) For a further discussion of examples of opposite conditionals with the same basic form but with some real structural differences, see Edgington, 1991, pp., 206–207, 1995a, pp. 293–299, and Bennett, 2001a, pp. 24–27. There is at least this much agreement about well-constructed stories of opposite or divergent conditionals: it is not the case that one is true and the other is false, otherwise the story is not well constructed. The opposite conditionals are both false, or they both lack truth value, or – the alternative Jackson and many others reject as inconsistent – they are both true.

RELATED TOPICS

Conditionals figure essentially in all the following topics. Recent discussions of these topics and the lines of recent research on conditionals I mention above tend to diverge from each other. I believe they have diverged too much.

Dispositions

A major reason the problem of counterfactual conditionals is important, according to Goodman, 1947, is to understand dispositions. The relation between dispositions such as 'This is water-soluble' and conditionals such as 'If this were to be put in water, it would dissolve' is more complicated than many philosophers used to assume. See Armstrong, 1996, and Lewis, 1994, for more recent developments.

Causation and Tracking

David Lewis introduced the notion of counterfactual dependence in Lewis, 1973a – see *If P, Then Q*, Chapter XI – to explain causation. It has been a central notion in discussions of causation ever since. It has also been important in the so-called externalist or reliablist accounts of knowledge. When one's belief that *p* counterfactually depends on the truth of *p*, then, as Robert Nozick put it, the belief tracks the truth. A belief that tracks the truth is (approximately) factual knowledge. See selections from D. M. Armstrong, Fred Dretske, Alvin Goldman, and Robert Nozick in Bernecker, 1999, for further references to this program in epistemology.

What Could Have Happened

In the Introduction of *If P, Then Q*, pp. 6–7, I quote two passage from Hume. The second summarizes Hume's 'reconciling project'. A pair of conditionals summarize what we mean by *liberty* or *the power of acting or not acting, according to the determinations of the will*: if we choose to remain at rest, we may; if we choose to move, we also may. In the first part of the twentieth century, G. E. Moore's version of the reconciling project was widely discussed and imitated. Later discussions of 'Free Will' in Moore, 1912, have been more critical. See for example, Chisholm, 1964, which discusses Moore and Austin together. J. L. Austin's discussion of Moore on 'if' and 'can', Austin, 1956, was, for a while, a center of attention; but the winds of philosophic fashion have shifted. Austin's essay does not appear in any of the bibliographies mentioned above except mine. (Lycan's omission is most puzzling, since the Appendix jointly written with Geis begins with a properly credited and one-time famous example from Austin, 1956: 'There are biscuits on the sideboard if you want them' (Lycan, 2001, p. 184)). Chisholm attacks the reconciling project. Attacks of several kinds on the reconciling project, and criticisms of the attacks, and defenses of the original project, have appeared frequently in the past twenty-five years, often turning on the logic of conditionals. See Ekstrom, 2002, for a summary of much of this activity plus her own position.

The earlier draft of *If P, Then Q* included a fuller illustration of the importance of conditionals to philosophical argument: Moore's version of the reconciling project, Chisholm's objection to it, Austin on Moore, Chisholm on Austin and Moore on 'ifs' and 'cans,' related problems connecting conditionals and dispositions, and phenomenalism. A revised version of some of this material, with additional treatment of Nozick on tracking, was my contribution to an American Philosophical Association symposium on the 'Philosophy of Language: Conditionals' with Donald Nute. Sanford, 1991, is an Abstract of this contribution.

The Direction of Causation

The general form of the explanation of causal asymmetry that appears in *If P, Then Q*, Chapter XIII, and in Sanford, 1988, receives much more detailed defense and development in Daniel M. Hausman's *Causal Asymmetries*, 1998. Although much of the discussion in this book is quite formal and abstract, Hausman keeps his basic topic always in view and keeps illustrating his points with fresh examples of real-word causation.

Supplementary Bibliography

Most of the authors listed here are also listed in the earlier Bibliography, pp. 254–62. Dorothy Edgington is a conspicuous exception.

Armstrong, D. M., Martin, C. B., and Place, U. T. (1996), *Dispositions: a Debate*, edited by Tim Crane, London, Routledge.

Bennett, J. (1988) 'Farewell to the phlogiston theory of conditionals', *Mind*, vol. 97, pp. 509–27.

Bennett, J. (1995) 'Classifying conditionals: the traditional way is right', *Mind*, vol. 104, pp. 331–54.

Bennett, J. (2001a) 'Conditionals and explanations', in *Fact and Value: Essays on Ethics and Metaphysics for Judith Jarvis Thomson*, edited by Byrne, A., Stalnaker, R., and Wedgwood, R., Cambridge, MA, MIT Press, 2001, pp. 1–28.

Bennett, J. (2001b) 'On forward and backward counterfactual conditionals', in *Reality and Humean Supervenience: Essays on the Philosophy of David Lewis*, edited by G. Preyer and F. Siebelt, London, Rowman & Littlefield, 2001, pp. 177–202.

Bennett, J. (2003) *A Guide to Conditionals*, Oxford, Oxford University Press.

Bernecker, S. and Dretske, F. (eds.)(2000) *Knowledge: Readings in Contemporary Epistemology*, Oxford, Oxford University Press.

Crocco, G., Fariñas del Cerro, L., and Herzig, A. (eds.) (1995) *Conditionals: from Philosophy to Computer Science*, Oxford, Oxford University Press.

Edgington, D. (1986) 'Do conditionals have truth-conditions?' *Critica*, vol. 18, pp. 3–30; reprinted in Jackson, 1991, pp. 176–201.

Edgington, D. (1991) 'The mystery of the missing matter of fact', *Proceedings of the Aristotelian Society Supplementary Volume*, vol. 65, pp. 185–209. This is the second paper in a symposium with Richard Jeffrey entitled 'Matter-of-fact conditionals'.

Edgington, D. (1995a) 'On conditionals', *Mind*, vol. 104, pp. 235–329.

Edgington, D. (1995b) 'Conditionals and the Ramsey test', *Proceedings of the Aristotelian Society Supplementary Volume*, vol. 69, pp. 67–86. This is the second paper of a symposium with Stephen Read.

Edgington, D. (1997) 'Commentary' in Woods, 1997, pp. 95–145.

Edgington, D. (2001a) 'Conditionals', *Stanford Encyclopedia of Philosophy*,

edited by Edward Zalta. Online. Available HTTP: <http://plato.
stanford.edu/entries/conditionals/> (accessed 29 July 2002).

Edgington, D. (2001b) 'Conditionals', *Blackwell Guide to Philosophical
Logic*, Lou Goble (ed.), Oxford, Blackwell, pp. 385–414.

Eells, E. and Skyrms, B. (eds.) (1994) *Probability and Conditionals: Belief
Revision and Rational Decision*, Cambridge, Cambridge University
Press.

Ekstrom, L. W. (2000) *Free Will: A Philosophical Study*, Boulder, Westview.

Dudman, V. H. (1991) 'Interpretations of "if"-sentences', in Jackson, 1991,
pp. 202–32.

Dudman, V. H. (1994) 'On conditionals', *Journal of Philosophy*, vol. 91,
pp. 113–28.

Hansson, S. O. (1995) 'The emperor's new clothes: some recurring problems
in the formal analysis of counterfactuals', in Crocco, 1995, pp. 13–31.

Hausman, D. M. (1998) *Causal Asymmetries*, Cambridge, Cambridge
University Press.

Jackson, F. (ed.) (1991) *Conditionals*, Oxford, Oxford University Press.

Jeffrey, R. (1991) 'Matter-of-fact conditionals', *Aristotelian Society Supplementary Volume*, vol. 65, pp. 161–83.

Kutach, D. (1999) 'References for conditionals," Online. Available HTTP:
<http://www.rci.rutgers.edu/-kutach/conditionals.html> (accessed 29 July
2002).

Lewis, D. (1997) 'Finkish dispositions', *Philosophical Quarterly*, vol. 47,
pp. 143–58.

Lycan, W. G. (2001) *Real Conditionals*, Oxford, Oxford University Press.

McGee, V. (1993) Critical Notice of D. H. Sanford, *If P, then Q, Philosophy
and Phenomenological Research*, vol. 53, pp. 239–42.

Nute, D. (1991) 'Historical necessity and conditionals', *Nous*, vol. 25,
pp. 161–75.

Nute, D. and Cross, C. B. (2002) 'Conditional logic', in *Handbook of
Philosophical Logic*, Second Edition, edited by D. M. Gabbay and
F. Guenthner, Dordrecht, Kluwer, 2002, pp. 1–98.

Sanford, D. H. (1991) 'Coulds, mights, ifs and cans, revisited' [Abstract],
Nous, vol. 25, pp. 208–11.

Sanford, D. H. (1994a) 'Causation and intelligibility', *Philosophy*, vol. 69,
pp. 55–67.

Sanford, D. H. (1994b) 'Causation', *A Companion to Metaphysics*, edited
by J. Kim and E. Sosa, Oxford and Cambridge, MA, Blackwell,
pp. 79–83.

Sanford, D. H. (1995) 'iff', *The Oxford Companion to Philosophy*, edited by
T. Honderich, Oxford, Oxford University Press, pp. 393–4.

Sanford, D. H. (1999a) 'Implication' and 'Inference', in *The Cambridge
Dictionary of Philosophy*, Second Edition, edited by R. Audi, Cambridge,
Cambridge University Press, pp. 419–20, 426–27.

Sanford, D. H. (1999b) Review of Woods, 1997, *Philosophical Books*, vol. 40,
pp. 119–122.

Sanford, D. H. (2001) Review of Hausman, 1998, *Philosophy and Phenomenological Research*, vol. 62, pp. 243–246.

Supplementary Bibliography

Stalnaker, R. (1975) 'Indicative conditionals," *Philosophia*, vol. 5, pp. 269–86. Reprinted in Harper, Stalnaker, and Pearce, 1981, pp. 193–210, and in Jackson, 1991, pp. 136–54.

Stalnaker, R. (1992) Book Review of D. H. Sanford, *If P, then Q, Notre Dame Journal of Formal Logic*, vol. 33, pp. 291–7.

Woods, M. (1997) *Conditionals*, edited by David Wiggins, with a commentary by Dorothy Edgington, Oxford, Oxford University Press.